By Walter Kerr

WALTER KERR

TRAGEDY

AND COMEDY

A Clarion Book

PUBLISHED BY SIMON AND SCHUSTER

FIRST PAPERBACK PRINTING 1968

LIBRARY OF CONGRESS CATALOG CARD NUMBER: 67–13031
MANUFACTURED IN THE UNITED STATES OF AMERICA
BY MURRAY PRINTING CO., FORGE VILLAGE, MASS.

ACKNOWLEDGMENTS

The *Oedipus Rex* of Sophocles: An English Version by Dudley Fitts and Robert Fitzgerald. Copyright 1949 by Harcourt, Brace & World, Inc. Reprinted by permission of Harcourt, Brace & World, Inc.

Sophocles' *Oedipus at Colonus:* An English Version by Robert Fitzgerald. Copyright 1941 by Harcourt, Brace & World, Inc. Reprinted by permission of Harcourt, Brace & World, Inc.

The *Antigone* of Sophocles: An English Version by Dudley Fitts and Robert Fitzgerald. Copyright 1939 by Harcourt, Brace & World, Inc. Reprinted by permission of Harcourt, Brace & World, Inc.

Aristophanes' *The Birds:* An English Version by Dudley Fitts. Copyright © 1957 by Harcourt, Brace & World, Inc. Reprinted by permission of Harcourt, Brace & World, Inc.

The Clouds by Aristophanes. From *The Complete Greek Drama*, Volume Two, edited by Whitney J. Oates and Eugene O'Neill, Jr. Copyright 1938 by Random House. Reprinted by permission of Random House.

The Bacchae by Euripides, translated by William Arrowsmith. Copyright © 1959 by the University of Chicago. Reprinted by permission of the University of Chicago Press.

The School for Wives by Molière, translated by Morris Bishop. From *Eight Plays by Molière*. Copyright © 1957 by Morris Bishop. Reprinted by permission of Random House.

Molière's *Tartuffe,* translated by Richard Wilbur. Copyright © 1961, 1962, 1963 by Richard Wilbur. Reprinted by permission of Harcourt, Brace & World, Inc.

The Misanthrope by Molière, translated by Richard Wilbur. Copyright 1954, © 1955 by Richard Wilbur. Reprinted by permission of Harcourt, Brace & World, Inc.

The Cherry Orchard by Anton Chekhov, translated by Stark Young. Copyright 1939, 1941, 1947, and 1950 by Stark Young; copyright © 1956 by Stark Young. Reprinted by permission of the Estate of Stark Young.

Luv by Murray Schisgal. Copyright 1963, 1965 by Murray Schisgal. Reprinted by permission of Coward-McCann, Inc.

for Phyllis

CONTENTS

1

INTRODUCTION

Wʜᴇɴ I first thought of writing this book, I thought of it as a book about comedy. It has not become that, because tragedy—most stubbornly—persisted in getting in the way.

It is odd that tragedy should have done that, particularly at this time in our theatrical lives. Tragedy, after all, has been pronounced dying or been declared dead as a working form for something like three hundred years, and no one professes to care very much, a few theorists excepted. Furthermore, this is not a time when forms as such concern us. We are interested in plays, not concepts, and the more violently a play shakes itself free of traditional concepts of any kind the more we are apt to admire it. We do not like to be bound by traditional habits of thought, we detest being hounded by categories. Let the event take place, and let us hope that it will be freshly exciting. The attempt to name it in advance might only lead us into making the same weary responses in advance; it might rule out real response altogether. The academies can, if they wish, speak of the past in the past's terms; our job is to develop experiences appropriate to a brand-new—if not always pleasant—world, to see that things happen in the present tense. Certainly these were some of the thoughts that rattled about in my head—as they may now be rattling about in yours—while I tried to fight off an ancient specter that seemed perversely determined to interrupt what I wanted to do.

Why did I want to write a book about comedy? For a simple and most unprofound reason. I love comedy immoderately. On the face of things, that is an idle statement. Doesn't everyone love comedy immoderately? Isn't comedy the one staple on the theatrical bill of fare, the one lure that is never resisted? While tragedy has been so long silent, comedy has continued to throw up its Sheridans and Wildes, its Shaws and Anouilhs; and just so long as it does, we are all content: the theater is still alive. Serious plays may fail to the right or succeed modestly to the left; but it is the newest *Odd Couple* that stirs an indecent haste to the box office. We are all partisans of comedy; who would dare lay claim to an excessive taste for it?

I would. I do. I have been a helpless prisoner of the form since I first saw Buster Keaton sink bravely to his death in three feet of water; and whenever the comic pressure becomes intense enough, I cry. Not everyone I know misses half his pleasure for weeping. That is a partial distinction. I also find that I am incapable of choosing among clowns. My acquaintances include those who admire Jack Benny but do not like Bert Lahr, who cherish Nichols and May but never could stomach Ed Wynn, who give Groucho Marx his due but remain indifferent to Phil Silvers. I love them all. Not admire. Love. There is a difference. Any fool can sit through a good routine, and laugh at it, the first time he sees it. It takes a fool of particular quality to sit through it five times, ten times, twenty times, long after he knows the laughs as well as the clown does and the trick of surprise has become an empty sleeve. I possess that quality, and can subsist on affection alone when the jests have ceased being jests and have become the things that of course this man does. I have seen Chaplin's film *The Gold Rush* not fewer than forty times, and naturally I no longer laugh at it. It simply warms me.

I think there is only one kind of clown I cannot tolerate,

and that is the kind who is himself uncommitted to what he is doing. A part of him is absent, listening, remembering, calculating. When Jacques Tati takes his hat and cane from a clothes-stand and manages to place the hat upon the cane instead of upon his head, I do not hate him because he is borrowing a piece of business from W. C. Fields. I hate him because he is so little involved with the business that he cannot do it well. He is outside comedy, making it; not inside comedy, being it. He doesn't believe that the problem is real. One evening I sat with a friend during a showing of Chaplin's *The Circus,* and when Charlie, having surreptitiously managed to eat the whole of a small child's hot-dog, soberly reached for a napkin and most thoughtfully wiped the child's lips, my friend clapped his hands in astonishment and fell back in his seat—I thought he was going to fall out of it—exclaiming, "He believes it! He *believes* it!"

But it was just this note of intense commitment on the part of the comedian that began to baffle me. Indeed, the clown's utter belief in what he is doing—because what he is doing is true and *not* a trick—is so much of the essence of comedy that the clown himself can become baffled by his own mood. I am told that Bert Lahr once hoped to persuade his colleagues to incorporate a new routine he had devised into a musical that was in rehearsal. He was fearful, almost certain, they wouldn't like it. But they agreed to listen to it. Lahr set up his props and, muttering feverishly to himself, went to work. Almost immediately there were chuckles. By the time the sketch had come to its climax the gathering was close to hysteria. At this point, and having got the last word out, Lahr turned on his obviously convulsed listeners, apoplectic. "All right!" he screamed at them, "*You* laugh! But that's funny!" The fierce seriousness of the gifted clown, so long a subject of romantic rumor, is not really in himself. It is in his material.

The more I attended to comedy the more I found it contradicting itself: what is funny had better not be laughed at, laughter is an inadequate response to what is truly funny.

Inside the lightest of jests there seemed to be a hard and resistant core that, even as it provoked laughter, wished desperately to discredit laughter. *Something* inside comedy is not funny. The form refuses to define itself on its own terms, defies explanation as an independent, self-contained eruption of high spirits, simply will not be claimed as an uncomplicated good companion. It does more than acknowledge an ache; it wishes to insist bluntly, even callously, on its often overlooked secret nature.

This may account for the mysterious distinction Groucho Marx once made between an amateur and a professional. An amateur thinks it's funny, Groucho said, if you dress a man up as an old lady, put him in a wheel chair, and give the wheel chair a push that sends it spinning down a slope toward a stone wall. The device, of course, has given us all our variations of *Charley's Aunt*. What is funny for a professional? "For a pro," Groucho said, "it's got to be a real old lady." The best comedy makes no waivers. It is *so*. And it is harsh.

The most frivolous of vaudeville jokes is in the end ambiguous, dependent at its center on no joke at all. We can sense, in a way, what Mr. Lahr meant by his outburst: laughter ignores the pain inherent in what is funny—not simply the pain of the man who has lived through, endured, the experience he has described for us. To be funny is to have been where agony was; let no one be casually cheerful about it. And I do think we sense that Groucho was right in pointing out that there is something terribly funny—something quite *terribly* funny—about the real old lady racing toward a wall that is missing from the female-impersonator variation with its emotional escape clause. We can laugh uninhibitedly at the female impersonator: he can take care of himself, and besides, he isn't real anyway. But what of the little old lady? Dare we laugh? We want to. The impulse is there, dark, beckoning, conspiratorial. We are even aware that *if* we can laugh, the laughter will be deeper, more centrally located, more candid.

But see here, now. The old lady may be hurt. She may be killed. Comedy at its most penetrating derives from what we normally regard as tragic.

I found myself forced, in the end, either to try to come at comedy through tragedy or to stand silent before this perpetual ambiguity. That is why what follows has at least as much to do with tragedy—and with tragedy *first*—as it does with comedy. Giving tragedy such priority may seem a bit gratuitous in an age that has seen comedy survive well enough in the absence of its elder brother, but I think we might pause to notice a peculiar event that has recently taken place. In the twentieth century an unexpected thing has happened to comedy. It has gradually turned black, spitting out—with a venom we think quite uncharacteristic—images and tirades that suggest a terrible impatience, inviting us to share what seems a very real insanity. It is almost as though the melancholy inside comedy that formerly tantalized and then eluded us had at last wholly overwhelmed it, pushing it to the wall—if only to Groucho's wall.

Now if there is actually a connection at root between tragedy and comedy, and if the doorway to comedy is truly a back door through tragedy, then the odd things that are happening in our theater today may in part be due to a quirk in the ancient nature of the forms as they were brought to birth and slowly separated from one another. The formal inquiry may be relevant, no matter where we go from here. It may even be necessary.

At this point I should mention that these pages contain both a deliberate limitation and a conscious disproportion. I mean to confine myself to comedy as a theatrical experience, partly because the term "comedy" came into being to describe a performing art and partly because dipping into Rabelais and Cervantes and *The Rape of the Lock* for illustration would encourage wanderlust without much altering the points at issue. I shall feel free to mention film, however, because what happens on film is once again performed; the clown's tribulations are enacted rather than reported. As for the disproportion, there are perhaps too many illustrations from the Greek for contemporary taste, from Aristophanes at the expense of Shaw, and from Sophocles when Shakespeare might have done. This is an imbalance intended to correct an imbalance. Because of certain inadequacies in present-day theatrical training, resulting in a lack of actors and directors equipped to deal with anything earlier than *Twelfth Night,* we almost never see on our stages the masterpieces that brought comedy and tragedy to birth—that brought them, in fact, to full maturity. We have very little direct experience of the plays that dictated the terms we use or that still continue to provoke, however subliminally, the responses we make in the theater. In trying to jog a race memory here and there, I am trying to compensate for an indifference that has sometimes grown into a misrepresentation. So much for waivers, or, if you wish, excuses.

The rest is argument.

2

THE TRAGIC SOURCE
OF COMEDY

COMEDY, it seems, is never the gaiety of things; it is the groan made gay. Laughter is not man's first impulse; he cries first. Comedy always comes second, late, after the fact and in spite of it or because of it. Comedy is really the underside of things, after the rock of our hearts has been lifted, with effort and only temporarily. It appears in the absence of something and as the absence of something. Man's primary concern is with the rock, with his heart, with tragedy; that is where his hope lies, strange though the taste of hope may be:

> In the desert
> I saw a creature, naked, bestial,
> Who, squatting upon the ground,
> Held his heart in his hands,
> And ate of it.
> I said, "Is it good, friend?"
> "It is bitter—bitter," he answered;
> "But I like it
> Because it is bitter,
> And because it is my heart."

Stephen Crane's aphoristic poem does not precisely speak of hope; it does suggest that only when he is eating his heart out is man truly happy. The forefront of man's mind, and any real future he can contemplate, is occupied with the curiously satisfying taste of the bitter. Sometimes he tires of tasting it, becomes aware of his own contrariness, in effect loses hope. He sees his activity as absurd and invites comedy to make a joke of it. Tossing his troublesome, acrid heart over his shoulder with a shrug, he looks about him for something easier to contend with—a handy melon from the melon patch, a woman in bed next to him, anything sweet. Indulging himself, and grinning devilishly as he does, he becomes a comic figure. He has abandoned hope and settled for what is here. He has chosen, for the time being, the lesser of two possible values, the ephemeral, the actual, the present and the passing, that which will leave him with no more than a rind. In the reflection of man's choices which drama gives off, tragedy is the positive and comedy is the negative.

So far as we know, comedy never has come first. It is something like the royal twin that is born five minutes later, astonishing everyone and deeply threatening the orderly succession of the house. It is the mistake of nature.

Such evidence as we have for the beginnings of dramatic form is scanty and confused. But some things seem clear enough and they make a pattern. The form called tragedy was given official standing in ancient Greece in 535 B.C. The form called comedy was not given such recognition until 486 B.C. Approximately fifty years elapsed between the apparent maturing of one form and the apparent maturing of the other. The presumption must be that tragedy drew naturally upon Greek energies until it had realized itself with some fullness; after that, there was more time for comedy. This is borne out, of course, by the plays we have. Aeschylus won his first victory in 484, Sophocles in 468, Euripides in 441. Aristophanes did not win a prize until 427. What plays of quality, by these and other writers, may have appeared and vanished betweentimes we cannot say; but it is fairly safe to assume, on the basis of prizes awarded and the fact that manuscripts were kept, that those we have were among the best produced. Assuming this, we can posit roughly a gap of thirty years between the creation of a tragic masterpiece like the *Antigone* and the production of a comic masterpiece like *The Birds.*

The gap is apparent, though in primitive miniature, again during the medieval rebirth of forms. Our difficulty with Greek drama is that we have so little primitive material; our difficulty with medieval drama is that we have so much, which means that we must follow a long trail before we come to anything like full tragedy or full comedy. But here we can at least see the seed, and the seed is beyond question serious, not comic. The first dim, gentle use of dramatic gesture and dialogue exchange occurs in a portion of the church liturgy which has to do with a visit to the tomb of the slain Christ. As the impulse expands, it embraces more and more of the passion of Christ, the bloody journey to death and resurrection. The impulse is also carried over from the events of Easter to the happier, though not comic, events of Christmas; perhaps significantly, it does not flourish nearly so much there. The first great growth centers about Calvary, the tomb, and the release from the tomb.

The first hint of dialogue and gesture is probably ninth century; by the end of the eleventh century expansion is rapid; by the end of the twelfth the expanded ritual can with some confidence be called a play. Comedy appears, in due course. On her way to the tomb, Mary Magdalen pauses to buy spices from a merchant, and you know—as medieval churchgoers did—what merchants are. A haggle ensues and it is meant to be funny. But we are now in the thirteenth century. No doubt it has not taken all of this time for some comic note to appear somewhere. Minstrels and folk dancers had surely seized upon the mimetic inspiration, combined it with the tricks of the trade and the capers of the dance, and made of the fusion a beginning secular folk play. But the clue had come from the cross.

I confess that when I am trying to imagine the rude beginnings of dramatic imitation I never imagine them in this way. Always, I imagine them as comic. I think of a woman imitating a neighbor's intolerable voice, or making a face to mock someone's perpetual poor-mouth, and of the family laughing shrilly in recognition; I think of a man doing his best to get drunk at the end of the work week and putting on his wife's bonnet to liven up the party; I imagine a relaxed folk situation in which genial mockery comes naturally. But, of course, a relaxed folk situation is already an aftermath; everything that is important, including all that is ritually and aesthetically important, has been taken care of earlier. There seem to be lyrical strokes, but no comic ones, on the painted walls of the Lascaux cave; most of what is there is terror, awe, and hope. At the bottom of a well lies a painted bird-man, dead. Small children almost never begin by mimicking their parents in sport; they mimic them in earnest, and what they mimic is their labor. Whatever one may imagine out of temperamental affinities, there are facts to be honored: Western drama, in its two evolutions, has given its first best attention to tragedy—or if not tragedy, then something gravely like it. In terms of time at least, man seems to have given a willing priority to what is tragic about him.

There is a further, perhaps more serious, sense in which comedy comes second. Comedy seems not only to follow tragedy but to derive from it. It is hard to be sure of our ground among the Greeks. Aristotle's account of the origins of comedy is baffling; though highly intelligent attempts have been made to clarify and correct it, it is unlikely that we shall ever be able to say firmly that *this* is the way Greek comedy came about. What we do know, however, is that when the art of tragedy was given official recognition it was an art divided into three parts, with a fourth assumed. Proper tragedies were trilogies: three related plays in which a first agony gave birth to a second and the second to a third, though it would seem from what we know that the third agony must have acted as an ultimate discharge of pain and responsibility, ending in reconciliation. The only complete trilogy we have is Aeschylus' *Oresteia*. In the first play, Clytemnestra murders her husband Agamemnon for both good and bad cause. In the second their son, Orestes, murders his mother to avenge his father. In the third Orestes is driven to near-madness by the Furies, who must punish him for the crime of matricide; at the end of this third play he is absolved and made whole again by Athena. Some of the single plays we have were to begin with parts of trilogies. Aeschylus' *The Suppliants* is the first play of a trilogy; we do not know how the last play ended. Aeschylus' *Prometheus* is the first play of a trilogy; we know that it ended in the reconciliation of the fire thief, Prometheus, with the Zeus he had robbed, but we do not have a text to analyze. Later, the requirement that tragedies be trilogies was dropped, and even such related plays as Sophocles' *Oedipus Tyrannus* and *Oedipus at Colonus* were conceived as separate plays.

But in the beginning, we are given to understand, the three-play tragedy was almost invariably followed in performance by a fourth piece, presumably written by the same author, in which the same material which he had been treating so tragically was suddenly seized by the bootstraps and turned upside down until apples and silverware and every sort of improper thing plummeted out of its pockets. This aftermath, or mocking of what had been so solemnly pursued, was called a satyr play, and we cannot really say that we know very much about it, even though our term "satire" has come from it. For one thing, we have only one extant text that is believed to be a true satyr play: Euripides' *Cyclops,* in which a sequence from the *Odyssey* is treated sportively. Here Odysseus comes to the island on which the one-eyed, man-eating Cyclops holds the aged Silenus and all his sons prisoners. Several of Odysseus' companions are slain and devoured. In revenge, and to fulfill a prophecy, Odysseus makes ready a burning brand with which he puts out the Cyclops' eye, after which he escapes, taking the Cyclops' slaves with him. The essential materials are much more than serious; they are horrifying. But Euripides' satyr play reduces everything that is momentous to malicious tomfoolery. Odysseus first gets the aged retainer, Silenus, thoroughly drunk. He proposes to do the same with the Cyclops. But Silenus is a fair-weather friend, a crafty old scamp, and to save his own skin he betrays Odysseus to the Cyclops. When Odysseus' companions are captured and turned on the spit, a detailed and delicate recipe for roasting humans is recited. In due time Odysseus does get the Cyclops as drunk as Silenus is, so much so that the Cyclops decides that his belly, now comfortably warmed, is "the greatest of deities." Indeed the Cyclops is so far gone in his cups that he begins to mistake the doddering Silenus for a very young boy and promptly carries him off to ravish him, preferring boys to girls as he does. Meantime Odysseus prepares his burning brand, though he can get no one among those he plans to rescue to help him assault the Cyclops. The most grateful of men turn cowards on the instant. One explains that he cannot help because "somehow or other I sprained my ankle, standing still." Odysseus does the job himself, and when the Cyclops emerges from his cave blinded, a cruel but essentially Chaplinesque sequence follows: everyone shouts false directions to the Cyclops while evading his clutches neatly. The concluding passage makes the very most of a pun. Odysseus, when asked by the Cyclops to identify himself, has called himself Noman. In his blinded rage, the Cyclops cries out that "Noman has undone me." His taunters promptly point out that in that case he is not undone. If he has been blinded by no man, then he can still see—and so forth. In the narrative structure of *The Cyclops* very little has been changed from the serious story as it appears in Homer. But every aspect of the serious story has been comically defaced.

Yet even *The Cyclops* comes a bit late for our purposes, too close in time to the full development of comedy under Aristophanes. What we should like, and don't have, is an

Aeschylean satyr play, the kind that might have followed on the heels and stepped on the heels of a *Prometheus* or an *Oresteia*. We should like to know what the relationship of three parts ache to one part frolic might have been. But though we cannot precisely know this relationship at the time of its first official establishment, there are still three simple things that may be deduced about the satyr play. It did not invent entirely new material for the occasion, but made use of material that had been treated extensively and most seriously beforehand. It mocked this material or at least made light of it. And, in performance, it followed rather than preceded it.

This is to say that it belonged to the material as a shadow does to the sun, and it erupts as the sun is going down. The two, shadow and sun, are almost one; certainly the second is unthinkable without the first. And the order of importance is clear: tragedy is the substance, the satyr play its irreverent reflection. The earliest comic fragments to have survived are parodies of serious passages from the *Iliad* and the *Odyssey*, and the very first playwright who can be identified as a comic playwright, Epicharmus, seems to have specialized in burlesquing heroic legend.

H. D. F. Kitto concludes that "if common sense and common experience are to be allowed any status in this debate, one would say that it is very much more likely that the lighthearted form of drama 'grew' out of the serious and strenuous one by way of parody, than that the serious one should have grown out of the other by rejecting everything in it which made it what it was."

There is a strong probability, then, that when the comic tone first became recognizable it became recognizable as burlesque of the solemn and sacred. That is what it is there for: to repair an omission. The solemn, the sacred, the tragic, in its upward strain invariably leaves something out.

To conceive of this relationship honestly we should have to imagine ourselves participating in the most elevating experience of which we are capable. We are vested, or our priests are. We are on the verge of touching the God we know. We have struck our breasts, acknowledged our venality, felt the venality washed away, ascended to the forgiveness we have freely been promised. We stand erect. There is no stain in the shared air. Then, at the altar, the priest burns his fingers on the incense pot and a small oath escapes him, as I once created a minor diversion myself by setting fire to the hair of the altar boy in front of me with the candle I so soberly carried. "A sparrow fluttering about a church is an antagonist which the most profound theologian in Europe is wholly unable to overcome," Sydney Smith once said.

Comedy insists upon the burn and the sparrow, and even upon the oath, not in order to give the lie to the occasion but to complete it. The occasion could not be entirely representative if one part of its truth were to be altogether suppressed. All truth is whole, one.

In this sense, comedy is tragedy's private diary. It records what may have been concealed, and quite properly concealed, while we were trying so desperately to maintain a social relationship with the gods. In a social relationship one tries to sustain the level of one's host. One does not scratch in public, no matter how unbearable the urge to scratch may be. But to say that there is no urge to scratch would be to falsify the real sum of reality. Comedy scratches freely in order to add the last necessary ounce of truth.

The forms are inseparable, then, one incomplete without the other. Tragedy is the forward or upward thrust, comedy is the drag or reminder. In the first Greek arrangement of plays we hear about, the two are balanced in just this way, with the satyr child being born directly of its tragic mother. In the medieval rediscovery of drama, the two-faced pattern is repeated. The first highly developed comic notes are developed not apart from, but out of, what has been presented as most terrifying.

Herod, in the medieval mystery cycles, is an obvious example. Herod is a murderer of infants and a direct threat to the newborn Christ. He is possessed of awesome power. He owns the dignity of a king. From him we should expect to derive fear, apprehension, suspense. But we cannot endure him as a pure symbol of threatening power. In our experience, no such thing exists. Power always has an untied shoelace, the very need to threaten suggests an obscure vulnerability. Herod thereupon becomes, to the delight of medieval audiences, an impotent ranter, something close to a clown, the other side of the kingly coin.

The devil is a better example. Of all the figures designed to beget fear among medieval audiences, the devil should logically be most threatening. A shudder should greet him; thoughts of eternity lost should prickle with his smoky entrance; for a Christian he is the tragic source, Lucifer the tragic type. How swiftly he becomes laughable, a derided and ultimately defeated buffoon! He is powerful indeed; but every inch of his flesh stings, he is eternally on hot coals. The image we quickly get of him is of a fool capering on the griddle. Damnation is real enough, but damnation itself dances on blistered feet.

Joseph the saint is seen as funny. Foster father of Christ, protector of Mary, celibate, worthy carpenter, intercessor at the throne of heaven, Joseph might be thought inviolate in his sanctity, gentle perhaps, but awesome in his self-sacrificing virtue. Joseph, however, is a man, and men are generally surprised to discover that their wives are about to have children they themselves did not beget. Men are humiliated and infuriated to think themselves cuckolds. They make scenes and try to identify the culprit and threaten to leave home. So Joseph does, in one of the most unexpected and charming of medieval inversions.

But the human need to notice that the priest has not shaved and that the judge who sentences us to death picks his nose did not end, in the Middle Ages, with observations about those deeply serious figures Herod, the devil, and Joseph. Ultimately it extended to include the Mass itself,

Christ's own gift and sacrifice as it is reenacted ritually. The
parodistic character of the celebrated Feast of Fools, together
with its various companion occasions of license, is well
known: instead of the Mass, the Ass. Earlier an ass might
have been introduced into church, during the devotional
mystery plays, by way of illustrating the flight of the Holy
Family into Egypt or, perhaps, Christ's entry into Jerusalem.
Now the ass took center stage in the same sanctified premises
and became the subject of a mock liturgy. Its praises were
chanted, altar boys brayed instead of responding in the usual
Latin, and swung censers gave off the odor of burning sau-
sages. Outrageous vestments were worn and abandoned revelry replaced all of the traditional gestures of adoration in
what Enid Welsford has called "a complete reversal of ordinary custom." Was this explosion of mockery a sign of essential disbelief? Was it a mere letting-off of steam under the
intolerable pressures of striving for sanctity? Or was it, instead, a necessary attempt to define more fully the nature of
the striving, to state an aspect of the sanctifying process without which the process could never be complete?

"It is a common mistake," Hazlitt says, "to suppose that
parodies degrade, or imply a stigma on the subject: on the
contrary, they in general imply something serious or sacred
in the originals."

Comedy is not a relief, it is the rest of the bitter truth, a
holy impropriety. The relief we find in it comes from its
having finished the sentence, having blurted out the one
thing that was on the tip of everyone's tongue but that everyone was refraining from mentioning. It is the proud criminal
finally throwing up his hands and "admitting everything,"
throwing himself upon the mercy of the court and so secur-
ing the fullness of justice.

There is no act in life that is not, when it is seen whole,
both tragic and comic at once. Our simplifying habit is to
split the cell so as to examine its properties separately. But we
are not, in practice, unaware of this simultaneity that will

hound us to our graves, where almost anything will cause the mourners to titter. "The consciousness," Hazlitt adds, "that there is something that we ought to look grave at, is almost always a signal for laughing outright: we can hardly keep our countenance at a sermon, a funeral, or a wedding."

In his autobiography Chaplin has explained the origins of some of the principal comic images in *The Gold Rush*. He had been reading a history of the Donner party, that unlucky band of pioneers who had lost their way to Oregon and become snowbound in the mountains. One hundred and sixty were trapped; eighteen survived. "Some resorted to cannibalism, eating their dead, others roasted their moccasins to relieve their hunger." From one of the most horrifying accidents of American history, Chaplin derived—by a mere trick of the light—a scene in which he boiled and ate a shoe and another in which his companion began to mistake him for an enormous chicken. It may be worth emphasizing again, in passing, that when we are first told the story of the Donner party, it is horror that fills our minds; comedy is some time coming, and without a comic genius to point out what is missing it might never, for most of us, come at all.

Yet comedy can come in a wink. There is probably no more traumatic myth permanently housed in the human psyche than the Oedipus myth. The fear that one will defile the sources of one's being is omnipresent. To kill one's father is to violate the chain of being upon which personal existence depends. To marry one's mother is to return to the womb and so turn the chain in upon itself, ending its productive extension. Though it is easy now to think of the Oedipus story as a dramatic convention or a primitive symbol, contrived as narrative and unnecessary as warning, we are not free of its content as nightmare. Far below the level of consciousness, fear and revulsion still stand at attention. When one of my children was eight or nine years old I permitted him to see a performance of Sophocles' play, wondering what he would make of it. When the performance was over, I asked him questions to see how much of the play's complexity he had been able to grasp. There was no immediate problem. With an accuracy that very much surprised me he was able to outline swiftly and easily the intricate details of the process by which the guilty man in Thebes was detected; he showed no difficulty in dealing with the several oracles which must be kept in mind or with the plot convolutions by means of which the infant Oedipus was passed from hand to hand to arrive at the destiny he had so carefully tried to avoid. The boy omitted only one thing in his account of the narrative: that Oedipus had married his mother. He did not evade this issue, sheepishly; he seemed simply to have forgotten it. A censor had acted so swiftly and at so deep a level that the suppression was unembarrassed.

A psychic shock as profound as that which the *Oedipus* generates in us would scarcely be thought susceptible of humorous or cavalier treatment. It has rarely been given such treatment. When, in Tony Richardson's film version of *Tom Jones*, we suddenly seemed to be approaching the possibility that Tom, in the course of his wenching, had wenched with his mother, our mouths dropped open. A beginning stir of astonishment, of disbelief that the film was actually proposing what it seemed to be proposing, moved across the audience. The audience sat up. Then the actress playing Tom's presumed mother turned directly into the camera, looking at us in close-up. The news was news to her, too. She made a surprised but philosophical grimace. In effect, the grimace said "Well, you never know where the next jolt's coming from, do you?" The audience exploded into laughter. Mother hadn't been the least bit upset after all. The force of the laughter came in part from our prepared astonishment. And in part it came from a discovery, a realization: Jocasta *might* not have hanged herself; she might have shrugged the whole thing off. We had been overlooking a possible truth. An audience will not laugh at what is not true.

The fact that, a few moments later, this lively wench was

discovered not to have been Tom's mother has no bearing on the issue. This new development was a mere dramatic politeness. Indeed, it became a further joke on the need for such social and dramatic politeness. The worst had already happened. We had looked at Oedipus and laughed, had found the comic in the tragic.

The order of events, and of our response to events, must be kept in mind in each of these instances: first seriousness, sanctity, dignity; then a light and somewhat insulting corrective. The tragic mask comes first in time and remains always first in importance. Further, it is as near an absolute as anything human can be. It is wholly tragic, completely a cry. The comic mask, assuming its defined shape somewhat later, is not wholly comic, not completely a laugh. A good comic mask, when you find one, is much more nearly a leer: the lips curved upward in merriment have some licentiousness in them, the mischievous eyes have some malice in them, the muscular strain of the grimace has some hurt in it. The comic mask is the tragic mask with the corners of the mouth forced upward as though by two fingers, and with the angle of vision altered.

It is the tragic mask, with a mouth turned down, that looks upward; comedy looks you right in the eye, ready to spit in it. Nietzsche speaks of that "union of god and goat," the satyr. The satyr's stroke is an afterstroke, a scratch across the face of tragedy, a grinning show of teeth in the face of death, of aspiration, of the agony that seeks transformation.

We have very good evidence, then, to show that comedy, in its fullness, comes after seriousness, after tragedy or its equivalent. And on somewhat lesser but nonetheless extremely provocative evidence, it seems likely that comedy comes *from* tragedy.

If these things are so, the two faces the theater shows us are in actuality the same face, worn by the same man, reporting the same event. Hercules will suffer and die after his labors; Hercules is a clown. Herod will slaughter the innocents;

Herod is funny. We shall never know what Socrates had in mind when he pronounced the two forms of theater identical:

. . . there remained only Socrates, Aristophanes, and Agathon, who were drinking out of a large goblet which they passed around, and Socrates was discoursing to them. Aristodemus was only half awake, and he did not hear the beginning of the discourse; the chief thing which he remembered was Socrates compelling the other two to acknowledge that the genius of comedy was the same with that of tragedy, and that the true artist in tragedy was an artist in comedy also. To this they were constrained to assent, being drowsy, and not quite following the argument. And first of all Aristophanes dropped off, then, when the day was already dawning, Agathon. Socrates, having laid them to sleep, rose to depart. . . . At the Lyceum he took a bath, and passed the day as usual.

Drink and drowsiness made a joke of Socrates' insistence that the joke was tragic and the tragedy funny. Something we do know for ourselves, however, and something we are constantly remarking on, is the swiftness with which a fine clown can slip into pathos. We are inclined to reserve our highest praise for those few clowns who are able to suspend the two faces before our eyes in such a way that we see they are one, as Marcel Marceau has most literally done in his pantomime *The Mask Maker*. Here the mask maker is trying on his various masks, quickly substituting one for another. But a particularly gleeful mask, sheer grin from ear to ear, becomes stuck. The mask maker tries to remove it, but cannot. His efforts are confident at first, then increasingly desperate. In due time we know that the real face behind the mask is a thing of maddened frustration, of unadulterated anguish. But all we can see is a perpetual smile. Because M. Marceau is a mime, he is using no real masks; we are looking directly at his face, in which the two expressions, one evident, one intimated, coincide. The fusion is absolute. The comic image dominates, because Marceau is essentially a comedian; yet we see and feel clearly what is behind it, even as it does so. Comedy stands on pathos, and its bandy legs are always giving way.

But, strangely, the reverse is not so. We do not admire most the tragic writer who is able to embrace in his tragedy the most substantial invasion of comedy. Comedy *can* be brought into tragedy; it is not intolerably false there. We are touched that Sophocles should have been kindly enough to make a shepherd gently amusing. We allow Shakespeare his drunken porter, and are grateful for Hamlet's wit. But our instinct does not ask for more. It asks, rather, whether quite so much should be there. That Marlowe should have thought it feasible to introduce so much into *Doctor Faustus* appalls us. And though we are deeply sorry to see Mercutio die, we sense that we are finally well rid of him. It does not distress us that the Fool should vanish from *Lear*. We banish him altogether in productions of *Othello*.

We are eager to welcome and to praise the discovery of seriousness in comedy, but our impulse is always to keep tragic form pure. We are nervous of the overimage, the shadow. We ask that tragedy represent us, as much as possible, in an uncomplicated and uncorrupted way. We ask that it remain bitter, because it is our heart. "The heart *prefers* to move against the grain of circumstance; perversity is the soul's very life," as John Updike has said. Of the two forms, tragedy and comedy, tragedy is the form we defend, protect from the incursions of its alter ego, hold firm and close to our breasts. It seems not to matter that it eats at our vitals; it was our identity to begin with, as it certainly shall be our end.

If the two forms are one, the one is tragedy. We insist upon this in practice, insist upon honoring tragedy as though it were the root, the mother, the matrix—perhaps not the whole story but certainly the main plot.

Our continuing instinct accords well enough with what can be deduced or conjectured about the religious rites which gave rise to the dramatic impulse. When scholars try to probe back beyond the first plays of Aeschylus or the surviving fragments of even earlier writers, into the now concealed and always mysterious womb of the mimetic instinct, some imagine comedy and tragedy as coming from a single rite capable of giving birth to both forms, though to comedy a moment later than tragedy. The primitive rite itself, in ancient Greece and elsewhere, was no doubt a variable, adapted to different religious and social functions at different times of the year. But at the heart of the rite, eternally repeated, is a knife, one central, unyielding concept: sacrifice, immolation.

There is a struggle, a combat, an *agon* implying agony, between two contending forces. The contention may be between the old year and the new, between summer and winter, between barrenness and fertility, between light and darkness, between the last king and the next, between any two champions elected to represent any two natural, necessarily exclusive forces.

The agony ends in a death. One party is slain and lamented. He is lamented because he has sacrificed himself in a necessary action. The action will, in the end, serve the common good of mankind.

Because the action has been necessary, because the good of mankind demanded this lamentable death, the slain figure is rewarded in one of several ways. The slain year may find itself fulfilled in the birth of the new year, to which it has contributed: the sacrifice is evolutionary in a simple sense. Or the sacrificial victim may be more personally rewarded, by resurrection or transfiguration, by what Gilbert Murray has called "his Epiphany in glory"; the sacrifice has been a purifying one.

The ritual ends in a feast, a celebration, a revel, perhaps in a spiritual marriage of the resurrected figure with one or another divine power. The impulse to comedy was thought by Francis Macdonald Cornford to reproduce all of these elements, even the agony and the sacrifice, in parodied form but to stress and elaborate the final feast and marriage. Tragedy tends to center its attention upon the contest and the death, curtailing and sometimes merely hinting at the transfiguration.

This outline is much simplified; it bypasses subtleties and ambiguities men will never finish discussing. But I think it may be taken as established that drama—all drama—grew from a sacrificial contest ending in a death and some sort of transfiguration. The proposition is given enormous reinforcement by our later medieval experience. From the sacrifice of the Mass—with its implications of agony, death, and resurrection—drama emerges all over again.

Agony is the heartbeat; death is the crucible; renewal is the goal. These are the three terms by which drama may be identified. They are all serious terms, and death stands at their center inflexible and indispensable, the key, the passport, the *sine qua non*. Whatever comedy is made must be made without blinking the terms or altering them fundamentally. One may see a joke in them but never outside them; they can be laughed at but not denied. They define our movement through space and time, in the theater and out of it. They describe our psychic thrust against the grain, beyond the pleasure principle; we meet in underground caves at Altamira, in cathedrals at Chartres, and in theaters, to repeat them. We rise in the morning to look for the transformations that will cleanse us and marry us to gods. We are not confused. The path is as deeply marked in our brains as the footprints that still climb the Acropolis, with such effort and so much promise of pain, toward Athena. Agony, death, transfiguration make up the compulsive rhythm of the only universe we know.

It is small wonder that with so powerful an instinct prodding us to repeat eternally these three simple but difficult gestures we should have given our first energies, and our deepest protective loyalties, to what we call tragedy. Tragedy must stand in the way. It *is* the way.

3
THE TRAGIC ENDING

TRAGEDY is the form that promises us a happy ending. It is also the form that is realistic about the matter.

Over several thousand years, and out of much bad theory, we have come to entertain casual assumptions which would not be borne out by even the sketchiest acquaintance with the plays we possess. It is strange that we should be able to maintain steadfastly, and even to make law of, principles that are in plain contradiction to much of the material on which they are said to rest. There are several commonly held principles that fly directly in the face of works they mean to describe, and we shall try to speak of them in some sort of orderly progression. At the moment suppose we focus on one: the notion that tragedy is largely defined by its unhappy ending and that comedy, in contrast, is defined by its happy one.

This is almost the simplest rule of thumb we know; schoolboys learn to repeat it quickly. But it is utterly inadequate even as a partial description of many of the greatest tragedies we have on hand to study. It not only fails to correspond to what happens at the conclusions of the plays; it directly falsifies what happens at the conclusions of the plays.

Of course any principle so simplified that schoolboys can parrot it is bound to lack something of subtlety. And we know, too, that much tragic theory as it was reformulated during the Italian Renaissance and imposed for a time upon all serious-minded playwrights was faulty. The Italians did not fully understand the Greeks when they came to their exhilarating rediscovery of ancient drama and Aristotelian principle. We learned to see the error of the Italian insistence upon unity of time and of place, for instance—although it took us several hundred years and a vast amount of experimental work in a contrary direction to decide that this could not have been quite what the Greeks meant. We know that dogmatic statements about tragedy have very often had flaws in them. Still, the general drift is right, isn't it? Tragedy is disaster, isn't it? We may have come to see that the tragic hero is often responsible for his own undoing, and so been able to reconcile ourselves to the dreadful fate that overtakes him, but the fate itself is death and destruction unredeemed, surely?

Never mind schoolboys. George Steiner, in *The Death of Tragedy,* finds true tragedy dead nowadays because Christianity, with its promise of salvation for any and all sinners who repent, has broken the back of the tragic assumption, which is that there is an "unaltering bias toward inhumanity and destruction in the drift of the world." For Mr. Steiner tragedy "is founded on the assumption that there are in nature and in the psyche occult, uncontrollable forces able to madden or destroy the mind" and "beyond the tragic, there lies no 'happy ending' in some other dimension of place or time. The wounds are not healed and the broken spirit is not mended. In the norm of tragedy, there can be no compensation."

To the same effect I. A. Richards: "Tragedy is only possible to a mind which is for the moment agnostic or Manichaean. The least touch of any theology which has a compensating Heaven to offer the tragic hero is fatal." The tragic vision, and particularly the Greek tragic vision, is bleak, final, implacable in its insistence upon Fate. The position is still critically respectable.

What is one to say of it in the light of plays we may read? We have only the *Oresteia* as an example of the earliest and most ample tragic form, the trilogy. After two plays of venom and unthinkable murder we come to a third, in which the venom is expelled, the guilt of the hero is washed away, and all warring forces are reconciled by the strict justice and transfiguring mercy of Athena. Mr. Steiner may insist that "where there is compensation, there is justice, not tragedy." But in the *Oresteia* every party to the long and exacerbating struggle is given careful compensation; the end of the trilogy blazes with a purifying justice. Is it possible to construct a theory, any theory, of tragedy without taking into serious account the content of this play?

The *Oresteia* moves, as John Jones has said, "in a bold arc . . . from tragic disquiet, through death and absence and sterile hatred, to fulfilment and blessing." Kitto adds that the Promethean trilogy, of which we have only the first play, obviously ended happily as Prometheus and Zeus moved "from enmity to a reconciliation in a new world order." Prometheus had stolen fire from heaven. The severity of his punishment, in the text we have, is exceeded only by the fury of his continued defiance of Zeus. Yet, hopeless as the situation seems to us in this first play of three, the trilogy is all the time curving in a direction that is, thematically speaking, "the right direction and one which hurts nobody, but rather removes hurt."

Can other trilogies have ended happily? Is it possible that *The Suppliants,* that play in which a bedeviled man seems to have no felicitous course of action open to him, ended happily? We cannot know. But on the basis of what we do know the presumption that all trilogies ended happily is actually better founded than the presumption that any trilogies ended unhappily.

The single-play form which later replaced the trilogy, and upon which so many of our structural concepts are founded, represented a foreshortened, though not inferior, accounting of the tragic span. It would be unreasonable in this more compressed form to look for any very extended development of the redemption motif. Aeschylus might have been able to give it one play out of three; but here, if the central sacrificial action is to be adequately dramatized, it cannot have so much as one third of the play. The contest and immolation must occupy the body of the play; they are its two active parts, whereas the transfiguration is essentially passive, a residue. At the same time, if there is any soundness in what we have been deducing about the full arc, the intention and ultimate significance of tragedy, we should, even in shorter plays, expect to find some hint of justice done or reconciliation achieved.

Of course we do find it. We find it in all sorts of degrees. Sophocles' *Philoctetes* is a play about the uses of power. The powerful bow and the magically accurate arrows of the hero-god Hercules are in the possession of poor Philoctetes, who has been unbearably wounded and then cast away upon an island. But the Trojan war cannot be won without these arms, and two Greek chieftains come to the island to deceive Philoctetes into surrendering them or, if necessary, to take them by force. Philoctetes, having earlier been betrayed by his own compatriots, refuses to part with his treasures; injured though he is, "he bends not to misfortune, but seems to brave it." He pleads, instead, to be returned to his homeland. One of his pursuers is so moved by Philoctetes' plight and by his firmness of mind that he gives over his effort to deceive him. The other is about to resort to violence. With the situation locked three ways, the dead hero Hercules, in his new role as a god, appears before the contestants "to turn thee from the paths thou meant to tread, and guide thy footsteps right." Making peace among them all, he warns:

> Thou too like me by toils must rise to glory—
> Thou too must suffer, ere thou canst be happy.

Thus one of the principals has found his own way to repentance and rectitude. The others are reconciled by Hercules in such a way that all are satisfied. The play is so deeply committed to human and divine concepts of justice that we sometimes wonder, in our latter-day rigor, whether or not we ought to call it a tragedy; but it is not a comedy and it is not, in its utter seriousness and singleness of tone, what we mean by tragicomedy. It can scarcely be doubted that Sophocles, understanding what he was doing, set out to write a tragedy in which emphasis was to fall upon the final, reconciliatory movement of the action. The play seeks and finds justice, finds it in the hearts of men first and then, to further purpose, in the wisdom of the immortals.

Sophocles wrote another play in which the emphasis was placed not necessarily upon justice but upon a moment of personal transfiguration. *Oedipus at Colonus* was written some years after *Oedipus Tyrannus* and the two, linked though they now are by the emergence of the second play, must be taken as separate and complete tragedies. The *Tyrannus* ends with Oedipus self-blinded and expelled, by his own law, from Thebes. The *Colonus* finds him being drawn, mystically, toward the earth on which he must die. His *agon* is not yet finished. There will be a desperate contest for possession of his body, even before life has left it. There is a quarrel under way between his two sons which will end in a curse being placed upon both of them. Almost to the last, Oedipus is pulled this way and that, a sacrificial victim. Then the time comes. There is thunder and lightning:

> Hear it cascading down the air!
> The God-thrown, the gigantic, holy sound!
> Terror crawls to the tips of my hair!

So sings the chorus. Oedipus speaks his last words to Theseus, King of Athens:

> . . . Most cherished friend!
> I pray that you and this your land and all

> Your people may be blessed: remember me,
> Be mindful of my death, and be
> Fortunate in all the time to come!

Theseus escorts the unseeing Oedipus to the secret place of summoning. Later a messenger reports the death:

> . . . It was not lightning,
> Bearing its fire from God, that took him off;
> No hurricane was blowing.
> But some attendant from the train of heaven
> Came for him; or else the underworld
> Opened in love the unlit door of earth.
> For he was taken without lamentation,
> Illness or suffering; indeed his end
> Was wonderful if mortal's ever was.

The chorus ends the play simply:

> Now let the weeping cease;
> Let no one mourn again.
> These things are in the hands of God.

Thus the end of the man who had killed his father, married his mother, torn out his eyes, cursed his sons, the man who—in an earlier play—had asked to be led from Thebes with the cry:

> . . . Lead the great wreck
> And hell of Oedipus, whom the gods hate.

A happy ending for Oedipus, stained by the "last evil that can be known to men: no tongue can say how evil"? Yes, a sanctified ending. But perhaps the *Colonus*, written at the end of Sophocles' life and produced after his death, represents a mellowing not only of the man but of the tragic form proper, a gentle falling-away of the power to face life starkly. I do not think that anyone who reads the play will raise this question; there is too much naked power in it, and the power is most overwhelming at the point of Oedipus' transfiguration. But it is a useful question, because it leads us back to another one: How hopelessly does the *Tyrannus* end?

I have had a peculiar experience with this play. I have seen a production in which the arrogance and the anger of Oedipus, together with his real dignity and his genuine determination to rid Thebes of its mysterious guilt, were vividly drawn. The pressure of his successive discoveries built fiercely. We were ready for his great cry and for his shattered flight into the palace. After the choral lamentation, he returned. But he was precisely as arrogant, with the blood streaming from his eyes, as he had been before. Where he had been angry with men, angry enough to accuse Creon of treachery and to strike the prophet Tiresias, he was now angry with the gods. Not Creon, not Tiresias, but the gods themselves had done this wholly unjust, unmerited thing to him, and he played out his leave-taking with bitter contempt for the heavens in his voice. The performance lost nothing in intensity. But it had suddenly become meaningless. Everything had changed for this man; and nothing had changed in him. We sensed, on the instant, a cipher, a vessel that could not be filled with new knowledge or affected by it. Why had he endured all of this, and why had we, to no purpose? The sacrifice had been made. And it had accomplished nothing.

What were we looking for, what silent expectation had not been fulfilled? At the simplest level, we had expected a change—a change of some sort, even for the worse perhaps, though it is doubtful that any tragedy has saved the worst for the last. We wanted to know how knowledge had altered Oedipus. And we expected, I think—even without close attention to the lines of the play—to see Oedipus cleansed in at least one strict and limited sense: cleansed of his ignorance. That limited cleansing would, in addition, most probably have provoked another: a man confronted with his own ignorance would very likely be cleansed of his arrogance.

And a man rid of both his ignorance and his arrogance, blinded though he be, would in some measure be a better man. No one would call him more fortunate, and no one ever has. But he would be better to just the degree that his mind and heart corresponded to the truth of things. If a man is not innocent he is better for knowing himself not innocent. If a man is not informed, he is better for knowing himself not informed. He may have gone through the fires of hell; but the fires have illuminated the world for him. However desolate his situation, a man is richer for truth. And with all of his regrets, with the pain still upon him, he knows he is richer. Illumination is what man seeks above all.

That some change has taken place in Oedipus is of course borne out by the text, and the actor was wrong. It could not be the change of the *Colonus;* not in these few minutes. And the change in the *Colonus* is in any case a redeeming gift of the gods. But Oedipus is no sooner out of the palace, in the text of the *Tyrannus,* than he is reaching out a hand to a "friend," the leader of the chorus; the chorus were formerly subjects. He asks for patience, and he says that "this punishment that I have laid upon myself is just." He cannot conceal his anguish and makes no attempt to; but he is swiftly humble before Creon, "whom I have deeply wronged." On Creon, as on his children, he asks the gods' blessing, and then he begs to be expelled from the city. He begins to speak of death but there is a hesitation upon his tongue:

> And yet I know
> Death will not ever come to me through sickness
> Or in any natural way: I have been preserved
> For some unthinkable fate. But let that be.

Yeats translates this alternately as:

I know that nothing can destroy me, for I wait some incredible fate.

It would be too much to suppose that Sophocles was here opening the door to the transfiguration of the *Colonus* as he would conceive it so many years later, though the root Oedipus legend, known to his audience, must already have supplied a suggestion of ultimate sanctity. The *Tyrannus* does not end in transfiguration or anything like it. But it does end in a beginning, a partial, purification. One man in Oedipus has died; another is being born. The eternal sacrifice continues to serve its gratifying purpose.

Jones would expand "our experience . . . of something decisively accomplished" in this play to embrace more than the newly awakened Oedipus:

His task is to find out what has angered heaven to the point of visiting Thebes with pestilence, and then to make amends; and this task he successfully performs. This last point (which has been almost totally ignored) is very relevant to the final sense of accomplishment. Thebes is put right with her gods, and the religious institutions of oracle and prophecy are vindicated.

I have not gone so far as to call the ending of *Oedipus Tyrranus* happy; that would fly too much in the face of our habits of thought and our casual, really unconsidered concept of happiness. What *is* a happy ending? Sophocles' *Electra* pursues, as a single play, the same bloody course of action that occupies the second play of Aeschylus' trilogy. Orestes returns to destroy his mother and her paramour for having murdered his father. He makes himself known to his sister, Electra, who has lived in shame and shadow the whole time and who is now at such a pitch of despair that she may take up the sword herself. Her discovery that her brother is alive and present is a joyous one; there is in the joy a promise of savagery to come, but the joy itself is very great. Orestes now makes plans to kill Clytemnestra first and then Aegisthus; it is a piece of "good luck" that the chorus approves and is willing to cooperate. The devious plan works perfectly.

Clytemnestra and Aegisthus are both slain. Orestes has achieved his purpose. A choral song ends the play:

"O house of Atreus, through how many sufferings hast thou come forth at last in freedom, crowned with good by this day's enterprise!"

There are no Furies here to hound the man who has killed his mother. Orestes does not consider himself hopelessly unclean, the chorus does not shudder at the prospect of an unbreakable chain of terror stretching into an unknowable future. Sophocles does not require another play—as Aeschylus had done—to bring the house of Atreus to rest and peace. Apparently the purification is accomplished. Because we are so familiar with the story as it appears in the second part of Aeschylus' trilogy, we tend to assume that Orestes cannot go scot free after his "crime," and we may be a bit bewildered that Sophocles should cut off the narrative on an assertion of triumph. The fact is that he does so. In this single play the "sympathetic" characters are wholly successful in their action, the guilty are properly punished, peace is restored to the community and the community is at once exultant. The outcome of the play is approximately the outcome we should expect of a good-guy, bad-guy, law-and-order Western. There is blood in the play, and we are horrified by it; but it is difficult to see how any ending could be more satisfying to the virtuous parties concerned.

Karl Jaspers, defending the position that the Christian promise of salvation stands in direct opposition to the unredeemed, unredeemable fatality of the Greek tragic vision, says that "the chance of being saved destroys the tragic sense of being trapped without chance of escape."

But Medea escapes rather too spectacularly. Having made a torch of Jason's intended bride, and having butchered the children she herself has had by him, this earth-demon is sent a chariot from heaven to accommodate her flight from human retribution and her mysterious—to us somewhat baffling —ascension:

> And the end men looked for cometh not,
> And a path is there where no man thought:
> So hath it fallen here.

In another play a sister discovers that, by divine decree, she must murder her brother in sacrifice. The sister and brother think out a means of escape and run to safety. That is Euripides' *Iphigenia in Tauris.* The same playwright's *Iphigenia in Aulis* ends with the heroine's immolation. But she chooses her immolation, which she might have avoided, as an act of public duty that will surely be blessed by the gods. This last play, which is a late one with emendations most likely contributed by Euripides' son, contains a passage that may or may not have concluded the original text. Its very existence, however, is most provocative for the link it makes with the religious rite out of which tragedy is thought to have sprung. Iphigenia is led away to the sacrificial altar. A messenger returns to describe her death:

> . . . And the priest prayed,
> Lifting the knife and gazing at her neck
> To see where he should strike. Then my heart failed me,
> I dropped my eyes, when lo, a sudden wonder!
> All might have heard the thud, but no man saw
> Where the maid vanished. Calchas cried aloud
> And all the army, marking a miracle,
> Unhoped-for, not to be believed, though seen.
> A panting hind lay in the victim's place,
> Most beautiful, and deer's blood stained the altar.

At the moment of sacrifice the animal victim and the human victim have become interchangeable, representing one another. Iphigenia's body becomes the hind's, in the play, as the hind's body has become Iphigenia's during the flowering of tragedy from its root. The source of tragedy and the later shape of tragedy seem to flicker across one another in a double image here, reminding and realizing at the same instant.

The purpose of the sacrifice remains the same: a burning-away of old life that a new may begin. It is through a reduction to ashes that an ascension to glory comes about:

> . . . She has risen
> Straight to the gods. So shall you lay aside
> Your grief and all your anger . . .
> The ways of the gods no mortal can foresee:
> They save the souls they love. And this one day
> Has known your daughter's death, your daughter's life.

We are not listening to a medieval miracle play; we are listening to a fragment of what was intended as Greek tragedy.

I shall not bother to list all of the Greek tragic endings that may be described as being in one way or another "happy." Nor do I wish to pretend that the plays mentioned here constitute the whole of Greek tragedy. They do constitute, however, so significant and varied a part of it that no understanding which fails to take them into account can possibly be considered adequate.

In each of them there is a central passage of suffering followed by a final assertion of triumph. The triumph may be blunt, swift, and virtually inexplicable, as in *Medea*. It may be a steady, "plotty" progression toward a good-over-evil climax, as in Sophocles' *Electra*. It may be melodramatically miraculous as in the *Iphigenia in Aulis* or it may blaze with the mystical dignity that seems to consume Oedipus at Colonus. However the note is struck, the reverberations it gives off are essentially, and often joyfully, transcendent. The victory is more than might have been hoped for.

That the sense of accomplishment which Mr. Jones insists upon in Greek tragedy has affixed itself to later tragedy, and certainly to Shakespearean tragedy, is so obvious to us that we are inclined to be flippant about it, impatient with it. We like to dismiss it as a bland convention. "Whatever became of that stalwart bore Fortinbras? Who eventually fixed *his* wagon?" asks one of J. D. Salinger's characters, dead certain that the healing at the end of *Hamlet* is so much lip service paid to a regulation piety.

We sometimes feel that Shakespeare himself must have been impatient with the "uplift" ending required of him. It is rather too bad, practically speaking, that an actor must be hired to pronounce so few words as the elevating Fortinbras is given. The coda of a Shakespearean tragedy, we may very well think, is often too easy, too pat, too dependent upon the soothing power of verse as verse, too literally a grace note appended to a vision essentially dour.

And there are perfectly good reasons why Shakespeare's "flights of angels" tags might have been written cursorily. Shakespeare was a long way away from his source in ritual: several thousands of years away from Greek sources he didn't know, four or five hundred years away from the medieval metamorphosis. The influence most directly exerted upon him was that of the Italian Renaissance, with its fondness for the Senecan blood bath, for Senecan stoicism in the face of disaster, for endings of some dignity but undisguised hopelessness. He had before him, ironically, an example of Christian tragedy more bleak in its implications than anything the Greeks could have devised: Marlowe's *Doctor Faustus*. Faustus is a Christian whose soul can be eternally damned, a prospect not precisely envisioned in Greek tragedy. As a Christian, he knows Christ's promise that repentance will earn him salvation; he begs the hours stand still "that Faustus may repent and save his soul." But the hours do not stand still and in their scurry he is left gasping, trying to repent but unable to feel that he has succeeded:

> O, I'll leap up to my God! Who pulls me down?
> See, see where Christ's blood streams in the firmament!
> One drop would save my soul—half a drop: ah, my Christ!
> . . . 'Tis gone. . . .

Faustus cannot catch hold of the mercy that has been promised him, possibly because his pact with Mephistopheles must be construed as an eternal pact to begin with, perhaps because the play is a Christian tragedy written by an atheist. This last combination, if combination it be, has surely produced the ultimate trap: damnation is possible but salvation is not. Shakespeare cannot have begun to write tragedy blandly assuming that the Christian promise of salvation had taken the teeth out of tragedy. He knew its teeth, and his own temperament may have made him especially sensitive to any drift in the world toward "inhumanity and destruction." The author of *King Lear* was no polite salvationmonger, and it should have been relatively easy for him to dispense with Fortinbras if he had wanted to.

The important matter, however, is not simply that Fortinbras is there, that at the end of *Macbeth* Malcolm should be saying "thanks to all at once and to each one," that a Capulet should at last be asking "O Brother Montague, give me thy hand," that Octavius should conclude the action we have followed with "let's away to part the glories of this happy day." If this were all, it would be cursory indeed.

What should be attended to more carefully is not the coda but the entire last movement of the play. Hamlet is one man for four acts. In the fifth he is another. Suddenly he is aware of a special providence in the fall of a sparrow. He has ceased being overwrought and has begun to sense that "the readiness is all." Readiness for what? For an essential role he is about to play, a role that is required of him and that is in some way ennobling. His dissatisfactions with himself drop away. With others he is newly courteous and forgiving. He moves to the duel, to the sacrifice of himself he is now honorably prepared to make, if need be. There is need, it seems, of the sacrifice, and he is mortally wounded. Dying, he is not bitter but, having forgiven Laertes, he begs Horatio to report his cause aright "to the unsatisfied." Why "aright," unless there was a right in it? Horatio is not to say that Denmark is rotten or that Hamlet was insanely slain. He is to give satisfaction, describe a rectitude of some sort. Good is to come of the

necessary journey through foulness. The whole last movement of the play, for all its violence, has been steeped in
reconciliation, a reconciliation which Hamlet's spirit has
intuited, sought, realized. We are not shocked to hear flights
of angels summoned for him.

The same long last swell is to be found in *Lear* as well, that
unlikeliest of places. I suppose no play ever written has
looked more directly into the eye of wantonness, has cried
out so passionately against the gods for killing men in sport.
Nor would I wish to make much of the goodness of Edgar,
the discovery of Gloucester that there is love in the world, the
fidelity of Kent. The great transformation is in Lear, mad.
The play is a torrent of madness, so much so that it seems
constantly on the verge of surrendering itself in willing
despair to the storm of unreason it has set loose; one madness
begets another until nearly all are drowned. The play's frame
of reference is unreason; whatever is to be done must be done
within it. Within it, Lear becomes the gentle and humble
man he had never been. It is in his madness that Lear is
transfigured; we would undo his buttons for him at the
sacrificial altar. We last hear him asking that other men look
with love upon the lips of the daughter he has wronged.

Shakespearean tragedy does not end in an abrupt, conventional, somewhat specious announcement that "All friends
shall taste the wages of their virtue, and all foes the cup of
their deservings." The announcement is invariably there, but
there has been a gathering of readiness, a ripening toward it,
for some time before. Prior to the ripening, no horror has
been kept from us; by far the greater part of the play is given
over to savagery and suffering. At the time of the ripening no
real miracles are worked. The groping toward reconciliation
has been subtle, one mysterious strand gradually making its
way through an almighty tangle; it has not been dwelt upon,
given a private room of its own. Strictly speaking, and most
paradoxically considering our habits of thought, there are
more miracles and more explicit transfigurations in Greek

tragedy than there are in Christian. Still, unmistakably, the strand of healing is there.

I have not proposed that there are no tragedies, Greek or Christian, that end bleakly. *Faustus* does end bleakly, though we are puzzled to say why it should. I would have a hard time trying to wash away for you the taste of despair that clings to the long falling movement of the *Antigone,* no matter how enlightened and repentant a man Creon is in process of becoming. Could anyone hold that *The Trojan Women* has the least trace of hope in it? I don't think so.

But *The Trojan Women* may suggest something to us. Let us waive the notion that Euripides' record of unadulterated sorrow is an exception to all rules, the notion that it is pure dirge, pure lyric lament; let us agree that it is some kind of play. Certainly, when it is well produced, it asserts itself as a play in the theater. Seeing it, we seek no excuses for it. Furthermore, its effect cannot be described as other than tragic.

What is the play about? It is not about Troy. Troy is already in ruins, Troy is done with. It is not about the heroes, tragic or otherwise, of Troy. They are all dead; only a child remains to be slain. The play is, of course, about the women who have survived both the city and its heroes. But it is about their survival.

I do not mean to hint that their survival is in any way happy. They do not regard it so, neither do we. The special emphasis of the play is upon the intolerable horror of continuing to live, of having to begin a new life when everything one has loved is in ashes. There is no choice here, no willingness to begin a new life. The disposition of the women will simply be made by the Greeks. It is made. Hecuba will be taken away by Odysseus. Cassandra is to become Agamemnon's concubine and will return with him to Mycenae. Achilles' son has claimed Andromache. Helen, not a woman of Troy but the cause of its fall, will be dealt with—harshly or weakly as the case may be—by her husband, Menelaus. Her fate is postponed until they shall have reached home again.

That is to say, for each of these women the possible action of the play is only beginning. This is not the end of them as it is the end of Troy. It is the first terrifying step out of the holocaust, and a step they would rather not have lived to take. But they must take it; that is what is happening in the play. Their very suffering depends upon the fact that they live and are being forced into motion. Life is not over. The play stands at the threshold of a dreaded new life.

It is, I think, a play of the threshold, of the introduction to the sacrifice. Until now these women have not been embroiled in the sacrifice; their husbands and sons and lovers have been enduring that. Now it is their turn to move to the altar and the knife, but the movement is far from complete. The sacrifice demanded of them will come nearer its peak as they arrive, slaves and concubines, in other houses. True immolation lies ahead. Within the confines of the play, we do not know what will become of them: how they will deal, how they will endure, how they will end.

Outside the play, with Greek legend as our guide, there are strange and contradictory hints. Cassandra quickly became a sacrifice to Clytemnestra's pride and jealousy, as we know; prophetess though she was, it would be difficult to see glory in her death. Andromache was loved by several men and bore them children; after a long life, she vanishes without definition, tragic or otherwise. Hecuba succeeded in avenging herself on her captors; thereafter she was transformed into an animal and escaped them. Helen lived happily with Menelaus and in one variation of her legend was, at the command of Zeus, carried off to Olympus on a cloud. After the time of sacrifice, the destinies of these women vary; almost any ending—of wanton slaughter or special sanctity—is possible. A shrine was erected to Helen.

I have stepped outside the play briefly for one reason only: to suggest what may have been in the minds of Greek audiences as they watched the initiatory movement of this play.

Within the play—and plays are best judged by staying entirely inside the boundaries so deliberately established by their authors—there is nothing but actual and anticipated agony. I would like to suggest that this is the case because Euripides has chosen a moment in time corresponding to the beginning of the *agon,* the onset of suffering, and confined himself to it. Because he has confined himself to it, we may say that the play has no ending, happy or unhappy, tragic or otherwise. It opens a door rather than closes one. It is not aftermath, which would indeed make it a mere dirge; it is the step into the furnace, with an outcome no man can foresee. In this light I would call the play a tragedy which is as yet too far from its ultimate resolution to know or say what its ending should be.

I think we must allow for the possibility of a genuinely tragic play which centers itself so tightly upon a single stage of the tragic movement that it cannot be held responsible for the full development, or even any development, of an earlier or later stage. Just as we have seen the *Oedipus at Colonus* devoting itself principally to the final stage, the stage of transfiguration, so I think we may see *The Trojan Women* devoting itself utterly to an early time in the agony. I do not think such intensity of focus need disqualify a play as a play, nor a tragedy as a tragedy. Neither do I think we are entitled to infer a happy ending for the Trojan women from the fact that the play limits itself so fiercely to a moment so far removed from any promise of spring. I think that we are obliged to say, simply, that the play refuses an ending. If *The Trojan Women* is one of the most despairing plays we know, it is also one of the least conclusive. Not one of its principals dies; not one even begins to see an end—of any kind—to her suffering. Euripides chose to write a play of dawn, black dawn.

The Greeks, by the way, did not know quite what to make of such an "unhappy ending." The presumption that the tragic cycle was meant to end on a note of benediction seems to have been so widespread that Aristotle was forced to take special pains to clear Euripides of the charge of having violated tragic form. We find the philosopher in the—to us—most peculiar position of fighting to make room, in tragedy, for the unhappy rather than the happy outcome.

"The critics," Aristotle argues, "are wrong who blame Euripides for taking this line in his tragedies, and giving many of them an unhappy ending. It is, as we have said, the right line to take. The best proof is this: on the stage, and in the public performances, such plays, properly worked out, are seen to be the most truly tragic; and Euripides, even if his execution be faulty in every other point, is seen to be nevertheless the most tragic certainly of the dramatists."

Because we cannot be certain how complete the text of the *Poetics* is, or even whether it has come directly from Aristotle's own hand, we are hesitant to say precisely what we think is meant here by "most tragic." There is some suspicion that the phrase simply means "most pathetic" in performance, most productive of tears. Nor does Aristotle's defense of the wholly sorrowful outcome constitute his only, or final, word on the subject. Later in the text he discusses the various kinds of plot incident that "strike one as horrible, or rather as piteous." Having rejected certain types of incident as essentially untragic, he moves on to those he thinks better. "But the best of all," he tells us, "is the last; what we have in *Cresphontes*, for example, where Merope, on the point of slaying her son, recognizes him in time; in *Iphigenia*, where sister and brother are in a like position; and in *Helle*, where the son recognizes his mother, when on the point of giving her up to her enemy." If he was willing to defend the unhappy ending, he seems not to have been willing to surrender certain preeminent virtues in happy ones.

"Aristotle's address to the question of happy and unhappy resolution," Jones concludes, "is utterly casual, and also self-contradictory. Once he says unhappy resolutions are preferable, once he says the opposite; he does not pause over the problem, or show himself at all concerned."

What are we to make of this apparent contradiction? Basically, I think, that one kind of ending—the happy ending —had been accepted as standard, that Aristotle continued to regard it highly in a number of instances, but that a new effort of understanding was required to account for another— though equally tragic—kind of play.

I would like to make a proposal here: that whenever the action of a tragedy is pressed forward to span its full possible length, whenever it works its way to an irreversible resolution, whenever it insists upon an absolute ending, its ending will be reconciliatory. Such plays as we have which see the matter wholly through, which force themselves beyond the mere experience of pain to the actuality of immolation —the *Oresteia,* the *Oedipus at Colonus,* the *Iphigenia in Aulis* —are plays of cleansing or transfiguration.

The tragic action, however, may be curtailed at will by the playwright, depending upon the segment of its arc he most wishes to display. As Kitto has said, with a pleasant trace of exasperation, " 'Tragedy' does not exist, except as an abstraction. Only *plays* exist, and the origin of these is the minds that make them." The minds that make "tragedy" do not always care to account for every last implication—or the very last implication—that may be read into the tragic span. There is no reason why they should be made to do so. The choice of field, of weapons, of the time, is theirs. It is up to us to understand that one third of a tragic movement is just as tragic as any other third.

Understanding this, accepting the proposition that a play may choose to complete itself before its tragic action has done so, we are still likely to listen for—and almost always to hear— the distant reverberation of the end that might have come. No matter how deeply tragedy plunges us into the world of doubt, Louis L. Martz insists, "it always seems to contain at least the Ghost of an affirmation." A happy ending, *some* happy ending, lies in wait, heard as a whisper.

I do not want to surmise too much. Let us say that, if we are forced to abandon our long-standing habit of thought which presupposes tragedy to be the theater's handmaiden of doom, we are still left with two choices. We are free to hold that the ending of tragedy is optional: it may be happy or unhappy. Or we may, if we wish, take a bolder step forward, not in total certainty but knowing that a difficult path to safety has existed and no doubt continues to exist. We may hold, on considerable evidence, that whenever the tragic action is disclosed to us in its fullness, we are likely to share the experience Nietzsche envisioned for the spectator: "he will have shuddered at the sufferings about to befall the hero and yet divined in them a higher, overmastering joy."

4

THE COMIC ENDING

B<small>UT</small> isn't joy the province of comedy? Not precisely; certainly not at bedtime.

We are accustomed to calling the endings of comedies happy endings, but that is simply a polite convention we have agreed upon. A moment's closer inspection would show us—perhaps to our astonishment—that the cheerful doling-out of futures which takes place at the conclusion of most comedies is not in any secure sense "happy." Rather, it is sublimely arbitrary.

Let us put to one side, for the moment, those comedies which have explicitly unhappy endings; they are true exceptions. *The Misanthrope*, in which a man who cannot abide ordinary social hypocrisy—above all in the woman he loves—turns his back upon society and the woman he loves to go his proud, cursing, solitary way into the uncorrupted desert, is a true exception. There is nothing else in comedy exactly like it. I would also except here that occasional comedy which puts off until tomorrow the worry of making up its mind. At the end of *Love's Labour's Lost* everyone decides to do nothing until he has taken a year to think matters through. That is a strangely attractive ending for *Love's Labour's Lost*, but it is not a characteristic solution for a comedy.

The characteristic solution for a comedy is for the playwright to clap hands and pack everyone off to bed, willy-nilly,

with or without love. It is as though a ringmaster, having
entertained us with his circus and knowing perfectly well
that a circus stops by the clock rather than by the exhaustion
of its possibilities, had assigned his animals cages, two by two,
much in the manner of Noah. Or as though the master of
ceremonies had taken a quick look at the collapsing revels
and had called out: "*You* take so-and-so, and *you* take so-and-
so (whom you may not have met—let me introduce you this
minute) and for heaven's sake pretend that you are going to
live happily ever after, *please* do." The happy endings of
comedy are no more than mere pretenses. Or rather they *are*
more. They are frauds.

Are we agreed that *Twelfth Night* is a representative, or at
least not untypical, comedy? In *Twelfth Night* Viola loves
the duke, whom she serves as a page boy. The duke, moon-
struck by the poetry of his own passion, madly loves Olivia.
Olivia, however, promptly falls in love with Viola, the page
boy and emissary sent to her. Each angle of a triangle adores
the one beyond it in a perpetual progression which prohibits
so much as a backward glance. A "happy" ending for these
three? Neither love nor logic could arrive at that. Who shall
be satisfied? Naturally we should like them all satisfied,
because we like them all. But here is what happens:

Olivia marries a total stranger, thinking him Viola. The
duke, now deprived of the Olivia who has inflamed his every
waking moment and no doubt his dreams, is informed that,
miserable though he be, *somebody* loves him. Viola, his page
boy, loves him. He turns to her—one can imagine the expression on his face—and finally speaks:

> . . . Give me thy hand;
> And let me see thee in thy woman's weeds.

It is assumed that once he has inspected the merchandise
he will accept it. The duke's two lines may not constitute the

curtest proposal ever offered a woman; surely they constitute the most resigned.

Viola, of course, does get the man she loves. One wishes her luck.

Resignation is the lot of many a "happy" clown. In *The Rivals* Bob Acres, Sir Lucius O'Trigger, and Mrs. Malaprop are all disappointed. Lydia Languish agrees to a compromise because she is assured that the man she thought she detested wasn't the man she thought she detested; he had only pretended to be, because of something rather detestable in her. And poor, dear Julia! Having forgiven Faulkland with a patience rare in saints, only to have him strike one last time like a scorpion that can never be housebroken, she comes to the eminently sensible conclusion that both the man and the cause are hopeless. But no. "There, marry him directly," she is instructed at curtain-fall, "you'll find he'll mend surprisingly!" Undoubtedly she does marry him. Poor, dear Julia.

Measure for Measure makes no bones about the matter. To begin with, it has an actual ringmaster: a duke who pretends to leave his city and who thereafter slips into a friar's robes, the better to eavesdrop on Angelo's lustful pursuit of Isabella, to help pull the strings that will put Mariana into Angelo's bed in place of Isabella, and, when expedient, to hear the confessions of the principals. He discloses himself at the end of the play with a magician's flourish, and then proceeds to put the rabbits into such hats as he thinks proper.

"I beseech your Highness, do not marry me to a whore" one character begs. "Upon mine honour, thou shalt marry her" the duke replies in what is essentially a high-minded and even magnanimous speech, after which he turns his attention to those others who are waiting to hear their loves disposed of:

> She, Claudio, that you wronged, look you restore.
> Joy to you, Mariana! Love her, Angelo.

I have confessed her, and I know her virtue.
. . . Dear Isabel,
I have a motion much imports your good;
Whereto if you'll a willing ear incline,
What's mine is yours, and what is yours is mine.

In short, Angelo, who has wanted Isabella, must make do
with Mariana, and Isabella, who has only wanted to help
Claudio, may help herself to the duke, if she cares to. Everybody gets what the duke wants.

Measure for Measure is a so-called "dark comedy" and may
be thought more cynical in the disposition of its available
hearts than a true light comedy would be. *As You Like It* is a
light comedy. It ends with the entrance of a master of ceremonies, Hymen, the god of marriage. Hymen manages the
situation efficiently:

Peace ho! I bar confusion.
'Tis I must make conclusion
          Of these most strange events.
Here's eight that must take hands
To join in Hymen's bands,
          If truth holds true contents.
          (*To Orlando and Rosalind*)
You and you no cross shall part.
          (*To Oliver and Celia*)
You and you are heart in heart.
          (*To Phebe*)
You to his love must accord,
Or have a woman to your lord.
          (*To Touchstone and Audrey*)
You and you are sure together,
As the winter to foul weather.
Whiles a wedlock-hymn we sing,
Feed yourselves with questioning,
That reason wonder may diminish
How thus we met, and these things finish.

If any of the characters has any questions about how he or she came to this pass, contrary to intentions and expectations, perhaps a few moments' reflection will persuade him or her to go quietly to the love couch. Phebe, who is given to Silvius, had better stop insisting upon her passion for Ganymede, for Ganymede is Rosalind and Rosalind is a girl. Orlando may very well express joy at having recovered his Rosalind, though in point of fact he has spent the entire evening in her company without recognizing her. What, by the way, will Rosalind think of this fellow when she has an idle hour to brood upon such matters, remembering how intensely he loved her *in absentia* and how little in the greenwood? Touchstone, of course, will raise no such questions. He is already philosophical: "A poor virgin, sir, an ill-favoured thing, sir, but mine own; a poor humour of mine, sir, to take that that no man else will."

It is interesting how often substitutes are cheerfully accepted in comedy, even substitutes of the wrong sex. Comedy is full of boys getting girls who were boys. Sometimes the substitution is retroactive. Bertram, in *All's Well That Ends Well,* is finally willing to accept the Helena he has spent so much time avoiding because he has already been to bed with a substitute: Helena. Helena has slipped between his sheets at night when it was Diana he wanted and thought he had. Somehow two chagrins make a grin.

Substitution, compromise, resignation—of such stuff is our merriment made. When the circus is over, the performing bears must perforce go back into cages. It really does not much matter whose.

Emotional victories in comedy are even rarer than right matches. Who wins, Petruchio or Kate? Strictly speaking, a "happy" ending for the play should show us Petruchio utter master of the shrew he has bargained to tame: that has been his goal all along, that has been what the earlier Kate deserved, that is the successful resolution of the action proposed by the playwright. And, on the surface of things, that is how the play does end. Kate submits utterly in her long last speech, urging all women to "place your hands below your husband's foot" and insisting that "Thy husband is thy lord, thy life, thy keeper, thy head, thy sovereign."

But few people—whether critics, playgoers or actresses—have ever been able to tolerate this ending when taken at face value. The moment we try to conceive Petruchio as literally and forever triumphant, the moment we try to accept Kate as literally and forever subdued, we bridle. We don't really believe that Kate means what she says, any more than Lucentio does as he leaves shaking his head and murmuring " 'Tis a wonder, by your leave, she will be tamed so."

Few actresses have ever allowed us to believe Kate wholly sincere. The speech of submission is most often read with a sweetness that deliberately passeth understanding. By being so bland, the actress lets us know she is being sly. Some actresses have come right out with it and winked; but the wink has generally been derided as obvious and unnecessary. It is plain enough to all of us what Kate is up to, no matter how straightforwardly Shakespeare seems to have written the scene.

Worse, we tend to turn against Petruchio altogether whenever we try to accept his victory as total and actual. Suddenly we see him as a boor. Petruchio "achieves only a false victory," H. B. Charlton cries out as he attempts to accept the ending of The Shrew as an uncontested happy ending for the man who is its hero. "He triumphs because he denies love. But his denial is simply a mark of his own limitation."

Mr. Charlton can scarcely contain his contempt for Petruchio regarded as victor. As it happens, most of us like the play's ending only so long as we think it an ambiguous one. Taken as a success story pure and simple, The Taming of the Shrew becomes distasteful, its conclusion sober and flat. Comedy creeps back into the ending only if Kate can bring it back. And Kate can bring it back only by casting doubt upon the outcome, only by hinting that Petruchio is not going to be quite so thoroughly "happy" as he supposes. Permitted to doubt, we smile again.

Now, it is not altogether proper to go prying into the possible or probable outcomes of the marriages comedy makes. The only true test of a play's ending must be made within the play: how many of the principals get what they want, how real or how artificial is the harmony imposed on the comic world at sunset? Comedies, like other plays, are meant to be self-contained; when the curtain falls, the issue is concluded, unless the playwright himself deliberately leaves us with insinuating, unanswered questions. And when unresolved matters do tantalize us—how much does Bassanio love Portia?—we are, after all, inclined to smirk knowingly and suppose that things will get themselves worked out somehow, more or less as they do in life. We shrug. The happiness to be got out of forced marriages, or arbitrarily contracted marriages, or the sighing acceptance of second-bests, may be a bit ambiguous. But let the bride be bright for the night, whoever takes her to bed.

Still, it is interesting that on one of the very few occasions when comedy itself has decided to go prying, it has come back with a discouraging report. Beaumarchais wrote two plays about the amorous Count Almaviva, his servant Figaro, and the girl Figaro helps him to get. In *The Barber of Seville* the Count is beside himself until he can possess his beloved; Figaro arranges matters. In *The Marriage of Figaro* the servant himself is now happily betrothed; the only thing that stands between him and his own bride is Count Almaviva, who has been decidedly unfaithful to the adorable girl he won earlier and who would now like to get his hands upon Figaro's. This, mind you, is not the aftermath of a mismatch; it is a blithe and casual comment on what has happened to true love. Once again a happy ending is managed: Figaro is free to claim his Suzanne because the Count is caught and embarrassed, whereupon he humbly and devotedly rejoins his wife. After two plays we may be forgiven the impolite question: forever after?

Indeed just before the curtain falls on the second play we are given a little reminder that the Countess has been doing some extracurricular daydreaming of her own. Can Beaumarchais have been planning a third play? No matter. If the charmed figures who now join hands and dance a few steps to proclaim the coming reign of happiness do not pause to leer at one another conspiratorially, we do. For we understand that the ending of a comedy, like everything else in it, is a joke.

It has been said that every comedy ends in a marriage, though "marriage" in this case signifies something more than the mere exchange of promises between two parties: it signifies a coming together of black and white and of wisdom and folly, a fusing of forces that have been playing tricks upon one another, a settlement, a subsiding, a silencing, which may mean gratification or may as readily mean a kind of death. There is very good reason why all comedies should end in marriages. Cornford long ago pointed out—persuasively, I think—that Aristophanic comedies generally end in arbitrary Sacred Marriages not because there is any logical or literary need for such marriages but because the form of comedy had derived from that portion of Greek ritual which sang "the hymeneal hymn" to fertility. As comedy found its footing, it kicked out at many things; but even as it took new and enlivening liberties, it continued to pay tribute—in its last few moments—to its ritual source.

The Aristophanic plots themselves, as Cornford says, "do not turn on the interests or fortunes of love. They are concerned with the rival merits of war and peace, the Athenian passion for serving on juries, the sex strike as a weapon in politics, the founding of a city in the air, the superiority of Aeschylus and the culture of his generation over the new culture of Euripides and the Sophists. No one, setting out to read a series of comedies dealing with social and literary themes of this sort and totally devoid of love-interest, would dream of expecting that nearly all of them would end with a *Komos*-procession and a marriage. There is in the nature and whole treatment of the subjects no reason whatever for such a termination."

Yet the Sacred Marriage and the *Komos* procession, which is an exuberantly phallic song and dance, are often there—as they are, say, at the end of *The Birds*. In *The Birds* a comic misanthropist who might in another century have been played by W. C. Fields succeeds in slapping away from him, as though they were so many gnats, the pompous, greedy, and obtuse fools who constitute the body of mankind on earth. He makes a pact with the birds of the air and establishes a walled-off kingdom of his own in the sky. Shortly new pests arrive to badger him: the gods, whose province the sky is. By cunningly playing on the weaknesses of the gods—all too human weaknesses—he bests them as well. "Divine Authority cedes the Sceptre," the delegate-god Poseidon admits. The action of the play might seem to be over. But:

Hold on! I nearly forgot.

Our clown-hero has had an afterthought.

The Birds are prepared to confirm Zeus' right to Hera,
but in return
they insist upon my having Basileia.

The victor has decided that he wants a goddess for his bride, though he has said nothing of wanting any bride before this. His request is of course granted, Basileia arrives to take his unfamiliar arm, and the procession begins as the chorus circles the pair, singing:

Eros flicked his golden wings
To be their charioteer,

> And through the swaying skies their car
> Darted in sweet career.
> *Round the royal pair we go:*
> *Hymen O! The wedding O!*

Any wedding will do so long as there *is* a wedding, that marriage which Cornford takes to be "the survival of one moment in a ritual action older than any form of comic literature." And it is the revel in celebration of this marriage —so often a forced marriage—that has apparently given us our word for comedy: *Komoìdia.*

"If Tragedy and Comedy are based on the same ritual outlines," Cornford concludes, "the Satyr-play at the end of the tetralogy must stand for the Sacred Marriage and its *Komos,* which form the finale of Comedy." But the point here, as it is very much Cornford's, is that the finale of comedy bears no organic relationship to the body of comedy. Historically regarded, it is an ancient echo, an obeisance. Practically regarded, it is an extraordinarily convenient device for cutting short an action that might have been improvised indefinitely and for swiftly imposing upon that action— at the very last moment—a boisterously "happy" atmosphere.

The inorganic and indeed slapdash structure of Aristophanes' comedies has bothered scholars for years upon end, and it is true that Aristophanic comedy tends to split into halves: in the first half a comic theme is established, and in the second half it is improvised upon almost at random.

That is not necessarily a bad way to construct a comedy; there may even be something in the nature of comedy that inclines toward roundabout improvisation rather than toward steady vertical progression. But we like things neater than that, and we have got them neater in much of our later comedy. Nevertheless, where the finale is concerned—that swiftly contrived, if not trumped-up, mating which enables us to part company for the evening with the sound of revelry in our ears—Aristophanes is not much more arbitrary or inorganic than Shakespeare. He may be less arbitrary than Molière, who devised a conclusion for *The Would-Be Gentleman* that has caused at least one translator, Morris Bishop, to give up cheerfully and close his text with a sassy note: *"As this has nothing to do with the previous action and characters, it is here omitted."*

Shakespeare smooths over his matchmaking and his final revels, rather; there is a gentleness in the apportioning and a balm in the verse that says in effect: what better solution? Molière treats his arbitrariness otherwise. He knows that it is there, he knows that nothing whatever can be done about it, and so he welcomes it with open arms for what it is.

Molière's endings have often caused students of the drama, and teachers of the drama, as much pain as Aristophanes'. One of two attitudes is normally taken toward them. Confronted with so many long-lost children restored to their parents, so many friends who have not met in twenty years meeting now, so many people who have been meeting daily without recognizing one another suddenly blinking twice and gasping "You!," so many secret documents so opportunely revealed, the man who would like all playwriting to be plausible simply throws up his hands in horror and decides that Molière was indeed a comic genius but that his genius did not extend to extricating his own people from his own plots.

The man who so loves Molière that he is unwilling to fault him in this way struggles harder. He proposes, as I have had teachers propose to me, that Molière's endings *are* plausible provided one is sufficiently immersed in the atmosphere of the period in which Molière wrote. Thus the ending of *Tartuffe* becomes a thoroughly reasonable one, in spite of the fact that the knot about the throats of the principals is tied so tightly that only a divination of the king, delivered by special messenger, can cut it. In this view, once it is understood that seventeenth-century France regarded the king as actually divine—or at least semidivine—and perfectly capable of arriving at right solutions for his subjects without bothering to interview them, the problem vanishes and the finale is appropriate, to the age if not to the play. I confess that even as a student I boggled over this answer. It was always possible that the common folk of seventeenth-century France regarded their king as divine in this sense, though I rather doubted it, but it seemed unlikely that Molière, so close to the king, could have counted on him for this sort of help. I thought Molière was pulling somebody's leg, if only Louis's.

But plausibility or implausibility has nothing to do with the matter. Molière did not write his endings to be believed in; he wrote them to let everyone go home. We may grant, for instance, that the arbitrary ending of *Tartuffe* is a curious one in that it may or may not be soberly spoken, in that it may be taken by the audience at face value or it may stir speculation about what the king might have said to Molière later when they were having a drink in private. We may take it in any light we like so long as we do remember how entirely arbitrary it is.

There is never any hint that any ending is possible until the very last phrase of Act Four. For four full acts Tartuffe has been gulling the credulous Orgon, dominating his household, lustfully advancing upon his wife, disinheriting his children. All of this activity has been essentially psychological; no mechanical structure has been building up inside it to insure Tartuffe's eventual overthrow. In fact, as things stand, there is no real possibility that Tartuffe can ever be overthrown or Orgon ever saved. Psychologically, Orgon is far too much of a muddlehead to contend successfully—even if his eyes should be opened—with the cunning confidence man who knows how to wrap him around his little finger. Those members of the family who have been able to see through Tartuffe have by this time been rendered impotent.

Then, at the end of Act Four, a vague hint of possible plot machinery is dropped, and dropped from the blue:

> "But one thing more is weighing on my mind."
> "What's that?"
> "I'll tell you; but first let's see if there's
> A certain strong-box in his room upstairs."

At this point playwriting purists perk up their ears in alarm. Is it conceivable that Molière is, in this appallingly obvious way and at this very late hour, finally planting a purely mechanical premise that will in some gratuitous way save Orgon? The purists shudder. Why they do not pause to think that if the author cared in the least about making his mechanics plausible he might with no trouble at all have smuggled this same piece of information into the comedy two acts earlier is one of the wonders of the critical world. Any journeyman, any hack, any amateur could do it—*if* he cared to. The obvious fact of the matter is that Molière, who possessed as much skill in plotting as any man who ever wrote comedy, is simply being cavalier.

As it happens, this hint is not particularly helpful, the mechanics that are now employed solve nothing, and in Act Five Tartuffe's victims are in a worse plight than ever. At last the moment comes to stop the nonsense and to patch the unpatchable. The king's delegate enters, a bolt from the purple:

> "Sir, all is well; rest easy, and be grateful.
> We serve a Prince to whom all sham is hateful,
> A Prince who sees into our inmost hearts,
> And can't be fooled by any trickster's arts.
> His royal soul, though generous and human,
> Views all things with discernment and acumen. . . .
> With one keen glance, the King perceived the whole
> Perverseness and corruption of his soul. . . .
> But to be brief: our sovereign was appalled
> By this man's treachery toward you, which he called
> The last, worst villainy of a vile career,
> And bade me follow the imposter here
> To see how gross his impudence could be,

> And force him to restore your property.
> Your private papers, by the King's command,
> I hereby seize and give into your hand.
> The King, by royal order, invalidates
> The deed which gave this rascal your estates. . . ."

and so on, into the rearranged night.

The situation has been hopeless. Without the intervention of a royal master of ceremonies it would have remained hopeless. Let the master of ceremonies come on and say whatever implausible thing is necessary. Molière is not bothered; that is how comedies end. Is the tone of the speech dignified, apparently serious? Apparently. To anyone who supposes that the endings of comedy must bear some deeply organic relationship to what has gone before, the ending of this one, as translator Richard Wilbur notes, "may seem both forced and flattering." There is even a sense in which the relatively sober tone of the speech in which Tartuffe is undone is justified by the *tone* of what has gone before. There is an unusually heavy undertow beneath such waves as dance in *Tartuffe:* the comedy is harsher than most, its title figure more villainously drawn than most. But however we take the ending—as gravely flattering, as perplexing, as agreeably devious—we still must take it as characteristically arbitrary. Molière always ended comedies by blowing a whistle.

Most often he did so more buoyantly. His general habit was to pack up the baggage of the evening with what might be called the magnetized ending—a flourish in which all of the confounded figures and all of the stray plot points are turned into so many iron filings which can, on the instant, be sucked toward a polarizing center with dizzying force. Such endings are, of course, preposterous. Molière knew that they were and, I think, loved them for it. *The Miser:*

ANSELME. . . . Learn to your confusion, that it is sixteen years at least since the man you speak of perished at sea with his wife and children . . .

VALÈRE. Yes; but learn, to your confusion, you, that his son, seven years of age, with a servant, was saved from the wreck by a Spanish vessel, and that this son, who was saved, is the person who speaks to you. . . .

ANSELME. But what other proofs . . . ?

VALÈRE. The Spanish captain; a ruby seal which belonged to my father; an agate bracelet which my mother had on her arm . . .

MARIANE. Alas! to your words I can answer, I, that you are not imposing, and all that you say shows me clearly that you are my brother.

VALÈRE. You, my sister!

MARIANE. Yes. My heart was touched the moment you opened your lips; and our mother, who will be overjoyed at seeing you, has thousands of times related to me the misfortunes of our family. Heaven also permitted us not to perish in this dreadful shipwreck; but our lives were saved only at the cost of our liberty; and they were pirates that picked us up, my mother and me, on a plank of our vessel. After ten years of slavery, a happy accident regained for us our freedom; and we returned to Naples, where we found all our property sold, without being able to gather any news of our father. . . .

ANSELME. O Heaven! how great is the evidence of thy power! . . . Embrace me, my children, and share your joys with those of your father.

VALÈRE. You are our father? . . .

ANSELME. Yes, my daughter, yes, my son; I am Don Thomas d'Alburci, whom Heaven saved from the waves, with all the money which he carried with him . . .

The embraces all round are marvelously mathematical, and the quick succession of passionate claspings is instantly capped by a new joke: now that everyone has been identified, the miser, Harpagon, knows just whom to sue for the re- covery of his lost money. Arbitrariness has been made into something very like a ballet.

The School for Wives is more complex still, in the same toy-magnet mood. Horace discovers that the friend to whom he has entrusted the girl he loves is in fact the enemy who has been trying to keep him from the girl he loves. At this same moment he discovers that the girl he has never wanted to marry is in fact the girl he wants to marry. And his enemy, still clutching at the girl he has reared as an orphan, discovers that he is talking to her father, just returned from a very long detour in the Indies. The characters' heads spin with their changing relationships, so swift is the turn of the fortune wheel; then the wheel stops, the world is righted by chance, the tangle dissolves as quickly as a street can be emptied in a speeded-up motion-picture film, and only the principal comedian is left defeated and alone.

What kind of endings are these? They are grinning endings, snap-of-the-finger endings, endings which seem to say in all candor: "No ending is possible, so let's make one up, shall we?" The very fun that is in them resides in the fact that they are patently not true. The moment one sees them played well in the theater one senses the gusto with which Molière approached them, the high heart and the wicked, bland smile with which he deployed all the artifices he was forced to make use of.

Molière was not a playwright who could not contrive an ending. He was a playwright who knew that in comedy all endings *must* be contrived. And so he went on to score his last point by making a point of the contrivance, no doubt while holding his sides. If anyone was happy at the ending of a Molière play, Molière was.

He spoke slyly of endings, in passing, when he took the trouble to fashion a playlet in answer to those who had dared criticize his *School for Wives:*

URANIE. . . . he doesn't care whether people criticize his plays, provided they come to see them.
DORANTE. Yes; but what ending could he find to it? For there can hardly be a marriage, or the discovery of a long-lost daughter. I don't know how one could finish off the dispute.

URANIE. We would have to think up some startling incident.
> (*Enter Galopin*)

GALOPIN. Madame, supper is on the table.

DORANTE. Why, that's just what we need for the denouement! We couldn't find anything more natural! We'll argue long and hotly, on both sides, as we have just done; and no one will give in. Then a little lackey will come to say supper is ready; we'll all stand up; and we will have supper.

URANIE. There couldn't be a better ending for a play. We will do well to stop right here.

Naturally, they stop right there. Comedy is not a form that reaches conclusions. It is a form that is interrupted—as a rule by something pleasant in itself, such as supper, or a rediscovered daughter, or a dance. The best comedy of all comes when the writer admits as much, when he refuses to strain for plausibility and dips instead into Oscar Wilde's hand-bag:

GWENDOLEN. This suspense is terrible. I hope it will last.
> (*Enter Jack with a handbag of black leather in his hand*)

JACK (*rushing over to Miss Prism*). Is this the hand-bag, Miss Prism? Examine it carefully before you speak. The happiness of more than one life depends on your answer.

MISS PRISM (*calmly*). It seems to be mine. Yes, here is the injury it received through the upsetting of a Gower Street omnibus in younger and happier days. Here is the stain on the lining caused by the explosion of a temperance beverage, an incident that occurred at Leamington. And here, on the lock, are my initials. I had forgotten that in an extravagant mood I had had them placed there. The bag is undoubtedly mine. I am delighted to have it so unexpectedly restored to me. It has been a great inconvenience being without it all these years.

JACK (*in a pathetic voice*). Miss Prism, more is restored to you than this hand-bag. I was the baby you placed in it.

MISS PRISM (*amazed*). You?

JACK (*embracing her*). Yes . . . mother!

MISS PRISM (*recoiling in indignant astonishment*). Mr. Worthing, I am unmarried!

JACK. Unmarried! I do not deny that is a serious blow. But after all, who has the right to cast a stone against one who has suffered? Cannot repentance wipe out an act of folly? Why should there be one law for men, and another for women? Mother, I forgive you. (*Tries to embrace her again.*)

MISS PRISM (*still more indignant*). Mr. Worthing, there is some error. (*Pointing to Lady Bracknell*) There is the lady who can tell you who you really are.

JACK (*after a pause*). Lady Bracknell, I hate to seem inquisitive, but would you kindly inform me who I am?

LADY BRACKNELL. I am afraid that the news I have to give you will not altogether please you. You are the son of my poor sister, Mrs. Moncrieff, and consequently Algernon's elder brother.

JACK. Algy's elder brother! Then I have a brother after all. I knew I had a brother! I always said I had a brother! . . . Algy, you young scoundrel, you will have to treat me with more respect in the future. You have never behaved to me like a brother in all your life.

It seems reasonable to assume that Molière would have enjoyed Wilde's ending. When Shakespeare is forced to contrive a quick conversion for one of the more villainous figures in *As You Like It*, he speaks most hastily of the repentance brought about by an "old religious man" whom we have never met, rather as though he wistfully hoped we might believe in it or at least would have the politeness to gloss over the matter. Molière is content that we shall disbelieve his happy endings; we are closer to the comic attitude when we do.

Happy endings on comedies are in a measure lies, a fact which becomes startlingly apparent to audiences whenever someone too solemnly pretends that they are not. I once attended a showing of the Louis Jouvet film version of Ben Jonson's *Volpone* after the film had been subjected to the scrutiny of the New York State board of censors. The censors had allowed the body of the film to remain reasonably intact; but, in the interests of public morality, they had appended to the final fade-out a subtitle which quickly recapitulated the fate of the principals: virtue had been rewarded and every last malefactor had been suitably punished. The audience with which I saw the film began to read the subtitle, gasped, and then broke into raucous laughter. Some of the laughter, no doubt, was due to an awareness of that censorial idiocy which had presumed to revise Ben Jonson's final thumb-to-nose. But perhaps not too much of it. The subtitle itself bore no indication that it had come from a censor's hand, it was professionally done, it might—for the majority of the audience, unaware of the situation—have belonged to the original film. But the laughter was universal. The comedy had established its own world of virtually unrelieved chicanery; a happy ending—a just ending—in such a world was unthinkable; the inherent contradiction of the afterword leaped from the screen with irresistible clarity. Scorn was all that could be granted it.

Comedies which do have happy endings—in the sense that the principal comedians achieve whatever it is they are after—are often exquisitely careful to avoid such scorn by anticipating it. When I was very much younger, so much younger that the comedians of silent films were my beloved mainstays, I often puzzled over an unvarying point of technique. The heroes of these feature-length comedies were bumblers, but successful bumblers: they did win the football games, however inadvertently, and they did rout the villains who were menacing the heroine or threatening the town. But they were never—*never*—permitted a triumphant fade-out, an ultimate glory.

Harold Lloyd might win the football game and then discover, by means of a note smuggled to him, that he had also won the girl. In his ecstasy he would lean against a shower faucet, drenching himself and his love letter. Fade-out and end of film. Buster Keaton might defeat an islandful of cannibals and then escape in a submarine, the girl clasped tightly in his arms. Having both arms so occupied he would lose his balance with the slight roll of the sea and tip against the submarine's control lever, sending himself, the girl, the crew, and every detachable object hurtling head over heels as the craft revolved in the water. The End. Harry Langdon might save the village minister and his blind daughter from the corrupting influence of big-city bootleggers, battering the local saloon to the ground with the help of a circus cannon. We would next see him married to the girl and established as the village policeman; as he carefully took the girl's arm to guide her along the sidewalk he would himself fall off the curb and land nose-down in the dust, waiting for the succor of the blind.

Chaplin's endings were, of course, more openly ambiguous than these, so much so that it became commonplace to speak of Chaplin's "unhappy endings"—though they were not quite that. At least twice in his career Chaplin completed a film with a so-called unhappy ending and then, for one reason or another, changed his mind, substituting a decisively happy ending. Both instances are instructive, for different reasons. In the case of a relatively early two-reeler, *The Vagabond,* the tramp figure had originally surrendered the Gypsy girl he loved to parents who had finally come to claim her; abandoned, he suicidally jumped into a lake which did not prove deep enough for his purposes. Perhaps the suicide motif proved too heavy a stroke for the texture of the short film as a whole. In any case, *The Vagabond* was finally shown with the girl and her parents returning for the tramp and whisking him into their fashionable automobile; when last seen he and the girl were staring raptly at each other as the car sped along. To this day the fade-out comes as a blow; we are left wondering what happened to the comedy. Because the film has an entirely happy ending, it seems not to have an ending or perhaps not to be a comedy; it is merely mysterious.

When, some years later, Chaplin decided that *The Gold Rush* had best end with the tramp winning the girl—though he had first planned a different ending—he was careful to insert a disclaimer. The last sequence of the film takes place on a ship from Alaska, bound for the United States. The tramp is now wealthy; but, being mistaken for a stowaway, he goes through a few familiar misadventures. Then he and the girl are reunited. Photographers are going to take a picture of the happy couple. As the photographers beg Chaplin to hold his pose, he slowly leans forward and kisses the girl. Immediately there is a subtitle: "Oh, you've spoiled the picture!"

The meaning is of course double. Literally, the photographers have cried out because he has not held his pose. Metaphorically, Chaplin is telling us that he knows what we know: ideally, the picture should not end in this way. The very fact that he tells us so cancels the effect of the ending; he has warned us that what he is doing is cheerful, but not true.

The "true" ending on a Chaplin film is not necessarily pathetic, though there is pathos in *The Circus* as we watch the circus train rumble away from the tramp, leaving him in the empty, burned-out circle where the tent once stood. The last image of *The Kid* is more typical. The child he has taken care of is finally restored to its mother: a door opens, the mother and child embrace. Then the mother makes a gesture suggesting that the tramp come into the house, too. For what? Tea? A reward? A permanent home? The door closes, and we never know.

The last image of *City Lights* is similar, though far more celebrated because it summarizes the Chaplin effect absolutely, too absolutely for some tastes.

The tramp has befriended a blind flower girl and fallen in love with her. Everything he has done in the film has been directed toward one end: finding the money that will pay for an operation to restore her sight. Now she can see again, and he comes toward her on the street. She has never before *seen* him. What will she think of him? She does not at first recognize him, of course. He cannot be certain whether or not he wants her to. He tips his shabby hat. In a close-up of the girl we become aware that, by touching his hand, she is gradually sensing the presence of the man she has known all along but whom she has imagined as handsome and a millionaire. In a counter-close-up of the tramp we see nothing but his enormous, expectant, fearful face. The film is over.

Plays of our own time are as careful to mar the negative of happiness, to make certain that it can never be printed as an undefaced positive, as films of the recent past or plays of the distant past have been. Perhaps the two best-known curtain lines of twentieth-century American comedy have been "Hey, Flagg! Wait for baby!" and "The son of a bitch stole my watch." In the first case, that of *What Price Glory?*, two men who have spent the evening quarreling over possession of a girl have decided to ditch the girl and stick together so that they can go on quarreling, which is what they really enjoy. In the case of *The Front Page,* an untrustworthy managing editor has only a few minutes earlier repented of his hardness of heart and generously let his star reporter leave town to get married. He has even given him a watch as a wedding present. At this moment, however, he is on the phone to the out-of-town police, charging the honeymooner with theft. The happy ending is rescinded, and it is the rescinding that is funny.

A happy ending must always be compromised. In *Arsenic and Old Lace* the hero, a drama critic, is unable to offer himself in marriage to the girl of his choice because it is extremely clear that there is insanity in his family. The difficulty is joyously resolved by the news that he is illegitimate. "I'm a bastard!" he cries exultantly, flinging himself into the heroine's arms. The laughter of the moment is made of many things, not least the remembered information that this fellow is a drama critic. But its most emphatic effect comes from the special double vision, the cross-eyed vision, of comedy: the hero's happiness depends upon his being socially unacceptable.

Compromise, resignation, doubt, frank disbelief on all

sides, the denial of dignity, the reminder that victory changes nothing and that the bumbler will go on bumbling—these are the indispensable ingredients of a comic "happy" ending. Without at least one of them, the ending will not be comic. To be comic, the ending must forcefully call into question the issues of "happiness" and "forever after." Comedy is not lyric, not rhapsodic, not reassuring; putting its last and best foot forward, it puts it squarely down in dung.

"And my ending is despair," Prospero says. Within comedy there is always despair, a despair of ever finding a right ending except by artifice and magic. Take away from the master of ceremonies his magical powers—his capacity for bringing about unreal solutions—and you have Prospero standing naked before his audience:

> Now my charms are all o'erthrown,
> And what strength I have's mine own,
> Which is most faint . . .

There is something about comedy that has no future.

5

THE TRAGIC GOOD

W<small>HY</small> should tragedy have more of a future than comedy? And why should comedy be happy enough without one?

As we look backward from the endings which conform so little to our casual expectations and into the struggle, the contest, the *agon* which occupies the center of each kind of play, we come upon a further curious circumstance. It is tragedy, not comedy, which sings the praises of man.

At the very heart of tragedy, with suffering at its most intense and with a shattering disclosure or even death lying in wait to put a capstone on all the pain, we are constantly hearing this:

> Numberless are the world's wonders, but none
> More wonderful than man; the stormgrey sea
> Yields to his prows, the huge crests bear him high;
> Earth, holy and inexhaustible, is graven
> With shining furrows where his plows have gone. . . .
> The lion on the hill, the wild horse windy-maned,
> Resign to him; and his blunt yoke has broken
> The sultry shoulders of the mountain bull.
> Words also, and thought as rapid as air,
> He fashions to his good use; statecraft is his,
> And his the skill that deflects the arrows of snow,
> The spears of winter rain . . .
> O clear intelligence, force beyond all measure!

That is the *Antigone* chorus singing. And it is in *Hamlet* that the hero, spying one corruption after another until the world seems wholly rotted, takes breath between anathemas to say:

What a piece of work is a man! how noble in reason! how infinite in faculties! in form and moving how express and admirable! in action how like an angel! in apprehension how like a god! the beauty of the world! the paragon of animals!

Tragedy never allows us to forget this vision. It is comedy, on the other hand, that speaks of the melancholy seven parts a man plays in his lifetime: mewling and puking infant, whining schoolboy, woeful lover, quarrelsome soldier, fat-bellied justice, piping ancient with shrunk shanks, and, as Jaques concludes:

> Last scene of all,
> That ends this strange eventful history,
> Is second childishness and mere oblivion,
> Sans teeth, sans eyes, sans taste, sans everything.

When comedy is at its most lyrical, as it is in Aristophanes, praise can be found, perhaps, for birds. But for man:

> Come now, let us consider the generations of Man,
> Compound of dust and clay, strengthless,
> Tentative, passing away as leaves in autumn
> Pass, shadows wingless, forlorn
> Phantoms deathbound, a dream.

Most of these lines and images are so familiar to us that we quite forget to notice that in each case they seem to appear in the wrong kind of play. But once we have made ourselves listen to them, and weighed them cumulatively, we cannot mistake the pattern: tragedy admires man, comedy feels sorry for him. We are somewhat startled to realize how regularly this is so.

Perhaps the bursts of rhapsodic praise which appear now and again between the accelerating throbs of pain in tragedy are no more than relieving grace notes, occasional unguents which are applied to make the next assault in a series bearable. Perhaps they are aesthetically motivated contrasts: black is blacker for a fissure of white. Perhaps they are designed to make the fall from grace greater: the nobler the toppling figure, the louder the crack of his breaking, Antony's death notwithstanding. Hamlet's apostrophe to the infinite capacities of man does occur in a speech composed mainly of maledictions; it is surrounded by a vision of this earth as a sterile promontory and a vision of man as the quintessence of dust.

But any serious examination of the full range of tragedy available to us must make it forcibly clear that the rhapsodic note is something more than craftsmanlike balm applied to an audience's nerves or craftsmanlike balance sought in the interests of aesthetic harmony. It is bolder than that, more pressing than that, more deeply imbedded than that. An assertion born with tragedy, it remains, forever after, the stuff of its bone.

The moment we turn from the strangely varied endings of tragedy to the central, fire-ringed area which the tragic figures enter and in which they are ravaged, we are face to face with two rich and desperate ambiguities. One of them is that we cannot be certain whether the figure entering the ring of fire is a man or a god. The other is that we cannot be certain whether the tragic act performed is a virtuous or an evil one, a right or a wrong one, a desirable or an undesirable one.

We dare not pretend that we can resolve these ambiguities easily. For instance, we are not free to say flatly that the tragic hero is a man and not a god; to do so, we should have to eliminate a great deal of Greek tragedy. Nor can we ever, with the celebrated tragic flaw in mind, say that the action carried forward is an undesirable or reprehensible action; to do so, not only should we have to eliminate some of the greatest of Greek plays but we should have to deny a complexity of motive and deed that persists in all tragedy.

One reason we are in such trouble with tragedy nowadays is that we are altogether too strict with it, stricter by far than the form as we have it permits us to be. Strictness comes naturally to us and in itself seems a virtue. We like to understand what impresses or tantalizes us, and understanding is best brought about by precision of thought. In the process of being precise, we reduce: we try to cut away whatever seems accidental or inessential or perhaps less than mature. We burrow for the typical, for the indispensable, for the fewest and clearest elements that can be said to make up tragedy. And we arrive at a formula.

We have help along the way. Aristotle said certain things about the form, and we fasten ourselves to those that can be made most explicit. Aristotle himself was not entirely explicit: we have seen that he was of several minds about tragic endings; he also showed a considerable flexibility in treating the character of the tragic hero and the character of his "error." Renaissance theorists, however, upon rediscovering Aristotle wished to make him more definite. They succeeded in making him more rigid—rigid about unities of time and place, rigid about endings, rigid about the flaw. Though they may not have been any nearer the essence of tragedy in their handling of the problems of the tragic ending and the tragic flaw than they were in their understanding of the unities, they were influential. Plays were written under the pressure of their findings; even Shakespeare's plays, free as they are, were written under an accumulating conceptual pressure. Tragedy was such-and-such; in part Shakespeare listened. The existence of new great plays written under such a pressure and out of such an understanding of course further hardened the concepts by seeming to validate them in their ever-increasing narrowness. We were arriving at a clean, finely detailed blueprint for a certain kind of play.

What kind of play? The kind—with *Oedipus* as its matrix,

certified by Aristotle, and with *Macbeth* as its easiest-to-grasp classroom illustration—in which a mortal man of some stature succumbs to a single powerful failing in his nature and is destroyed by it. Oedipus is accomplished, but Oedipus is proud; he lets his pride drive him to anger and rashness and he ends a blind outcast. Macbeth is accomplished, but Macbeth is ambitious; his ambition hurries him on to a justly ignominious death. I confess that as a young teacher I began my classroom lectures with just such a definition. As I glance at textbooks today, I see that this image of tragedy remains the standard academic image.

The perils of approaching tragedy with a format already laid out—a format that is partly inherited but may be newly narrowed by a desire to be more precise than the last man—should be obvious. First attention, and intense attention, is given to plays which are described as mature, fully representative, typical—to *Oedipus, Macbeth,* and *Othello,* no doubt—with the more puzzling plays reserved for discussion later on. Next an effort is made to move outward from the pinpointed center toward those somewhat disturbing examples of the form which may, with an imaginative stretching of the mind and just a bit of strain, be *made* to conform to the tight definition already offered. Scholars have put their lives and their labors to showing that *Romeo and Juliet* does accommodate itself to the traditional tragic pattern and that Romeo's flaw is "fury." A flaw has been found for Antigone, and I am not at all certain that it is not there; before it can be assigned her, though, there must be a thorough discrediting of all those commentators who have found her a saint.

When these strays have been rounded up, there is still work to be done. Invariably a number of plays remain which simply cannot be coaxed into submission to the formula at hand. Indeed some of them seem to defy any formula that has ever been projected as a working formula for tragedy. What is to be done with these? As a rule, nothing at all—except to deny them admission into the tragic canon. The play that does not conform to one's definition of tragedy is simply called not a tragedy.

Justifications can always be offered for the rejection of an intractible play. The *Prometheus Bound* chains its god-hero to a rock and leaves him there, immobile, for the duration of the narrative; the play is static. Among the figures who speak to him are Force, Violence, and Ocean; these are abstractions. Stasis and abstraction are marks of primitive dramatic work, aren't they? The *Prometheus* can safely be put to one side as a "primitive." It is a great work of its kind, yes. Aeschylus, it seems, could not do less than great work. But it is not work of the kind we are here concerned with. The principal figure in *The Suppliants* lacks a flaw and there is no providing him with one. Fortunately, *The Suppliants* may be the earliest of Aeschylus' extant plays, and its antagonist is not a person but a chorus of fifty women. Another "primitive."

Should the play be a late one, so late that its aberrations cannot be attributed to the birth pangs of drama, other explanations for its failure—as tragedy—can be advanced. Euripides was the last of the great Greek dramatists whose work we possess, and *The Bacchae* was very likely the last play he wrote. *The Bacchae* pits a vain, foolish, quite helpless mortal against an attractive god who first toys with him and then, in appallingly cold rectitude, destroys him. The god is the hero of the play, he is both benevolent and cruel, and he is not shown as having any definable weakness. The play defies us to understand it as we wish to understand *Oedipus* or *Othello*. It has, as a result, been dismissed variously as a satyr play, as an antireligious tract, as a cringing return to religious belief on the part of Euripides the exile, as a bold reaffirmation of religious belief on the part of Euripides the mystic, and as a text so corrupt, disorganized and baffling as to constitute no play at all, much less a tragedy.

The classroom is not alone in its practice of ruling out what it cannot trap in a baited definition. Critics are often willing to make surprising exclusions—or to maintain curious silences—as they set about erecting and defending tragic boundaries. If a critic holds that the ultimate experience of tragedy is an experience of the "unrelenting and absurd," he will probably not bother to discuss any apparently tragic plays in which the forces that have hounded the tragic victim do relent or in which an orderly and just accommodation of all interests is reached.

One man will draw up a list of "works which we cannot admit among tragedies," and the list will include Aeschylus' *Agamemnon*, Sophocles' *Electra* and *Oedipus at Colonus*, Euripides' *The Trojan Women* and *Andromache*. Another will tell us, with a most admirable directness, that "*Lear, Othello, Coriolanus, Julius Caesar, Timon of Athens* are inadequate tragedies, if we take that form seriously." In each of these cases the critic will acknowledge that a form called tragedy does, or did, exist, he will name the particular plays which accord with his definition of it, and he will accept the consequences of his definition by being candid about what he must reject. In making his rejections, he is generally careful to point out that he is not calling the abandoned plays bad ones. They remain good and interesting plays, to be placed in categories which may be called failed tragedies, or paratrage-dies, or perhaps metaplays. They are excluded only from the tragic heartland.

But the exclusions are too many to leave the heartland vitally populated. We may overlook the habit tight defini-tions have of canceling one another out: what is central for one man becomes peripheral for another, and *Lear* fluctuates from being the archetype here to being a third thumb there. What is truly troubling is that each effort at reducing tragedy to a straight and narrow line necessarily waves to one side, and helps to obscure from our view, anything curved. In many cases from one third to one half of the felt tragic canon is brushed away as technically untragic. In all cases one or another "masterpiece" is, however reluctantly, dismissed. Indeed it might quite safely be said that there is *no* tragedy which is not in some way curved, in some way sufficiently irregular to deviate from the straight line proposed for it. No one tragedy really fits to perfection any one definition of the form, not even a definition substantially derived from it; *every* tragedy has its puzzle, its inexplicable loose end: Iago is strangely motivated, Hamlet can be taken as resolute or irresolute or both, Oedipus has striven so hard to keep himself free from stain that it is scarcely just or plausible that he should stain himself so absolutely.

Something more might be suggested. It is possible that tragedy is not, in its nature, anything like a straight line, that its temper and thrust are altogether against narrowness, that it never can be plotted between two points on a graph. Tragedy may not be a quivering vertical; it may *not* be an arrow throbbing from the force of its flight but already, and permanently, imbedded in the fixed heart or earth it has struck. It may instead be fan-shaped, endlessly opening. The nature of tragedy may itself be open, constantly expanding, exploratory, evolutionary.

The suggestion is premature. For the moment we had best content ourselves with a question. If, in defining tragedy, we find ourselves forced to part with even one distinguished play which has for any length of time been considered a tragedy, do we dare think that we have succeeded in identifying tragedy? Or have we merely arrived at one man's ideal of the form, subject to swift challenge by another man's ideal? Do we dare be less open than the form actually is?

I would rather lose a definition than a tragedy. Put to it, I would rather attempt to construct a theory of tragedy by beginning with the outposts of tragedy—throwing a girdle wide enough to encompass the most difficult, the most bizarre, the most intractable of plays—than by striving mightily to drive a stake through its heart. I would rather circle the city walls, staring up at those watchtowers which face toward the desert—*The Bacchae, Prometheus, The Suppliants, King Lear*—than lay claim to knowing the city from an inspection of the shrine at its hub. I do not think we can say that we have described a form if we have admittedly failed to embrace it in all of its existential fullness.

For the moment, then, I prefer to suppose that any play written as a tragedy by a man known to be capable of writing tragedy and accepted as a tragedy in the rough-and-ready course of popular tradition *is* a tragedy. That is a loose statement, certainly; but it is perhaps no looser than the behavior of the form.

Facing the form, in its looseness, in its fullness, as it is, we are first forced to deal with its primary energies. Instead of looking for the weakness that may or may not defeat a tragic hero, we must look for the strength that makes him move. What is it that tragedy so admires about man? Why is it that tragedy is so often, and so surprisingly, willing to bestow upon man a happy ending? What powers are at work here?

Godlike powers are at work. Hamlet says it, but we are reluctant to take him literally. Does "godlike" have a meaning, except in a polite, perhaps overenthusiastic, poetic sense? For the Greeks, for tragedy sprung fresh from the root, calling a man a god was no mere metaphor. It was a statement about blood lines, about a claim of kinship that might be exercised at any time. And if we are, or were, dealing with something like a god in tragedy, we had best look at the matter hard. It may have consequences.

Nowadays we are often puzzled to find Greek tragedy shuttling so freely between plays that are about men and plays that are about gods. We exercise no such freedom ourselves, nor did we when our society was more conventionally religious than it is at this twentieth-century moment. Looking backward out of our own tradition, we find it most curious that any tragic dramatist should ever have exercised so easy an option. The Greek tragic dramatist might write a play centrally concerned with human beings, he might write a play centrally concerned with gods, and he might write a play mingling the two—if not as equals then as free contestants. Furthermore, the three kinds of play are all one kind of play; there is no sense of difficulty in moving from one to another, no sense that the playwright is having to force his hand because he is writing in an unnatural vein, no real sense of anachronism.

The most obvious explanation for this odd state of affairs lies in the rumored origins of drama. So far as we know the original tragic hero was a god. So far as we know the religious ritual which transformed itself into tragedy at the foot of an Athenian hillside began with a chorus of worshipers singing the praises of the god, dancing in honor of the god, narrating the deeds of the god. Then one unforeseen day a worshiper who may have been Thespis broke out of the choral grouping to speak for himself. His impulse may have compelled him to say something on the order of "I, Dionysus, bring you these gifts . . ." or "I, Dionysus, command you to dance. . . ."

This is coarse guesswork. Still, there is *The Bacchae* at hand, an extant play in which the god Dionysus is the central figure and in which he first appears as an ordinary mortal:

> And here I stand, a god incognito,
> disguised as man. . . .

Translator William Arrowsmith is willing to describe this play as "Euripides' re-enactment of a myth which doubtlessly embodied Dionysiac ritual." Mr. Kitto is not so certain that the origins of drama were necessarily Dionysiac; the impulse may have come from some other, or any other, choral honoring of a god. Nevertheless—and allowing for the fact that a developing ritual in honor of one god may easily have passed its developments along to a ritual honoring another—it is possible that we are here in the presence of an echo of that first vital moment of transformation in which an actor declared himself the god and in which the god, as a result, was forced to present himself as a man.

Thespis had said, in effect, "I *am* the god," and an inter-play of identities had begun. Tragedy seems to have begun, too, on these terms. Hereafter man would not be simply someone in the orchestra describing, in the third person, the qualities and achievements of the god. He would assume, in the first person, the god's person.

Why wasn't the act thought blasphemous, so blasphemous that it must immediately be suppressed? Two thousand years after the death of Christ we are still extremely skittish about permitting an actor to assume the role of Christ. As it happens, some members of the Greek community do seem to have been shocked. According to Plutarch, the lawgiver Solon was greatly disturbed:

Thespis, at this time, beginning to act tragedies, and the thing, because it was new, taking very much with the multitude, though it was not yet made a matter of competition, Solon, being by nature fond of hearing and learning something new, and now, in his old age, living idly, and enjoying himself, indeed, with music and with wine, went to see Thespis himself, as the ancient custom was, act: and after the play was done, he addressed him, and asked him if he was not ashamed to tell so many lies before such a number of people; and Thespis replying that it was no harm to say or do so in play, Solon vehemently struck his staff against the ground: "Ah," said he, "if we honour and commend such play as this, we shall find it some day in our business."

Solon, however, seems to have been as much out of step as he was out of patience. The practice of seeing the man as god and the god as man had already taken "very much with the multitude," which seems not to have found the two-way substitution seriously inappropriate. Man was accepted as an adequate stand-in for the god, just as the god was accepted as a representative—if not indeed the primary—tragic hero.

Thus far we are relying upon legend, conjecture, and the pleasant gossip of Plutarch to try to forge for ourselves an image of the god-man upon whom tragedy rests; since it is legend, conjecture, and gossip, we are not absolutely obliged to accept any of it. What we must take into account, however, if we are to understand the first great body of tragedy given to us, is the casual, continuing presence of gods upon the stage throughout the whole range of Greek drama. Wherever Greek tragedy came from, it is capable to the end of housing gods.

If we think of the gods who appear in Greek tragedy at all, we no doubt most often think of them as steadily dwindling anachronisms, as vestigial figures soon lost and well lost. We like to imagine that at the very beginning of things tragedy quite naturally leaned upon the religious ritual from which it had taken its first leap forward, accepting—while it was still in a formative state—the god who had been invoked as the necessary god of the action; that it rather quickly discovered it could make use of man as the tragic hero with greater freedom, greater intimacy, and greater plausibility than it could the god; and that once this "natural" step had been taken, the step was irreversible. If the god is to survive as Greek drama advances, we say to ourselves, he will survive as no more than a "god from the machine," that power who appears—so routinely, so miraculously—for a very few moments at the end of the play to sever only such knots as are clearly beyond human management. Even so brief an appearance disturbs us: we suspect a weakness in the playwright's plotting.

But we are inventing, or falsifying, a chronology. The god is not a figure who appears importantly in a few early plays and who then finds less and less room made for him. He appears, full-bodied, whenever the playwright pleases. The use of the god-hero survives as something at hand, an unforgotten understanding, which a playwright—whether as relatively early as Aeschylus or as relatively late as Euripides—could employ without further ado whenever he chose.

We like to call the *Prometheus* a "primitive." But it isn't.
It is neither an early nor a formative play. When Aeschylus
selected a god for his central figure he was simply exercising
his right of choice. He had long since successfully dramatized
not only the human figures of legend but even—in a bold
innovation—the human figures of contemporary history. He
would return to human figures again, though without feeling
himself in any way barred from introducing Athena as an
exceptionally important "goddess from the machine" in the
Oresteia.

It is not enough to call *The Bacchae* a late play. *The
Bacchae*, with its insulted and vengeful god-hero, is very
likely the last play written in the great succession from
Aeschylus to Sophocles to Euripides, the final signature of the
form in its Greek display. With its echoes of the very beginning of Greek drama, it comes at the very end of Greek
drama. Meantime, Sophocles had written a play about
Hercules, suffering son of Zeus and first worshiped as a god
by the Athenians, at a relatively late date in his career, and
Euripides had written another at about the middle of his. It
is in and out among these full-bodied uses that the less
central "gods from the machine" appear. Certainly human
figures outnumber gods in Greek tragedy; but they never do
supersede them.

At this point, however, we are forced to ask another question: What was a god to a Greek? We have just mentioned
three gods who serve as central subjects for tragedies—Prometheus, Hercules, Dionysus. In each case the god's claim to
divinity is clear—on the paternal side. Dionysus and Hercules
are both sons of Zeus. Prometheus is the son of Iapetus, a
Titan or sun-god. But as we turn to the mothers who bore
these gods, the matter of lineage is somewhat compromised,
or at least confused. Legend has never said firmly whether the
mother of Prometheus was Themis, a Titaness, or Clymene, a
nymph. Where legend is firm, as in the case of Hercules and

Dionysus, the mothers are human mothers. Dionysus is the son of Semele, a mortal, as Hercules is the son of Alcmene, another mortal.

That is to say, at least two of these figures are god-men. They inhabit two worlds, poised between the divine and the earthly. They are in some sense infinite and finite at once. The hero may be a god; but he generally has something of man in him.

But the reverse is also true. Because a god—Zeus himself most often—has bestowed his seed upon mortal women, mortals may claim a considerable degree of divinity for themselves. In the principal Greek legends, nearly every hero traces his ancestry back to one or another divine visitation; if a god has not actually mingled his blood with the human line, he has taken a mortal under his special protection and has often thereafter raised him to semidivine status. The alarm of the chorus, addressing the gods of earth and sun, as Medea goes into the house to murder her children is more than a natural or merely human alarm:

> For lo! these are the offspring
> Of thine own golden seed, and I fear
> That divine blood may now be shed by men!

Schlegel held that it was "the distinctive aim of tragedy . . . to establish the claims of the mind to a divine origin." In any case, where the hero of a tragedy was a man, he generally had something of a god in him.

God-men and men-gods: it should not be difficult to see why a playwright might move from one to the other without apparent hesitation. Where blood lines are intermingled, heroes become interchangeable.

At the same time the intermingled blood lines produce peculiar tensions. The god may feel it necessary to *prove* himself divine, as Dionysus does in *The Bacchae*. There have been rumors:

> They said that Dionysus was no son of Zeus,
> but Semele had slept beside a man in love
> and fathered off her shame on Zeus—a fraud, they sneered,
> contrived by Cadmus to protect his daughter's name.

Thus, Dionysus is quickly outraged by Pentheus, the ruler

> who now revolts against divinity, in *me;*
> thrusts *me* from his offerings; forgets *my* name
> in his prayers. Therefore I shall *prove* to him
> and every man in Thebes that I am god
> indeed.

Or the god, being in some sense a lesser god, may suffer severely at the hands of a greater. Prometheus suffers for having stolen fire from Zeus, to whom he is not equal. Hercules is driven mad by the goddess Hera and compelled, in his madness, to slaughter his own children. Near the end of this play, looking at what he has done, Hercules, a demigod, permits himself to doubt whether the gods exist.

The tension is as great, or greater, in man. Aware of his partial divinity, man is terrified of exceeding his role. He can never know the precise point at which he will claim or dare too much. For how much of him *is* god, and where does his godlikeness end?

In Greek legend Oedipus is a descendant of Cadmus, who married a daughter of the gods; gods came from Olympus to attend the wedding. Yet when a priest addresses Oedipus at the opening of the *Tyrannus* he phrases his words carefully:

> You are not one of the immortal gods, we know;
> Yet we have come to you to make our prayer
> As to the man of all men best in adversity
> And wisest in the ways of God.

A moment later, though, remembering Oedipus' victory over the Sphinx, he permits himself this:

> It was some god breathed in you to set us free.

Agamemnon's grandfather was himself a grandson of Zeus. The royal line of the house of Atreus has divine seed in it. Yet when Clytemnestra proposes to Agamemnon that he walk the "bright carpet" that has been laid at his feet, he recoils:

> Such state becomes the gods, and none beside.
> I am a mortal, a man; I cannot trample upon
> these tinted splendors without fear thrown in my path.
> I tell you, as a man, not god, to reverence me.

Agamemnon does walk the path, but he walks it in fear. The Greek byword—"Avoid excess," "Nothing too much," "Observe the mean," however one wishes to phrase it—reflects the man-god's uneasiness about the precise nature of his heritage. "No poet speaks so much as Sophocles," Kitto says, "of the need for *phronesis,* 'wisdom.' 'Phronesis' implies knowing what you are, knowing your place in the world." Man, the hero, has been warned: he is godlike but not God.

When he assumes too much he is guilty of *hubris,* "of the Insolence that brings vengeance on itself." But at what point does a legitimate claim to divine power become an insolent claim to divine power? The question is—and perhaps in the nature of things must be—an unresolved one. *Is* Agamemnon punished for walking a path properly reserved for the gods? Or is he punished for having sacrificed a daughter needlessly? Or is he not punished in any true sense but simply slain by a vindictive wife? Agamemnon's uncertainty about the prerogatives he may assume is reflected in our own uncertainty about the prerogatives he has, or has not, assumed. The question stands open, the issue ambiguous.

It is possible that there is *no* point at which a man must necessarily halt, provided he is willing to accept the costs of going forward. Lionel Abel has offered us a helpful insight here. Upon occasion the Greek tragic hero seems to assume to himself, or to display, the powers of a daemon. *The New*

Century Classical Handbook describes a daemon as either "a supernatural agent or intelligence, lower in rank than a god; a spirit holding a middle place between gods and men," or "a ministering spirit, sometimes regarded as including the souls of deceased persons." Certainly Medea is, or possesses, a daemon; that is why, no matter what she has done, she can rise aloft in triumph at the end of her earthly course. Other tragic figures are not so patently possessed of magical powers as Medea is; yet they behave, in their arrogance, as though some sort of supernatural intelligence were their birthright.

"The character who acts as if he or she had the power of a daemon will be destroyed," Mr. Abel tells us. But "after such destruction may come daemonic powers. *Hubris,* then, is a claim to a certain kind of divinity which may or may not be granted."

What is startling in this—and looking back over Greek tragedy we see that it is true—is the fact that the so arrogant claim, the reckless equating of oneself with a god, the rash and presumably fatal usurpation of near-divine authority is fatal only in the sense that it will bring pain. In the end the excessive powers which the tragic hero assumes or demands may very well be his. Arrogance, even *hubris,* may—after a searing period of transformation—end in sanctification, as it does with Oedipus. A possible pattern, even when we are talking about the most reckless assumption a man may make, is this: dare, suffer, achieve.

"The glorious power to *do,*" Nietzsche says, "which is possessed by great genius, and for which even eternal suffering is not too high a price to pay . . . is of the very essence of Aeschylean poetry, while Sophocles in his *Oedipus* intones a paean to a *saint.*"

Thus, Mr. Abel concludes, "*hubris* is ambiguous. It can lead to destruction; it can also lead to what, for the Greek mind at least, amounts to something like grace."

Whatever the outcome of a given play must be—and the tragic hero, like Agamemnon, may fall far short of grace, may simply die—we cannot deal with Greek tragedy in general unless we are prepared to deal with god-men and men-gods, with central figures whose power transcends the purely natural. Greek tragedy is peopled by degrees of divinity.

Christian tragedy—or, better, tragedy written in the Christian era—removes something of the literal power and also something of its ambiguity. Man is man now, made by God but not born of him. God is God, a spirit wholly other than his creatures. God's blood does not flow in men's veins, though his spirit moves in their hearts. Men are not gods nor are they becoming God. They retain their identities while striving to become one with Him. Where Greek heroes were literally children of the gods, Christian heroes—insofar as they are Christian—aspire to become brides of God. The difference is vast.

Yet the capacities of the tragic hero remain surprisingly undiminished. Anyone who has listened to Hegel's insistence that "the true theme of primitive tragedy is the godlike" will find himself readily at home with Hamlet's emphasis upon man's "godlike reason." Man is like a god to Hamlet; Hamlet sees his father's brow as god-sealed; Hamlet himself, Maynard Mack remarks, "has sought to play at God." The first great trumpet blast of Elizabethan tragedy heralds the Herculean exploits of a Tamburlaine; Faustus bargains with the devil to make himself still more godlike; Shakespeare's heroes, as everyone has noticed, are all of them outsize, capable, like Lear, of playing at God the Father.

Because the Christian tradition holds that man is made in the image and likeness of God, the *likeness* is once more exploited. The particular powers which tragedy seems, in its beginnings, to have attributed to man and to have required of man continue to be exercised.

It has been remarked that at one time to be a king was to be half a god. We sometimes suppose, in our contemporary eagerness to arrive at a tragedy of the common man, that the "aristocratic" bent of tragedy is a tiresome and out-of-date legacy from a particular social order which has vanished: when kings were kings it must have seemed advisable to write about them; now that there are so few kings we might very well lower our sights. But tragedy did not employ imaginary kings in order to please real ones. The first flowering of tragedy took place in a society which described itself as a democracy. Later tragedy, in the Elizabethan period and in Racine's France, was looking for the same heroic qualities— for extraordinary capacities, for powers beyond the norm— and in the institution of kingship, inflated by its claim to "divine right," it found what it needed. What is aristocratic about tragedy is not social but spiritual. Shakespeare, to quote two contemporary editors of Hegel, "has endowed his characters with a degree of intelligence and imagination that 'makes them free artists' in themselves," and it is this freedom and power—wherever it may most likely be found—that tragedy seems to seize upon.

The degree to which an Elizabethan tragic hero is raised toward a kind of supernature cannot really be measured in any practical way; there is no specifically divine lineage to be reported, and we are forced to fall back, vaguely, upon what we feel. Perhaps there is one trick of the light that might be watched, though. Every so often the truly supernatural walks the stage. There is a ghost come for Hamlet, a Hecate for Macbeth, a Mephistopheles for Faustus. The very fact of these visitations suggests that we are playing out the action on a plane somewhere between heaven and earth, god and man. But how naturally is the hero able to receive his visitor, how much can he seem his familiar? Faustus and Mephistopheles are familiars so quickly that their exchanges are admired as the first successful use of an easy conversational tone in English blank verse. Before the ghost is gone, Hamlet is calling him "old mole," and we should scarcely be surprised at this point to see him give the shadow's beard a tweak. Hamlet experiences great difficulty in determining the ghost's identity; but he shows no difficulty at all in sharing a stage with him. Macbeth converses with witches as though witches might well wish to converse with Macbeth. Today we are puzzled that ghosts and witches should appear in such "human" plays, and we are forever asking ourselves how the Elizabethans could have been so credulous. But we are looking at only one half of the stage. What we forget is that the Elizabethans were equally credulous about Hamlet, Macbeth, and Faustus, and that they thought them capable of walking where ghosts walked. The world of the play is single: Hamlet does not become a displaced person upon his dead father's entrance. Man and Mephistopheles meet as equals, even though they do not finish so.

In seventeenth-century France the situation in this respect is no different, though Racine has come at tragedy on a radically different trajectory: he has gone directly back to the Greek tragic sources, including what was supernatural in those sources, for his materials. Racine was a Christian, as his audiences were Christian. What conceivable credit could they give, in a plausible play, to sun-gods? "The seventeenth-century spectator," George Steiner says, "did not literally believe that Phèdre was a descendant of the sun, but the implications of magic and daemonic chaos in the blood which such a legend conveys were still acceptable. It was one of those miracles of afterlife which sometimes occur in art." A changed theological view did not change the response man made to tragedy—even when tragedy called attention to the changed theology. Phèdre was in some sense godlike; that could be understood.

What tragedy has constantly said of its heroes and heroines, in each of its three principal appearances on this earth, is that its heroes and heroines commanded exceptional, to some degree supernatural, powers—powers that might be used in working toward a desired goal.

What sort of goal? Not only desired but desirable. The second source of tragedy's admiration of man is the purity, the worthiness, the absolute value of the thing he seeks. What the tragic hero is trying to catch in his fist is in itself a good.

We have already mentioned one critic's firm insistence that what Oedipus set out to do was to purify Thebes, a task he successfully accomplished. If we tend to ignore this accomplishment in our discussions of the play and if, habitually, we fail to take much notice of what is *right* about the tragic act being performed, it is no doubt because our minds are so sympathetically transfixed by the pain of the man performing it. But the truth that fills Oedipus with such pain is also the truth that saves Thebes. In effect, Oedipus has sacrificed himself for the good of the community. We might very well ask why he should not—sometime—be rewarded. And we might ask ourselves which we should have preferred—that he spare his city or that he spare himself.

There is no time in the play, or in the past that is made present in the play, when Oedipus' intentions are not wholly honorable. The past that is revealed to us shows us a man who has quite literally gone to the ends of his earth in order to avoid committing the crimes prophesied for him. When he comes to Thebes he comes as her savior, and is made tyrant for the good he has done her. Apparently he has been, and is, an excellent ruler. Confronted with a plague in Thebes, he acts vigorously, ingeniously, devoutly. Hearing from the oracle that it is the murderer of the old king who has defiled the city and so brought the plague to it, he pledges himself, under his own curse, to uncover and to expel that murderer. His first blaze of anger is at a man who seems to be willfully concealing facts of the utmost importance, thus further imperiling the health of Thebes. It is true that when Oedipus is told that it is he who is the tainted one, he blazes with anger again; he cannot conceive himself guilty as another man might be guilty, and this is a fault in him. The fault leads him to foolish excesses.

But it is perhaps even more important to notice that, as the evidence continues to close about him, he does not, in his mounting apprehension, attempt to evade the issue. A less forthright ruler, beginning to suspect what Oedipus begins to suspect, might very well decide that the time had come to suppress such an investigation. Oedipus makes no move of this sort. On the contrary, the more dangerous the investigation becomes the more fiercely does he pursue it. He would, of course, like to prove himself innocent, if that is possible. He would like even more to know the truth. When he does know it, he does nothing to avoid its consequences; he accepts the consequences, and he begins his expiation by punishing himself. On his own showing, he is a very good man who cannot be deflected from a most desirable goal: knowledge, and the general health that will come of knowledge.

There is no need to dwell upon what is admirable in Antigone's purpose: she is serving, with her life, an "immutable law of the gods." Pelasgus in *The Suppliants,* staring at the insoluble problem before him, wishes nothing more than to serve justice absolutely. Orestes does not like doing what he is called upon to do; but until he has done it, and suffered in the doing, his world cannot find its way to the song:

> Peace to you, peace of a happy communion,
> People of Pallas. Zeus who beholdeth
> All with the Fates is at last reconciled.
>   O sing at the end Alleluia!

Hamlet does not like doing what he is called upon to do, either. But what he seeks is clear enough: justice and rest for his father's shade, honor for his mother, an end to all that is rotten in Denmark. If he makes a mistake, it is the mistake of trying to correct too much: he wants all friends as honest as Horatio, all women purer than his mother, all foul vapors that rise from the earth quenched. If he delays, it is for fear of himself doing something wrong and so adding to the general pestilence; he would be judicious as he would have all men judicious. The image he holds in his head, and by which he measures those about him, is that of his father: "a combination and a form indeed, where every god did seem to set his seal to give the world assurance of a man." If Hamlet is sick, he is sick with a passion for perfection.

In each of these instances the tragic goal is not only admirable, it is a goal which the tragic hero is bound in conscience to seek. A command has been laid upon him; in pursuing the action he is doing no more than his duty.

There are other, quite different instances in which the hero thrusts his own way into the situation, possibly daring or demanding too much. Yet the goal itself retains its abstract purity. Zeus holds that Prometheus has dared too much; Prometheus, nails driven through his feet, continues to insist that his only crime has been to benefit mankind: "all arts, all goods, have come to men from me." Othello is asking too much to demand that his wife be faithful to him *beyond any possible shadow of suspicion*. But absolute fidelity, which is what Othello asks, is in itself an absolute good. Every man would think it a good to be certain of a love which could not be corrupted. What most men accept, and what Othello is unable to accept, is a relative certainty, a certainty that is part hope and part faith. The absolute, in the view of most men, is unattainable. Othello insists upon it. In doing so, he destroys himself and the woman whose never-to-be-questioned love he wants. But he is asking for more of a good, not less. He, too, is bent on perfection.

Lear wants love and he wants it out loud, he wants it constantly demonstrated; having shattered his mind in the attempt to seize it by force, he finds it, at the end, freely given. He has demanded a good in a somewhat mistaken way; it is still a good when it comes to him.

Phèdre is not entitled to the love she demands; neither is Macbeth entitled—just now—to the kingship. Here we have gone beyond the impulsive thrusting of oneself into a situation or a compulsive insistence upon perfection. So far from having any obligation to do what they do, Phèdre and Macbeth cannot even claim to have invented beneficent roles for

themselves. They have usurped the roles of others. That is a
crime or a sin. But what they desire is no less desirable for the
improper means they have taken to seize it. Love itself
cannot be conceived as less than a good, either in the minds
of the characters or in the minds of the audience. Neither can
the kingship be taken as anything less than absolutely desirable. The crown as such is something to be honored by all
men; always we wish to see the best man, the just man, the
virtuous man wear it. Whether or not power tends to corrupt, and no matter how cynical we may grow—with or
without Shakespeare's help—about the processes of politics,
we continue on our own election days to consider the be-
stowal of power a compliment to quality, to some sort of
virtue. To rule, to possess power, is to be in a position to do
good. That is still our estimate; and we work very hard to put
in positions of power the men who, in our opinion, will do
the most good. If Macbeth must be driven from the kingship
and destroyed, it is precisely because the purity of the kingship must be maintained. Macbeth has been willing to do an
evil in order to possess a good, and that has been an error of
judgment on his part. The error of judgment marks him for
failure; it does not tarnish the crown. Macbeth has not
aspired to something less than worthy of him, but to something more.

Not to blink what is perhaps most difficult, the goal of
Dionysus in *The Bacchae* is to let human beings know the
person and the power of the god who *is*. Dionysus has been
taken captive and led before Pentheus, the youthfully arrogant ruler of Thebes.

> PENTHEUS.   But *I* say: chain him.
> And I am the stronger here.
> DIONYSUS.   You do not know
> the limits of your strength. You do not know
> what you do . . .
> When you set chains on me, you manacle the god.

Pentheus the unbeliever does more than manacle the god. In a sacrilegious excess of venom, he shears away the god's curls. Thus far Dionysus suffers the insults heaped upon him, but he warns that Pentheus

> shall come to know
> Dionysus, son of Zeus, consummate god,
> most terrible, and yet most gentle, to mankind.

Pentheus does come to know the strength of the god, and in a way that is "most terrible." Dionysus' gentleness is something we hear about in the play. What is terrible in him we see. In a vast sweep of destruction, the god's power is revealed. That power is, by human standards, appalling; and we are appalled by it, literally sickened by it. Although we hear the human admission that "justly—too, too justly" has the god Dionysus "destroyed us all, every one," we are still sickened; the idea of justice does not ease the ache. Although we raise our eyes to the roof of the palace to see the god appear "in epiphany" and understand that he is now disclosing himself to us in the fullness of his glory, we are still sickened; the glory is not easy to look upon. There is no sort of comfort in it. There is not even any grasping this glory. "Elusive, complex and compelling," William Arrowsmith writes, "the play constantly recedes before one's grasp, advancing, not retreating, steadily into deeper chaos and larger order, coming finally to rest only god knows where—which is to say, where it matters."

Dionysus has achieved his objective. He has displayed himself. What we feel about what we see—whether we are revolted by it, whether we would prefer never to have looked —is beside the point. The power of a god *is,* and it is awful. Now we stand before it in awe. However we may feel, there is no way in which we can regard the demonstration of what *is* as anything other than a good. The divine, and direct knowledge of divinity, are by definition desirable.

Though Faustus severs himself from God and makes a pact with the devil, there is no questioning the good of what he seeks: he seeks knowledge. Prometheus steals knowledge for man, Faustus buys knowledge for himself, Dionysus drops knowledge upon the earth like a bolt of lightning. The road taken may be devious or unwise or unexpectedly terrifying; but there is never anything mean or undignified or undesirable in the goal.

Though we do find secondary figures in tragedy whose aspirations are base—the inexplicable Iago, Edmund in *Lear,* perhaps the shadowy Aegisthus—these are surprisingly few. Even the presumed "villains" or fierce antagonists of most encounters hold a good in their minds. Claudius, like Macbeth, has done what he has done in order to own a good; and he is sufficiently distressed by what he has done to try to pray. Clytemnestra makes a case for herself that is to some degree persuasive: she has wished to vindicate the claims of the family, and of human life, against Agamemnon's wanton sacrifice of Iphigenia. Edmund's dying gesture is a generous one. There is a bias toward good in the turn of the tragic wheel.

The matter goes further than that. Tragedy never comes into existence because an undesirable goal is sought; neither does it ever consist in a clash between two despicable aspirations. But one of the greatest of tragic effects—with the *Antigone* as supreme example—is the clash between two virtuous intentions. "The essentially tragic fact," Hegel said, is "not so much the war of good with evil as the war of good with good." In the *Antigone* Creon is no simple-minded dictator trying to ride roughshod over the world of spirit. He is rather, in Hegel's words, "really a moral power; Creon is not in the wrong; he maintains that the law of the State, the authority of government, is to be held in respect, and that punishment follows the infraction of the law." Creon has refused burial to the body of Polynices because Polynices had attacked his own city and "no traitor is going to be honored

with the loyal man." Having made his decision, he is bound
to enforce it or let the state slip into anarchy. This last threat
is constantly and—I think we may take it—honestly in his
mind:

> Anarchy, anarchy! Show me a greater evil!
> This is why cities tumble and the great houses rain down,
> This is what scatters armies!
> No, no: good lives are made so by discipline.

The leader of the chorus, having heard out this particular
speech, concludes that:

> Unless time has rusted my wits,
> What you say, King, is said with point and dignity.

We may take every sort of exception to Creon's position
and say that this is authoritarianism speaking; we may, as we
have done, make Creon over into a fascist. We may notice, in
passing, that the choral leader's defense is no defense; leader
and chorus both are forever blowing hot and cold in the
Antigone, supporting now this figure and now that. Nor do I
think there is much doubt in anyone's mind that Antigone's
loyalty to the ancient law of the tribal gods is meant to be an
appealing loyalty. But if Creon is authoritarian, he is under a
special obligation to uphold authority. If the chorus blows
hot and cold, the wavering need not be due to anything
sycophantic in the people of Thebes—the chorus has nothing
to gain from supporting Antigone, little to gain from supporting Haemon—but to the fact that the listeners, the members of the community, are naturally and genuinely torn this
way and that. The listeners are present at an irreconcilable
clash between valid objectives, between independently admirable goals.

In Racine's *Berenice* the clash between equally desirable
objectives is not public and unilateral—with one force up-

holding one virtue, the other force another—but private and, in the privacy, fiercely doubled. Titus and Berenice love one another honorably. But another honor intervenes. Roman law demands, upon Titus' accession to the throne, that he renounce Berenice. In each of the two principals, now, there begins an agony of contending goods: love and honor, or love and *gloire*—which Kenneth Muir defines as "intrinsic virtue"—compete with one another for possession of the principals' wills. The tragedy simply details the ascendancy—the very painful ascendancy—of one good over another.

We began these comments by speaking of the good sought by Oedipus. But Oedipus is not the only figure in the *Tyrannus* whose motives are pure. In all of the play there is not one unworthy intention. Oedipus does accuse Creon of having plotted against him in reporting the oracle. But this is one of Oedipus' mistakes: Creon has actually done nothing but tell the truth. Oedipus does accuse Tiresias of having been an accomplice in the murder of the old king when Tiresias refuses to speak of that murder. But this is another of Oedipus' mistakes: Tiresias has kept silent only to spare Oedipus pain. And that messenger who brings the worst news has hopefully meant to bring the best. Five or six independently desirable goals cross lines to make a web that snares a man; but there is no strand to the web that is not honorable—even generous—in purpose, and the web, when it is finished, upholds Thebes.

A tragic figure may possibly falter in one of a dozen, or a hundred, ways; but there is no questioning the objective desirability of the goal that has set him in motion.

At the heart of tragedy, feeding it energy, stands godlike man passionately desiring a state of affairs more perfect than any that now exists.

6

THE TRAGIC CRISIS

Bᴜᴛ we are too hopeful. *Isn't* the godlike tragic figure flawed, flawed in such a way that no matter how high his aims or how great his capacities he is certain to make a misstep? Isn't it precisely the burden of tragedy to report how the great must inevitably destroy themselves?

We answer "yes" to these questions almost by reflex. The tragic hero is a flawed man, we say, a man so possessed by jealousy, pride, ambition or any other of the deadly sins that his blind, raging course must bring him earthward in blood. There was a goddess among the Greeks named Nemesis whose function it was to exact divine retribution for certain human excesses, especially insolence and presumption, or what we have always called *hubris,* and the generalized concept of Nemesis has continued to lie in wait for the too bold tragic hero. The scale of a man's arrogance accounts for the scale of his suffering. For a great crime, great punishment: that is the point that tragedy makes.

But tragedy, taken as a whole, makes no such point. Even if it did, we should still be no nearer arriving at a distinction between tragedy and comedy. The comic hero—especially in that boldest and clearest comic form we call farce—is every bit as flawed as the tragic hero. Avarice is a flaw in Harpagon, lust in Tartuffe, gluttony in Sir Justice Greedy, pompousness in Dogberry, hypocrisy in Joseph Surface, and when one begins to think of the corrupt passions that *become* the characters in any play by Ben Jonson a cataract of flaws roars over the broken dike. In lighter forms of comedy there is less outright venality, but there is nearly always a substitute for it: the obtuseness of a lover or the incompetence of a do-gooder. Out of the goodness of his heart, or out of sheer love of chicanery, Harlequin is always trying to help someone; the mess he makes in the process is dizzying. Buster Keaton is always ready with solutions to problems: when his boat springs a leak in its side, he drills a hole in the bottom to let the water out. Aristotle spoke of a flaw *or* an error in tragedy. Where comedy does not have a flaw, it is a comedy of errors.

More important than noticing that the flaw is not peculiar to tragedy, however, is noticing that the flaw does not always exist in tragedy—and that tragedy cannot be defined or explained by it. There are certainly tragic heroes who possess flaws. There are tragic heroes who *seem* in some way flawed, though we have great difficulty in saying just what has flawed them. And there are tragic heroes who seem altogether unstained but suffer nonetheless; some of them have been defended by some commentators as saints.

The range of possibilities is very great. If we generally refuse to see that a great many different kinds of tragic figures exist, that they are brought to their pain by very different paths, and that they naturally and logically arrive at endings that are not in the least uniform, it is because as we pretend to look at the plays we have in hand we begin our investigations with a flaw in our eye, with *the* flaw in our eye. Our predetermined focus is again narrower than the form that is being investigated.

We have come by this particular narrowness naturally enough. We are bound to attend Aristotle; he is not only a great philosopher-critic, he is the only philosopher-critic to have written extensively about tragedy while tragedy was first in process of defining itself. And in speaking of the kind of dramatic figure who suited the plotting of tragedy best, he gave us the clue which we have hardened into "flaw," though he never does incorporate this clue into any of his explicit definitions of tragedy as such. The figure who serves the tragic plot most satisfactorily, he tells us, is a man whose misfortune "is brought upon him not by vice and depravity but by some error of judgment."

Actually, it has taken some forcing to make "flaw" out of that. An error of judgment need not stem from a character weakness, as we are perfectly well aware. Geniuses make errors of judgment. Wholly virtuous men make errors of judgment. In practice, we have had to play down the pure "error of judgment" as a possible cause of the tragic crisis, or assume that by "error of judgment" Aristotle really meant an aberration brought about by one or another form of self-indulgence, in order to make the "flaw" concept stick. Still, we like to be reasonable about things, to arrange them as neatly as is possible in direct cause-and-effect relationships, and it is not *un*reasonable to say that when a man who is in no sense vicious or depraved makes a serious error of judgment he is probably failing to control an innate—and hitherto suppressed—tendency in himself toward just this sort of error. Furthermore, Aristotle vastly admired the *Oedipus,* as we do, and the *Oedipus* seems to offer us a fairly clear case of the flaw in action: it is the hero's pride—driving him to anger and rashness—that propels him so swiftly toward catastrophe. If there is no greater play than the *Oedipus,* may not its greatness in part be due to the precision with which it charts the course of what the chorus calls "insolence"?

The flaw was a clean and comfortable way of explaining the tragic progression when it came time, during the Renaissance, to renew the bloodlines of the form; it fitted, furthermore, the Christian conceptual pattern of sin and punishment very readily. Unsurprisingly, drama after the Renaissance—fastening upon the Aristotelian "flaw" and making a canon of it—does actually display the flawed hero more regularly and more explicitly than Greek drama ever did. The

seven deadly sins become, for a time, the virtual calendar of
tragedy: we have little trouble seeing the pride in Coriolanus, the jealousy in Othello, the ambition in Macbeth.
Macbeth is even more clearly a walking flaw than Oedipus is;
with fresh evidence added, the presumed pattern becomes
firmer.

Its firmness was reinforced, and is reinforced, by our tendency to think of tragedy as moral illustration. The temptation is hard to resist. Before us on the stage is a suffering man.
But the projected universe in which he suffers is sensed, or
stated, to be an orderly one. The world itself is in balance or
will come into balance through a sufficient number of expia-
tory deaths; rectitude is its nature. If this is so, however, the
universe cannot be responsible for having initiated the man's
suffering: *he* must be. He has done something wrong for
which he is being punished; he has himself put the time out
of joint and must pay for it.

What the play seems to be saying—and what it occasionally
is saying—closely coincides with what the moralist is so tirelessly, and for that matter so accurately, saying from his
pulpit: surrender to your temptation, whatever it may be,
and you will suffer for it. The moralist likes the "flaw" theory
because it helps him in his own work: he can quote act and
verse, as evidence, from the stage. The listener, moving back
and forth from stage to pulpit, carries baggage with him both
ways. The habit of identifying the exhortation with the
image, the image with the exhortation, becomes easier and
easier. Many distinctions are lost, some of them essential; but
the "flaw," surviving both ways, becomes more strongly en-
trenched in the corridors of the mind.

Out of good and bad tradition, out of moral anxiety, out of
unquestioned habit, really, we have come to imagine the flaw
as *creating* tragedy, as being responsible for each private
doom or public dilemma. Yet the flaw is a concept that
becomes maddeningly elusive under the most cursory examination of actual plays.

It is elusive where it should be most obvious. Yes, of course *Macbeth, Othello,* and the *Oedipus* adapt themselves easily to the standard schoolbook formula for tragedy. They do, provided we ask no impolite questions. Macbeth is surely ambitious, Othello jealous, Oedipus proud and rash.

But, although Macbeth does seem some sort of second cousin to the symbol Ambition in a medieval morality play, there is very little in Shakespeare's text to show that Macbeth himself is ambitious. He does not invent for himself his kingly future; it is suggested to him by prophecy. Even after he has heard, and wistfully half believed, the prophecy, he does not behave ambitiously; it is all his wife can do to chart the necessary deed for him and set him to performing it. There are many eager usurpers in Shakespeare, but Macbeth is not really one of them. Is Othello innately jealous? Or is jealousy an emotion created for him and imposed upon him by the suffocating presence of an Iago whose purpose has never been made plain? If jealousy is Othello's natural flaw, why does it require an extraordinarily malevolent master-mind three long acts to light a fire in his mind? Who is flawed—Othello or Iago? And if both are flawed, which flaw is the more active? Oedipus is indeed what his chorus calls "insolent," but to what degree is his pride "wrong," consider-ing the pains he has taken to do always what is right?

These are the "easy" plays and they are not so easy. Still, their ambiguities are tolerable. We are not altogether de-prived of the sense of watching some sort of flaw chart its course: the plays, taken as wholes, do show us ambition overreaching itself, jealousy destroying its object, pride come tumbling down.

More serious difficulty begins as we try to catch in our hands a flaw, say, for Lear. Ask a student, or for that matter as sophisticated a man as Graham Greene, to name the flaw in *King Lear* and he will readily answer, "Ingratitude," though that is a flaw in Regan, Goneril, and Edmund, not in the principal character—in which case what has become of the flawed tragic hero? A further search can be made to find a flaw in the old king himself, certainly in the play's early scenes, where Lear is, to say the least, highhanded and obtuse. John F. Danby discovers him guilty of something more serious still: he has willfully broken the bond of nature. Mr. Danby examines in detail the medieval Christian concept of the "bond of nature" which relates children to parents, the community as a whole to the king, and the king in turn to that divine order perceptible in Nature which serves as a model for the structure of human society. These relations fuse to create a web of unified responsibility; so long as children, community, and king perform their roles properly a general harmony is assured. But Lear violates his role first by fragmenting his kingdom, for which he is personally and symbolically responsible, and then by rejecting his daughter Cordelia, who most perfectly represents the sense of fully honored obligation. Lear has been led into this double error by age and arrogance.

But even with this illuminating world view as a guide to the play, the matter of "flaw" remains far from single or simple. Goneril and Regan break the bond of nature at least as fully as Lear does, and Edmund directly challenges it by denying its existence. Furthermore, Lear "is a good king"— not an idealized good king, but one on the human-natural scale, "capable of corruption, error, rescue, and regeneration." If his initial lapse is "inward, and the upset in the outer world of the body politic follows as a consequence," it is at the same time true that inner goodness, in order to sustain itself and function effectively, "needs a community of goodness." Lear cannot find such a community of goodness, and the flaw is once more distributed, the responsibility diffused. Arrogance and age initiate, but do not account for, all that happens after. Least of all do they account for the fact that Lear, in his madness, becomes what he has never been before: humble and knowing. These qualities grow in him during the most substantial and impressive portion of the play, almost as though it required the complete shattering of man's projected world in order to bring a man peace.

Indeed, as the play advances deeply into near-uniform madness, questions of right and wrong seem to vanish for Lear, Gloucester, and Edgar, who now become the firm center of our attention, the true principals of the play. From reasoning about right and wrong the principals turn to investigating the unreason of reason. If there is a flaw at the last it is a universal flaw, one that may involve the entire social and divine fabric as men understand it; that is not a comfortable concept for most academic definitions of tragedy to accommodate, though it does have an overtone of Kitto's "flaw in the universe."

Hamlet is baffling in so many ways that I scarcely wish to name him here. But the much-debated issue of whether he is resolute or irresolute cannot be untangled without creating another tangle: which is the flaw? If the play is a revenge tragedy, then resoluteness—the thirst for vengeance—would be the flaw that brings Hamlet down. If the play is a play about a sensitive intellectual unable to get on with things, then irresoluteness would be the flaw that cripples him. We have a choice of flaws which is, in effect, a cancellation of flaw.

However, we understand that *something* is the matter with Hamlet. It is not clear that anything is the matter with Antigone. "Antigone has from the time of Goethe been the subject of a 'stainless soul' school of commentary," John Jones reminds us, while calling attention on his own part to what is "ignoble" in certain of the stances she takes. I must confess that I can myself never read her as altogether un-flawed: Antigone seems self-important to me, nearly as much as Creon is power-important, and when the chorus links her to her father, Oedipus, by proclaiming them "both head-strong, deaf to reason," I feel a chill wind of arrogance behind the manifestly good deed. But for many, perhaps most, readers Antigone is more nearly a saint, a martyr sacrificing herself to principle. Her flaw, if she has one, is so subtle that later generations have been unable to agree upon it. And she may not have one. Creon is more certainly flawed, though also tantalizingly within his rights; but we neither see nor read the play as the tragedy of Creon, and we are generally surprised and disturbed by the prolonged attention given him toward the close of the play.

Clytemnestra kills Agamemnon in part out of old hatred and new lust. But when Orestes returns to avenge his father and kill Clytemnestra, does he come out of weakness, or out of *hubris,* or in error? He comes at the explicit command of a god, whose distasteful order he is dutifully carrying out. Aeschylus ultimately clears him of any stain; Sophocles does not suggest that he has ever been stained.

"The guilt of Orestes," Werner Jaeger insists, "is not founded on his character. Aeschylus does not consider him to be a man whose nature destines him to commit matricide. He is merely the unfortunate son who is bound to avenge his father: at the moment when he enters manhood, he is faced by the dreadful deed which will destroy him before he even tastes life, and to which the god of Delphi constrains him again and again whenever he shrinks from the fixed end."

Prometheus, in stealing fire from Zeus to give it to mankind, certainly offends Zeus; but has he acted out of weakness or out of strength?

"I dared it, I saved men," he says.

Bound fast to his rock, Prometheus persistently denies any personal guilt.

> . . . Let the very air
> be rent by thunder-crash.
> Savage winds convulse the sky,
> hurricanes shake the earth from its foundations,
> the waves of the sea rise up and drown the stars,
> and let me be swept down to hell,
> caught in the cruel whirlpool of necessity . . .
> It does not make me tremble.

O holy Mother Earth, O air and sun,
behold me. I am wronged.

"I am wronged" are the last words we hear. To be sure,
this is the first play of a trilogy, and perhaps these are the
words of a stubborn hero blindly disowning a guilt he has
actually incurred. Perhaps this is *hubris* in action, defiant and
unresolved at a point that is only one third along the way.
We know, however, that Prometheus was ultimately released
and then reconciled with Zeus. *Was* his cause just, then? Or
more just than not? Can a man write a play in which it is
considered an "error of judgment" for a god to have saved
men? Perhaps. But that is again something more subtle than
a flaw earning punishment. And an ultimate resolution of a
quarrel between a god and a god over the survival of man is
something subtler still, subtler and more difficult than simply
bowing before a flaw in the universe.

Professor Kitto has been forced to posit a flaw in the
universe precisely because he has been unable to find a flaw
in a man. The play at issue is *The Suppliants,* the man is
Pelasgus, King of Argos. To Argos have come the fifty daughters of Danaüs, refugees asking asylum. If Pelasgus gives
them asylum he risks war with the nation they have fled. If he
does not give them asylum, he perforce offends the gods. His
situation is intolerable, and he has done nothing to bring it
into being. Pelasgus himself is "a perfectly innocent man,"
but however he acts he must bring some disaster upon himself and his country. "Through no Aristotelian flaw of character," Kitto says, "through no deficiency of sense, intellect or
morality, has the King fallen suddenly into this awful
dilemma."

Yet the play is a tragedy. Professor Kitto admires the play
enormously as "one form of Tragedy, and that perhaps the
profoundest . . . the spectacle of the hero isolated before
some awful rift in the universe, looking, like Pelasgus, into
the chasm that must engulf him." Because the notion of an

utterly innocent man so caught corresponds very poorly with one of our most widespread concepts of tragedy, Kitto must work hard to persuade us that there is a tragic type for which we have really had no previous name: he calls it the tragedy of the virtuous man in the "cleft stick." Lacking a flaw in the man, we must—if we are to maintain our most cherished explanation for disaster—find one somewhere else. We find it in the natural order, in the cosmos itself. "A disharmony in the make-up of things, and a perfectly innocent man is broken." Contending pressures originating altogether outside the tragic hero converge to engulf him; thus a loving and acute critic finds his own way of reclaiming a nonconformist play. Whether one agrees that the flaw in tragedy may be envisioned as cosmic rather than personal, or whether one goes on to wonder if the term "flaw" is appropriate to the play at all, an uncontested fact remains. Pelasgus is without guilt.

The difficulty is so intense in Racine that Roland Barthes has felt compelled to offer an even more striking suggestion. The universe, especially as it is represented by the figure of the Father, is transparently unjust. In order to justify the universe, the Father, the God who set all things into motion, man must see himself as retroactively guilty, must *invent* a guilt for himself in order to make sense of the world: "if man is pure, then God is impure, and the world falls apart." Therefore the tragic hero is engaged in a kind of inverted redemption: "We might say that every tragic hero is born innocent: he becomes guilty in order to save God." If this is an accurate description of what some Racinian tragic figures actually do, it is an even more accurate description of what *we* do to many tragic heroes. We provide them with a guilt which will soothe our understandings.

Prometheus' "I am wronged" is a phrase that may well ring in our ears as we watch a number of plays—as we watch Orestes being flayed by Furies for an act he was ordered to do by a god; as we watch Pelasgus weigh the intolerable alterna-

tives upon which he must act through no error of his own; as
we listen to Antigone go to her death:

> And yet, as men's hearts know, I have done no wrong,
> I have not sinned before God. Or if I have,
> I shall know the truth in death. . . .
> Thebes, and you my fathers' gods,
> And rulers of Thebes, you see me now, the last
> Unhappy daughter of a line of kings,
> Your kings, led away to death. You will remember
> What things I suffer, and at what men's hands,
> Because I would not transgress the laws of heaven.

How curious it is that we should see Prometheus suffering
because he has transgressed a law of heaven and Antigone
suffering because she has not! Tragedy's span of vision would
seem to be wide enough to admit strange contradictions.

The questions I have been raising here about individual
plays are, of course, not new ones. What college student has
not been puzzled by *Lear,* and what high-school student has
not looked twice—rather irreverently—at Macbeth? Who has
not noticed that Othello, so far from being a walking deadly
sin, describes himself as a man "not easily jealous"? Our
usual practice, however, is to raise questions about plays one
at a time, as though *this* tragedy had certain problems causing it to deviate from a norm represented by all other, or
most other, tragedies. We imagine a norm because we are, for
the moment, not looking at it. The moment we turn to
another play, focusing our minds upon it exclusively, *it*
becomes the problem play, while the last difficult play examined slips quietly into the norm again. The fact of the matter
is that there is no tragedy which cannot be called into
question or at least subjected to hot debate where the "flaw"
is concerned.

The flaw is always ambiguous, even in such an apparently
cut-and-dried case as *Macbeth.* It is sometimes strangely distributed, to be found—if it must be found—more apparent in

Lear's daughters or Antigone's opponent than in Lear or Antigone. It must sometimes be conceived as a flaw in the universe rather than a flaw in any of the characters, because all of the characters are patently innocent, though this assumption raises the further, unanswered question of "What *is* the flaw in the universe?" and also runs directly counter to our strong sense that tragedy asserts the balance of things, that it sounds—in Nietzsche's phrase—"the gospel of universal harmony." And sometimes the flaw is simply absent. It is difficult to see either flawed protagonists or a hostile universe in Sophocles' *Electra*. Jones goes so far as to say that "the *Persians* is the one play in the entire extant literature—not just in Aeschylus—which is genuinely and fully founded upon *hubris*." We have fastened ourselves to too simple an explanation of the tragic agony.

In general, we have fastened ourselves to the flaw because we were looking for an explanation of the disastrous end that overtakes tragic figures. We thought we saw death everywhere and we searched for a weakness or an error or a sin that might account for it. We sought a beginning negation in order to explain an ultimate negation. But neither negation is uniformly present. Tragedies do not all end in disaster or death; many end most satisfactorily for their principals. And the sin or error or flaw that might demand death, or necessarily produce disaster, is not consistently visible, either; a number of tragic figures seem wholly uncorrupted.

We are forced to look elsewhere for a term that will describe the nature of the tragic action while accommodating its extraordinary range of gestures.

7

THE TRAGIC MEANING

IN TRAGEDY man's aim is high and his thrust is strong. With no *necessary* character weakness to impede him, he should achieve his objective more often than not. In fact, the real puzzle of tragedy is not that some heroes should achieve their objectives or that some heroes should go on to an explicit glory. Given the goodness of the goal and the exceptional powers of the man pursuing it, the puzzle of tragedy is that its heroes should ever fail. On the face of things, the odds would seem to favor success.

We know that tragedy sometimes confers success. We know —to summarize briefly—that the course of events in the central tragic action can take an astonishing variety of turns. Some tragic heroes, like Othello and Faustus and Macbeth, stumble and destroy themselves without achieving their goals or without achieving them in ways that can satisfy them. Others, like Orestes, endure a prolonged period of pain but emerge in time with the goal achieved and the pain removed. And a few, like Sophocles' other Orestes or Euripides' Dionysus, suffer relatively little pain and win through to quick satisfaction.

We are required, I think, to explain—or at least to face— two conundrums. Why should the tragic action and the tragic outcome vary so radically from instance to instance? And, taking into consideration the two strong values which argue for success, why should one of the tragic experiences be flat failure?

In order to contend with these puzzles, I shall have to say what I take tragedy to be. Tragedy seems to me to be an investigation of the possibilities of human *freedom*.

Whatever is free about man is examined, given work to do, invited to assert itself and to assert itself utterly. "I shall follow this thing to the end," Medea says, putting into so many words what Oedipus and Orestes and Pelasgus and Antigone and Hamlet and Lear and Phèdre are all determined to do.

The end is not known. The limits of human freedom are not known. There is no defining these limits beforehand, because the terms of the definition are themselves indefinite: we speak of human but mean superhuman; we probe a godlike freedom without being able to measure what is godlike.

This freedom can be measured only in the doing and only in the dark. Exercised, it may provoke good or evil or good after evil or both at once. With each exercise of a godlike freedom we are required to follow where the freedom leads, without set expectation, without any sort of certainty, prepared only for discovery and ready for surprise:

> The expected does not always happen,
> And God makes a way for the unexpected.
> So ends this action.

The *Alcestis* closes on that note, the *Medea* on this:

> Many the things we think will happen,
> Yet never happen.
> And many the things we thought could never be,
> Yet the gods contrive.

The *Hippolytus* chorus says of the play's ending that "it came unlooked for." Shakespeare, as a rule, does not pause to express surprise; but who could have looked for the ending of *Lear?*

Tragedy proposes that the door is open and that man may walk through it. It does not say what is on the other side until it sees what is on the other side. Orestes, on the other side, discovers not only the means of his own purification but the means of resolving a contest between gods and daemons that has ravaged the world. Lear, on the other side, finds nothing, the "no thing" that so terrifies him.

Tragedy seems to me an exploratory form, not an illustrative one. It does not begin by saying that thus and thus is *so* and then proceed to show us why. It begins by asking: What is possible? It asks: What may man do, and what may come of what he does? Then it moves forward to find out.

The form never tires of citing man's past accomplishments—possibilities that have become actualities—because it is girding itself to press on to new possibilities. Again and again a Greek chorus cries out the litany of man's gains, adds up once more the conquests made by his astonishing powers, his superb flexibility. What has defeated him, bound him? Not the sea, not the soil, not the horn of the massive bull, not fire, not "the spears of winter rain," not even the malice man sometimes feels for man—"All are tamed, tamed in the net of his mind."

The freedom is in man's mind. It exists, to begin with, in man's godlike capacity for manufacturing the symbols of language and mathematics which Prometheus is so proud to have handed down. With these powers man is free to move among the stars and to name, in his philosophy, the things he cannot see.

The powers are multiplied, the freedom extended, by man's capacity to store his accumulated knowledge in his brain. Because man can hold his knowledge in his head he holds the cosmos in his hand.

But he is freer still. Beyond knowledge, beyond memory,

beyond reason, he can still act. Man has a vast freedom to know and then—when he does not know—to choose. A kind of terror enters here. When he has not knowledge, man has choice. Blinded, he can yet move, over Dover cliff with Gloucester or into the heart of God with Oedipus. He is his own arbiter, mover of himself, a creature loosed into the universe with a power to change it irrevocably. Nothing can resist the movement of his mind, in his mind.

O clear intelligence, force beyond all measure!

Beyond all measure. Man is the paragon of animals because his faculties are infinite, Hamlet says. Surely "infinite" is too strong a term, even for the faculties of a creature who has downed the sky. But it is not. "Infinite" may be taken literally, not simply because man does not yet know how far his thought and will may carry him, but because he knows he is free to declare himself independent, if he chooses, of the infinite God who made him. Man is free to defy Zeus or to renounce Christ, free to free himself of obeisance to any other, all other, power. The degree to which this freedom may be exercised is insisted upon by Judas in Yeats's brief pageant-play, *Calvary*. Meeting Christ carrying the cross, Judas proclaims himself the one man in the world no longer subject to Him.

> CHRIST. My father put all men into my hands.
> JUDAS. That was the very thought that drove me wild.
> I could not bear to think you had but to whistle
> And I must do; but after that I thought
> Whatever man betrays Him will be free;
> And life grew bearable again. And now
> Is there a secret left I do not know,
> Knowing that if a man betrays a God
> He is the stronger of the two?

Judas exults in his total freedom:

> . . . I did it,
> I, Judas, and no other man, and now
> You cannot even save me.

Man's freedom is in this sense absolute. Man can declare himself law. The chance—the probability—that he will suffer for such a decision is beside the point. The decision is his to make, if he wishes; when he makes it, it cannot be altered by Anyone.

Judas has never been made the central figure of a major tragedy. Within tragedy, Prometheus is the archetype of this ultimate freedom of mind and will, and he is so precisely because his body is bound. Chained, he is free to challenge Zeus for as long as he likes. In the end Zeus must arrange a compromise, for there is no way in which Prometheus' intellectual and spiritual independence can be breached.

Moral issues must be put to one side here. Moral issues come into being as a consequence of man's freedom, as moral principles come into being as a guide to man in his use of his freedom. They do not alter the fact of his freedom. Man is free to love to the point where he must kill his love in order to have it all and forever. He is free to know what he wishes to know; he is free to know sin. He is free to pursue reason into madness, perfection into corruption, vengeance into glory. He is free to will nothing but good. Tragedy reports the *fact* of his freedom in each case, the freedom in each case having been exercised "all the way."

Because tragedy is the form that dares pursue each of its actions to the fullness of man's capacity, it cannot commit itself too soon to determining matters of right and wrong: to do so would be to inhibit the free forward movement. Certainly temperance, prudence, the mean, is praised in tragedy. Creon will tell Oedipus, "Do not seek to be master." And when Creon has had his own taste of being master the chorus will say of him:

> There is no happiness where there is no wisdom. . . .
> Big words are always punished,
> And proud men in old age learn to be wise.

But most praise of the mean will come from the chorus, as this last counsel does, as this next counsel does:

> . . . unwise are those who aspire,
> who outrange the limits of man.
> Briefly, we live. Briefly,
> then die. Wherefore, I say,
> he who hunts a glory, he who tracks
> some boundless, superhuman dream,
> may lose his harvest here and now
> and garner death.

The chorus, however, is—nearly always—the *inactive* agent in a Greek play. The chorus is not the hero; it is all the rest of us, those of us who lead lives of relative security because we dare nothing. The chorus may well praise the mean because—in its passive, reflective, undecided way—it is hoping for stability, frightened when great deeds are done. It does not necessarily lack wisdom; it does lack the will to action which brings tragedy about.

Otherwise, questions of right and wrong, when they are touched upon, are either rendered ambiguous or raised as mere aftermath. The chorus wavers between Creon and Antigone, refusing to side morally with either contender; we waver in the same way between Coriolanus and the unthinking mob he rightly-wrongly despises.

And when Creon speaks so wisely to Oedipus he is speaking from hindsight, after the assault upon heaven is over: "Do not seek to be master; you won the mastery but could not keep it to the end." Moral homilies, even profound moral observations, are possible once the deed is done.

But tragedy is generally forced to treat questions of right and wrong ambiguously or as aftermath because questions of right and wrong, of explicit innocence or guilt, are not the questions it means to pose. "On the contrary," Hegel said of the Greek tragic heroes, "it is their fame to have done what they have done. One can in fact urge nothing more intolerable against a hero of this type than by saying that he has acted innocently. It is a point of honour with such great characters that they are guilty." They are guilty, that is to say, of having *acted,* of having acted to the limits of their powers without pausing to count consequences. So far as moral guilt or innocence is concerned, "the heroes of tragedy are quite as much under one category as the other."

Phèdre does feel shame. "But her sense of shame," Henri Peyre stresses, "is not followed by true repentance. Not once in the play does Racine write the word 'sin.' Phèdre's last cry is one of regret for never having enjoyed the fulfillment of the criminal love for which she must nevertheless atone." At the end Phèdre would have more freedom, and more. It might have been said of her, though Mary McCarthy said it of Lady Macbeth, that "the unimpeded exercise of her will is the voluptuous end she seeks."

Oedipus comes to his ultimate confrontation with God, according to Kitto, feeling that "there was no sin." Oedipus "has nothing with which he can reproach himself; repentance is not in the picture at all."

The master-image of tragedy, then, is not a moral one. "The master-image," in Jones's phrase, "is that of playing with fire 'out there' in the objective scheme of nature." Fire may destroy or cleanse; no matter. Tragedy must play with it. The possible must be investigated.

This is the openness—for good or for ill—which tragedy dares walk into. As a rule, man's ability to walk forward into the infinite is regarded as a good; it is difficult for man to regard his freedom otherwise. But there are occasions when freedom itself acquires teeth. The power to choose suddenly becomes an obligation to choose, and we are immediately caught up in the tragedy of the "cleft stick." Because Pelasgus, in *The Suppliants*, is both free to choose and forced by his position as king to choose, he finds himself in a vise created by his freedom. Here are his alternatives, just the two of them. Neither can be elected without pain. One must be elected. The power to do becomes the necessity of doing. The torn principals of Racine's *Berenice* are similarly trapped in their right of choice: both are free to set love above honor or honor above love, and it is this freedom that creates the tragic action. "All that is serious in life comes from our freedom," Bergson said.

Thus man's very possession of freedom gives no single answer: it is a good; it is an intolerable burden. On the one hand it permits us to pursue what Schlegel called "that longing for the infinite which is inherent in our being." On the other it draws us into a dilemma which A. C. Bradley has described in his discussion of *Hamlet*. Of all of Shakespeare's tragedies, Bradley says, "*Hamlet* most brings home to us at once the sense of the soul's infinity, and the sense of the doom which not only circumscribes that infinity but appears to be its offspring." Doom may be born of our experience of the infinite. If Oedipus is embraced by the infinite, Hamlet is destroyed by it.

Tragedy returns so many different answers because it must keep itself free to report what freedom finds. It cannot be narrower than the area it invades. Tragedy is *in* the area: not in the flaw, not in the hero, not in any moral conclusions which may be drawn from a difficult experience, not in sadness or suffering or fate. Tragedy is a terrain, vast, unmapped in advance, waiting for the impress of feet which will not break stride until the last possible step has been taken. In the full tragic experience, I. A. Richards has said, "there is no suppression. The mind does not shy away from anything." The tragic area is boundless; the tragic will is unfettered; the tragic end will be whatever it happens to be in this particular case, that is all. Tragedy occurs when man uses his freedom without reservation.

We have a habit of thinking that "tragic" means "sorry" or "doomed" or "morally guilty"; it means "free."

If it is easy enough to see why tragedy should provide us with a variety of courses and a variety of outcomes, it is still not easy to understand the persistence, within the tragic variety, of one kind of play—the kind that simply shipwrecks the man who has acted. We learn to expect a certain spiritual surprise of tragedy: Oedipus is granted the daemonic glory he seems so wrongly to have insisted upon; Orestes discovers that he can murder his mother and still be given absolution; Hamlet, in spite of all he has done or not done, deserves flights of angels to see him to his rest. Or, when surprise is absent, it is absent for very good reason: Macbeth may be shipwrecked, but no one is surprised that he should be; it is clear to us from the outset that in using his freedom to kill the king he is embarking on a course he himself holds improper, not navigable.

But there are some few tragedies which are truly bleak, tragedies which give the effect of being irrationally, irredeemably bleak; *Lear* is the king of them. And it is these that bring us close to Bradley's terrible paradox: the infinity that is open to man may itself doom him, the exercise of freedom may end in the loss of all freedom, may end in total and arbitrary disaster. Why, in some instances, should freedom kill freedom? Why should Lear begin by exercising his kingly freedom to the full and end by being thrown on the earth to rot?

Inch by inch Lear is stripped of his freedoms, stripped by his daughters, stripped by his Fool, stripped by the elements, stripped by the gods who play with men for sport—until finally he is stripped of the freedom that begot his freedoms: the use of his mind. Darkness comes down. Nothing is. If in the darkness Lear finds a degree of peace that light never allowed him, if he is offered an evidence of love better than any he has known before, the small comforts that come to him have no power to heal. The man cannot be restored. Breath leaves him, and the universe is silent. A man of generally good intentions, of exceptional capacities, and of no very appalling failings has been deprived of his powers by a "wanton" hand. The universe has not so much punished him as rejected him utterly, humiliated him and cast him away. That was Lear. He is nothing now.

When we come upon such a play—a play in which the malignant effects of the action seem far in excess of anything the hero has done to provoke them—we generally say that we are in the presence of an inscrutable Necessity, a Necessity to which we are as blind as Oedipus is, before which we are as helpless as Lear is. The concept of a last Necessity supposes that the universe exists in a certain way which may be challenged but cannot be changed, which is right but cannot be reasoned about. Man may be free to move into the infinite; but because he does not know the "necessary" nature of the infinite—"necessary" simply because it *is*—he may make a false step without warning and fall to his doom without further cause. The infinite is not required to explain to man why its footholds were insecure.

The idea that the universe behaves according to certain irresistible laws of its own does not always, or automatically, eliminate the other idea that the tragic hero is responsible for what happens to him. Sometimes the two ideas coexist, run parallel, as Bernard Knox has demonstrated in his exceptionally helpful comment on the ending of the *Oedipus Tyrannus:*

The overthrow of the tyrannos is complete. When Oedipus returns from the palace he is blind, and, by the terms of his own proclamation, an outcast. It is a terrible reversal, and it raises the question, "Is it deserved? How far is he responsible for what he has done? Were the actions for which he is now paying not predestined?" No. They were committed in ignorance, but they were not predestined, merely predicted. An essential distinction, as essential for Milton's Adam as for Sophocles' Oedipus. His will was free, his actions his own, but the pattern of his action is the same as that of the Delphic prophecy. The relation between the prophecy and Oedipus' actions is not that of cause and effect.

Mr. Knox goes on to say that the relation between what Oedipus has done and what the oracle said he would do is that of a metaphor. It equates two things which are themselves utterly independent of one another. Man makes the outcome without prompting from Necessity; but Necessity knew what it would be all the time.

Yet there are tragedies in which man's contribution to disaster seems an insufficient one, and it is in these that we feel ourselves most at Necessity's mercy. An apparently indifferent hand has struck a mortal blow and has given no signs of caring whether or not the remains were buried. Some human residue is rubbish.

Even in these plays we make an astonishing assumption: that Necessity is just. It is not just in man's way; man's justice cannot account for it. But because we have come from, say, the rubbish heap of *Lear* not filled with disgust but filled instead with an inexpressible satisfaction, we acknowledge that Necessity is somehow just in its own way. What is, is. And whatever perfectly satisfies its own requirements must be said to possess perfect rectitude. That man should sometimes be crushed by the requirements of a rectitude he can neither anticipate nor fully understand is very hard; but the fact has been observed and so must be recorded. "It may be hard," Kitto says in discussing the burdening of innocents, "but Aeschylus never pretended that life was easy, or that Zeus was simple, or that only the guilty are tortured."

Still, to say that Necessity must be honored, or that whatever is hard must indeed be accepted, does not fully reconcile the tragedy of extraordinary harshness with the affirmative pressures which we have found existing in all tragedy. It is all very well to say, with D. D. Raphael, that "we do not feel that *man* is lowly, is dust and ashes, when confronted by the greatness of that which he opposes and by which he is crushed. He is defeated, but he remains great, sublime, in his fall." How does he? Why should he? What is sublime about an apparently irrational extinction?

I do not think sufficient attention has yet been given to a hint which might be taken from Kitto and applied not only to a handful of plays but to the entire tragic range.

In discussing the *Prometheus,* Professor Kitto suggests that Aeschylus is displaying for us a conflict between Zeus, who stands for a kind of rigid authoritarianism that exercises power in the interests of stability, and Prometheus, who stands for the questing and not quite containable intelligence. "Both have to concede something, and assimilate something," he says, "before they are reconciled in the later perfect cosmic order of Zeus." The two, that is to say, are in opposition now, but in testing their opposition to the full they will arrive at an advanced state of understanding, a richer and higher order, later. "Such an evolutionary theme explains the prominence given to the evolution of civilization in our play [Prometheus' proud boasts about the advances he has arranged for man], and it accords very well with the evolutionary theme which becomes prominent in the *Oresteia."*

The key word here is "evolutionary," and it provides us, I think, with the hint we need if we are to answer our last and most perplexing questions. In the case of the *Prometheus,* Professor Kitto can only "suggest" an evolutionary theme, because the trilogy, as we have it, is incomplete. But the complete *Oresteia* leaves no room for doubt. It offers, as its content, no fewer than three evolutionary processes which result in evolutionary advances.

On a personal plane there is the spiritual transformation of Orestes from an avenger who can say to one of his victims, "I must make sure that death is bitter for you," into an ennobled figure, "taught in the school of suffering," who knows that

> The blood upon my hands has sunk to sleep,
> The matricidal stain is washed away.

On a social plane there is evolved, before our eyes, a judicial concept by means of which Athens will henceforth be able to rule itself in such a way that

> Ne'er, I pray, ne'er may that
> Root of evil, civil strife,
> Rage within her boundaries.

And on the supernatural plane there is an even greater evolutionary achievement. An ultimate accommodation is reached between the daemonic powers of the Furies and the Olympian powers of Zeus, Apollo, Athena. The ancient dark forces that controlled the human subconscious and the new forces urging the cause of social reason are to fuse their energies in a divine harmony wholly beneficial to man. The heavens are now filled with "a song of faultless victory" as the Furies, who formerly terrorized mankind, pray

> . . . that no harm
> Befall the offspring of humanity;
> And prosper too the fruit of righteous hearts.

All of the gods, having made peace among themselves, are now friendly to man, just as Oedipus, having passed through the fires of his own evolutionary transformation, finds himself in harmony with powers that formerly eluded and tormented him:

> For I come here as one endowed with grace
> By those who are over Nature . . .

The evolutionary thrust of tragedy—or at least of some tragedies—has been intimated elsewhere. Harvey Cox, coming at the matter not from a dramatic but from a social and religious viewpoint, readily adopts an evolutionary reading for the *Antigone*. Antigone, in this view, is "the tragic figure who symbolizes the painful transition from tribe to town, from kinship to civic loyalties." She defends an old and valid way of life: a society held together by intense adherence to bloodlines. But at the time of her gesture a new and larger order is in process of being forged: that of the community composed of many families and assuming authority, as a community, over any one of them. Creon is the new man, the social rather than the tribal being. In the end, his new way of life must win, superseding but not necessarily discrediting the old. However one may feel about the two participants in this struggle, and no matter what pain is imposed upon both, a forward movement is recorded; man enters a more complex state of being, the social structure extends its reach.

Similarly, in using the *Andromache* to pinpoint a recurring strain in the tragedies of Racine, Roland Barthes finds one of the play's heroes seeking "to choose in himself and for himself between Past and Future, between the oppressive comfort of an old legality and the risk of a new legality. For him the problem is to live, to be born to a new order, a new age. This birth can only be violent. . . ." The conflict of the play is not confined to a private struggle between hatred and love; rather, "it is much more harshly (and justly) between what has been and what seeks to be." But all of the play's central figures are engaged in just such a conflict, and in Andromache's case the struggle is rewarded. "The outcome of the play is unambiguous. . . . Andromache has made her conversion, she is free."

We have seen Iphigenia's body vanish under the knife and the body of a hind appear in its place almost as a relic of Iphigenia's former state; the image of evolutionary ascent is virtually literal.

But we are speaking here only of what might be called evolutionary successes. In an evolutionary context, why should we confine ourselves to those tragedies which make either a spiritual or a physical transformation explicit, which display in plain view an accomplished mutation?

It seems to me conceivable, gathering the evidence we have, that *all* tragedy is directly engaged in exploring the evolutionary thrust forward, and that it is just this participation in the processes of change that impels every tragic hero to exercise his godlike freedom "out there," to test the universe for what is possible with all the force he commands. It seems to me conceivable that tragedy puts man on the path to becoming more than man, to doing "more than man may do," and then watches—hopefully, fearfully—to see what will happen to him.

From an evolutionary point of view, every sort of thing may happen to him. Whether we are speaking of that spiritual evolution of the individual which was understood by Greek and Christian alike or of that evolution of species which was understood by no one until the nineteenth century, it can never have been supposed by anyone that all evolutionary advance was immediately, uniformly discernible or that successful mutation was the one event to be looked for. Christians have known failed saints, as the Greeks knew failed heroes, as we know failed species. Successful mutation, genuine transformation that is also an advance, is possible. In species, it is also so rare that we have taught ourselves to think casually in terms of millions of years. Man, the creature, was once some other kind of creature; at some future time he will no doubt be yet another kind. But we must make our reckonings long. In individuals, spiritual transformation seems less rare; there is quite a full callendar of Christian saints. In order to arrive at the calendar, however, it has been necessary to think in terms of, and to wave to one side, more than millions.

It is to be expected that a dramatic form devoting itself generally to the most intense pitch of things should, if setting itself to render an account of evolutionary possibility, show us possibility triumphant, transformation achieved. Tragedy does this, as we have seen. But it should also show us a great many other things.

At least three other things come immediately to mind. If tragedy means to account for the entire spectrum of evolutionary activity, it should certainly show us the near-miss, the advance that is within finger-tip reach but that fails for want of strength in the fingers, as though a man had succeeded in reaching the uppermost ledge of a wall and then, through fatigue or a miscalculation on his part, lost his hold.

It should show us what seems stalemate but later proves an advance. The resistance offered to man as he makes his fierce thrust forward is very great, so great that it must often seem that an individual hero has failed, when in fact he has made matters easier for those coming after him. As Karl Jaspers says, "The mighty breakthrough of the new is bound at first to fail against the staying power and coherence of the old way of life not yet exhausted. Transition is the zone of tragedy."

And tragedy should also show us—if it is to be entirely honest—the evolutionary dead end we know to be possible. It should take into account the change that does not prove an advance at all but ends in dry bone on the beach—in the gutted frame of a Tyrannosaurus rex called Lear.

In short, tragedy should report every conceivable experience man can have as he exercises his freedom totally in the hope of arriving at a new state of being. In order to get at these possibilities, and to see how they are reflected in tragedy, we need some sort of image, however crudely literal and insufficiently subtle it may be. Suppose we imagine the evolutionary opportunity "out there" as a vast and invisible, though granite-tough, honeycomb over the face of which man clambers in search of a fissure that will let him through. Most of its cells are solidly blocked; the man who batters his head stubbornly against any of these can only end by breaking his head. Some few cells—a very, very few—are open enough to permit relatively easy passage; a degree of ingenuity will twist a man through. And some other few are blocked but vulnerable; there are cracks in the granite which may, after painful effort, be scratched wider and deeper until the barrier crumbles and passage becomes possible. On the other side, for those who achieve the other side, lies a new degree of freedom greater than the freedom which has thus far been exercised.

If this image is at all a tolerable one, it may help to unravel certain puzzles which have pursued us like Furies. We ask why man, in the process of exercising his godlike freedoms, should nearly always be ravaged and sometimes destroyed utterly. But the exercise of a freedom toward an evolutionary end must always be painful; change is painful, mutation is painful, because old traits must be sheared away and new ones grown. A child does not acquire a second set of teeth without pain; an older child does not pass through adolescence without pain; an adult does not make a marriage without pain. The achievement of any new state of being entails both severe loss and difficult experiment, by trial and error, to discover precisely what the new state of being may be. And if change is painful, so is the attempt to avoid it. Pelasgus, like Titus and Berenice, would prefer not to be forced into choosing the change that must come; but there is a need—a Necessity—of making the change. The pain is not only in the doing; it is in the pressure that insists on the deed being done. Lear begins his play by making the most radical of changes; thereafter he resists, in fury, the consequences of the very changes he has made. But change will not be resisted. The evolutionary pressure will not be resisted. It will burn in a man, it will alter a man, it will drive a man into altering other things, whether he wishes or no.

There is a further, deeper sense in which the evolutionary process requires something like destruction. Because man is now in the process of becoming more than man, man as we know him *must* be destroyed. The birth of the new requires the death of the old, as, in the supposed origins of the tragic rite, the birth of the new year required the death of the old, the making of a new king required the unmaking of the old. The rites which seem to have given us the impulse to tragedy are themselves plainly evolutionary, in however intuited a sense. The original tragic rite included "celebrations of the mystery of individual growth and development," Francis Fergusson tells us, pointing out that at the same time it was "a prayer for the welfare of the whole City; and this welfare was understood not only as material prosperity, but also as the natural order of the family, the ancestors, the present members, and the generations still to come." If the Greeks were unaware of the evolutionary process as the nineteenth century came to know it, they were by no means unaware of the transitional position of man; at one end of the scale they dressed him in the skins of his animal origins, at the other they called him god-seeded and advanced him to daemonic powers.

The necessary death of one kind of nature if another is to supersede it means more than passing pain; it means a kind of dissolution. The paleontologist-philosopher Teilhard de Chardin does not expect that we shall ever find the "missing links" we are looking for between man and his predecessors. When a transformation has been achieved, the old husk is thrown off—and husks rot. Rotted husks are not likely to be discovered by scientists. But the moment tragedy is conceived as an evolutionary form, the spectacle of the rotting husk readily becomes one of its logical images.

Indeed I think that we may, without difficulty, conceive of the evolutionary process itself as Necessity. Here are the stern circumstances under which man advances or fails to advance. There are no guarantees, only opportunities.

The image I have suggested above may help us to understand not only the tragedy of the abandoned husk but also the tragedy of the free act which kills freedom. The one indispensable requisite of evolutionary advance is flexibility —the sustained capacity to deal with change, to be responsive to new possibilities. An openness is wanted, must be maintained at all costs; the man or species striving toward a new state must be forever supple before the prevailing winds:

> In flood time you can see how some trees bend,
> And because they bend, even their twigs are safe,
> While stubborn trees are torn up, roots and all.

The open man, the flexible man, probes the surface before him experimentally, looking for the faint crack in it that will make the granite give way beneath his fingers. Where he finds no opportunity, he moves on, with increasing fatigue perhaps, but without impatience. He tries another part of the surface, and another; he recognizes the reality of the barrier before him and adapts himself to it. He husbands his strength as best he can and holds himself ready for the assault that will have to be made when an actual fissure responds to his touch. He is able and he is free to explore possibility; at the same time he conforms himself, curves himself, to the nature of the surface on which he must work. When an evolutionary advance is finally made, he is the kind of man who will make it.

There is another kind of man—at least one other kind of man—who begins by attacking the inviting, invisible honeycomb with intentions as noble as his powers. For a time he works over its face judiciously, testing here and there with some caution. After a while, though, he makes a judgment: *this* is the place I *shall* go through. Where a flexible man might feel his way indefinitely, this firmer man fixes his sights upon a single course and commits himself to it irrevocably; he will go through with his fists, or his head, if need be.

He has made a judgment. In evolutionary terms, he has made an error of judgment. For by his own free act he has lost his freedom. By fastening himself to the single free act envisaged he has made himself incapable of further free acts. He is no longer flexible, open to other possibility. He has said to his God, or to Necessity, "not thy will, but my will, be done."

His will is locked. What has happened here might best be described as a thrombosis of the psyche. In exercising itself the will has knotted and thereby lost its suppleness. The man with the locked will is now not only unable to adapt himself to the rest of the infinite face before him. He will be unable to adapt himself to his failure when he fails. He will spend himself in his fixed position, ever more frustrated as he is ever more committed, and he will fall.

The tragedy of the locked will is essentially an ironic form, perfected by Sophocles; its root irony lurks in the elected free act which closes off the possibility of any other free act. Antigone cannot be budged from her course. Creon cannot be budged from his. Two locked wills lock horns. No alternative is ever considered by either power. The possibility of an accommodation by means of which both might advance to an understanding or a greater freedom, as opposed forces in the *Oresteia* do advance to understanding and increased freedom, is excluded not by the nature of tragedy but by the nature of the principals in this particular tragedy. Antigone is, by her own hand, an evolutionary suicide. Yet the irony is doubled: an evolutionary advance comes about in any case, and it comes about *because of and in spite of* Antigone and Creon. Both principals help to produce this advance; but they do it at such great cost to themselves because they are equally intransigent. They create the future by unnecessarily immolating themselves.

Because Sophocles developed the tragedy of the locked will, both in the *Antigone* and in the *Oedipus Tyrannus,* with such consummate skill, and perhaps because Aristotle— in his deep and just admiration—so often centered his attention upon it, men have often in later times treated it as though it were *the* tragic experience, tragedy exclusive, the norm, the pattern par excellence. The tragedy of the locked will does provide us, of course, with the pattern most often handed down in schoolroom definitions today. As we have seen, it is simply one of the marvelously varied tragic possibilities. But if tragedy is imagined as dealing with the evolutionary inclination of man's freedom, the tragedy of the locked will becomes—once again—a natural and even necessary variation upon the general theme. Here a possible advance has been slowed, or perhaps frustrated, or forced to call for a general holocaust, because a man has proved inflexible.

This evolutionary view of the tragic content gathers together, and I think justifies, the whole puzzling spectrum of presences which simultaneously inhabit and haunt tragedy: the admiration of man which is constantly expressed, the insistence upon man's near-divinity, the display of freedom carried forward "all the way," the yearning for infinity, the triumphant achievement of new states calling for paeans of joy, the painful passing through the crucible of men later transformed, the shattering failure of great men whose errors of judgment have bound them to themselves and locked them out of the advance, the harrowing dissolution of men gone up blind alleys and left there to disintegrate and to vanish, the conviction that persists at the end of every tragic experience that no matter what has happened it has all happened as part of a process which is in itself exalting.

Even the failed and abandoned have been participants in a forward journey; they sense an ending they cannot see, and so do we. Hegel speaks of heroes who "appear to be violently destroying the laws" and who are either vanquished or savagely punished. But they are "the heroes through whom a new world commences," for the disaster which overtakes them as persons does not diminish the ends they sought, the moving principle that drove them. The principle itself "will penetrate later, if in another form" and elevate itself into that momentum of spirit which urges the general advance.

In the light of an evolutionary understanding, Nietzsche may no longer seem quite so romantic as he once did:

Now we see the struggle, the pain, the destruction of appearances, as necessary, because of the constant proliferation of forms pushing into life, because of the extravagant fecundity of the world will. We feel the furious prodding of this travail in the very moment in which we become one with the immense lust for life and are made aware of the eternity and indestructibility of that lust. Pity and terror notwithstanding, we realize our great good fortune in having life—not as individuals, but as part of the life force with whose procreative lust we have become one.

Nietzsche was speaking directly of tragedy. The twentieth-century paleontologist Abbé Henri Breuil was speaking more generally when he noted that life tends to throw up a certain "psychic force" whenever there happen to be stimulating circumstances. In attempting to describe "the nature of this inaccessible reality which is so supremely active," Breuil maintains that the psychic forces which move us are, and perhaps forever will be,

outside our comprehension. We are ourselves contained in them . . . the truth is that the cosmos is an indivisible cosmic fact, a single reality, inside which swarm . . . individual beings in their infinite variety. The cosmos is not God. It feels its way, as it were, with a sort of freedom of adaptation . . . making a thousand experiments of which only some succeed, and some much fewer still (such as human intelligence) modify, locally at least, the setting and framework of things.

What is this unit, more essential than any one of us? This cosmos of which the dust of life is the blossom, the face of which only one known being, Man, is able to contemplate . . . himself creating art, beauty, imagination, or troubling it, in his humble way, with erratic and excessive passions? . . . For Man, as far as his thought can grasp it, the cosmos is a large body moved and organized by a single law, an Energy beside which all others are as ripples.

That inaccessible, enveloping, groping and unrelenting Energy of which Breuil speaks seems to me the essential tragic energy, its varied and unpredictable behavior the characteristic tragic behavior. If this should be the case, tragedy as a form is as inexhaustible as the process it reflects, capable of development beyond anything we can now see; we are simply being blind to possibility when we speak of the "death" of tragedy, and we shall have to account for our failure to produce satisfactory tragedy during the past three hundred years or so in some other way—but that is an accounting which must be reserved for a later chapter.

That the contemporary world feels a ferment which is very like the evolutionary tragic ferment I have just been trying to describe seems to me clear from a remark of Lionel Trilling's:

I venture to say that the idea of losing oneself up to the point of self-destruction, of surrendering oneself to experience without regard to self-interest or conventional morality, of escaping wholly from the societal bonds, is an "element" somewhere in the mind of every modern person who dares to think of what Arnold in his unaffected Victorian way called "the fulness of spiritual perfection."

Tragic man's quest for a state of spiritual perfection which will make him even more godlike than he now is does engage him, inevitably, in a break with those of his fellow men whose concern is mainly for security, in a surrender of his person to the painful experience of fully exercising his freedom, in an act of self-destruction which may end as mere destruction, or as sacrificial immolation, or as new birth.

That is the course elected by the man "who hunts a glory, he who tracks some boundless, superhuman dream."

Now this suggestion that *all* tragedy reflects one or another phase—individual or universal, successful or unsuccessful—of the evolutionary process under which men groan toward a glory dimly sensed is simply a suggestion of my own. What cannot be doubted, I think, is tragedy's commitment to freedom, to the unflinching exploration of the possible. We may wish to say no more of tragedy than what Henry Adams said of art: that it is "a fairly large field where no one need jostle his neighbor, and no one need shut himself up in a corner." But we are obliged to recognize, in the plays we already possess, not only a boundless variety in what is done but a boundless confidence in man's capacity for doing. It is man's extraordinary freedom of action which brings the play into being and thereafter defines it as tragic.

> Has the fight begun? May it begin!
> The presentiment enchants my mind . . .

So sings the chorus of the *Oedipus at Colonus,* nerving itself to its bold, repeated chant:

> *For God will see some noble thing*
> *Before this day is over.*
>
> Forevisioning the fight, and proud,
> Would God I were a soaring dove
> Circling the tall cloud;
> So might I gaze down from above
> On the melee I love.
>
> *For God will see some noble thing*
> *Before this day is over. . . .*
>
> Stern Pallas, hear us! Apollo, hear!
> Hunter and sister who give chase
> To the swift and dappled deer:
> Be our protectors! Lend your grace
> To our land and our race!
>
> *And you shall see some noble thing*
> *Before this day is over.*

8

THE COMIC
INCONGRUITY

TRAGEDY makes a great curved arc into the heavens, sometimes falling short of its sought goal like a Roman candle exploded too soon, sometimes crowning the universe and then vanishing "God knows where" in a burst of glory. Comedy never leaves the ground.

Its vision is not low. Squatting on the ground, it does not look downward to concentrate upon a universe that is either anthill or dungheap. It is not, as the inchoate notes left us in the name of Aristotle would have it, concerned with creatures "beneath us." Its glance is not superior but leveling.

Comedy cocks an eye upward at the very same man who is straining to divinize himself and notices that he is packing a little extra weight. Though he is on his way to infinity, he has a ham sandwich in his pocket and a bandage on one big toe. Man may free himself of the earth, but—as things stand just now—he carries a little bit of the earth with him wherever he goes, and so he must carry whatever is required to nourish or soothe it. He must render unto matter the things that are matter's. He can free himself of God but not of the need for a haircut.

King of infinite space, man is in fact bounded in a nutshell, and while the physical reality of the nutshell does not deny man his intellectual and spiritual mobility it does constitute baggage, baggage for which no other porter can be found. The baggage is heavy and in some measure humiliating. A bishop should not have to go to the bathroom. A weightless astronaut in space should not have to worry about making an appointment with his dentist. An ambassador busy on an important mission for his country should not have to pause over his scheduled appointments and soberly reshuffle a few to leave time for sex. The situation in each case is more than inconvenient; it is preposterous.

But that is the basic joke, the one incongruity upon which all other incongruities rest. That a being so entirely free should be so little free is absurd. That a creature capable of transcending himself should at the same time be incapable of controlling himself is hilarious. Hilarity is a gasp, a shock, a shriek of disbelief at what is plainly evident. There the creature is, and the creature cannot be. "He's impossible," we say of a fool who has made us laugh, as we wipe away our tears. We do often cry when we laugh.

We cry because the disparity is unthinkable, and we laugh because there is no other thing we can do about it. Laughter always erupts precisely as the situation becomes hopeless: nothing in the world now can stop the old lady in the wheel chair from crashing into the wall, Charley's Aunt doesn't realize he has lost his skirts and is going to be found out, the cabin is slipping over the cliff. Or, in James Agee's much-quoted example, "Laurel and Hardy are trying to move a piano across a narrow suspension bridge. The bridge is slung over a sickening chasm, between a couple of Alps. Midway they meet a gorilla."

In tragedy there is always hope, up to the last minute and beyond it, some kind of hope; we rarely laugh. We are serious so long as there is a way out. Comedy occurs when there is no way out. A popular cartoon of recent years shows two starved, bearded, manacled men at the base of a towering room. Thirty feet above the chains that bind them is a barred

window too small for either to pass through. There is nothing else in the chamber. One of the gaunt men is saying to
the other, "Now, here's my plan . . ."

The men have hope, and we know better, and that is
comedy. Comedy depends upon tragedy, because it would
have no disparity with which to shock us, it could not say how
preposterous man is, if tragedy did not first and fully display
man's extraordinary freedoms. Comedy listens, nods, does not
deny. In the end, it simply points. It points to the thousand
ways in which the admittedly free man is not free. It keeps an
echo of freedom about, because if it did not there would be
no joke; in the cartoon the bearded man's freedom to plan is
the echo. But its own province is the province of chains; it
spends its hours counting—blandly, almost without comment
—the manacles that cannot be got rid of. It walks through a
world paved with flypaper.

Tragedy speaks always of freedom. Comedy will speak of
nothing but limitation.

If tragedy opens a possible door to the infinite, comedy
tries to slam it shut, catching tragedy's finite fingers in the
process. In the first fully developed comedy we know, Aristophanes' *The Acharnians,* a demigod appears, the same sort
of demigod who has figured so prominently in tragedy.

> "Who are you and what?"
> "Amphitheus the Demigod."
> "Not a Man?"
> "No, I'm immortal."

The demigod quickly ticks off his lineage to make good his
claim that there is "immortality in our family." He then
indicates that he is at present on a divine mission, just as
surely as Orestes was.

> The Gods moreover have dispatched me here
> Commissioned specially to arrange a peace
> Betwixt this City and Sparta. . . .

Semidivine status, god-given goal. This is our man from tragedy, all right, not altogether some other creature. However, there is a hitch.

> . . . notwithstanding
> I find myself rather in want at present
> Of a little ready money for my journey.

Even a demigod needs cash if he is to get anything done in *this* world. The universe in which he now appears is peculiarly constructed: it acknowledges his freedom to come and go as a god, but only on condition that he come and go as a paying guest. On earth, the infinite is taxed.

"Dear me. Even Hell's gone commercial," mutters Dionysus, another demigod, in *The Frogs*. But this particular demigod is subject to a good bit more in the way of material humiliation than the demand that he pay two pennies for his passage to Hades. First he must row his own way across the infernal lake, with a chorus of frogs singing its "koax, koax" as he labors. "My arse is sore, koax, koax," he finally adds to the lyric.

Arriving at Pluto's gate, he is severely frightened by an underworld apparition. His embarrassment is duly noted by Xanthias, his slave.

"What's the matter?"
"I seem to have soiled myself. . . . Bring me a sponge and apply it to my heart."
"Here you are. Apply it yourself. . . . Merciful God, is *that* where your heart is?"

Before entering Hell poor Dionysus is horsewhipped.
"You cannot torture me. I am a god," he protests. But he has, in a fit of cowardice, exchanged clothes with his slave, and now it is impossible for the guardians of Hell to tell which of them is truly the god. A test by horsewhip will determine the issue, for, after all, gods don't cry. When an

"Oooh! Oooh!" escapes him under the whip, he is wistfully eager to explain it away.

"Then why the tears?"

"Some onions popped into my mind."

Other things pop into godlike minds along the way. One demigod to another:

> "Tell me, O Herakles:
> Hast ever been seized by a craving for pea soup?"
> "Over and over again . . . I see pea soup
> in my mind's eye."

A solo voice in the chorus sings:

> I just glimpsed the prettiest girl in this part of the town,
> And a pink little nipple popped through a rip in her gown!

The demigod, all too temptable, is at once heard to volunteer, "I'd like to play with that pink little nipple," though that is not what he came to Hell for. He came to Hell for a most noble purpose: to find a first-rate poet and restore him to earth again.

The godlike power and the noble purpose are here repeated from the tragic landscape. The tragic landscape, a thing of boundless freedoms, is accepted as the basic landscape. Over it a transparency has been laid, a transparency covered with graffiti—with scrawled reminders that no demigod is quite godly enough to count himself free of a sore hide, loose bowels, unbidden erections, or a passion for pea soup. Whatever mankind cannot escape, comedy puts into its sketchbook.

But we had best try to deal with the graffiti of comedy—the chalk marks superimposed upon the tragic vision—in some sort of order, for there is an order in them and it is an ascending one, ascending at the last to the point where it is *almost* impossible to say which is the background and which the foreground, which tragedy, which comedy.

We are most obviously dealing with comedy when we are

most preoccupied with man's physical limitations. Though comedy's vision is not low in the sense that all aspiration is ignored, there is still such a thing as low comedy. Low comedy comes into being whenever the aspiration of the necessary background is kept to the barest possible minimum and when the staggering imperatives of the foreground are hurled at us with such force that we grow wide-eyed at the very size of them. It is comedy in its first state of shock.

Low comedy is a birth experience, and for a time traumatic. It consists in the discovery that we have a backside and that it is going to be slapped. Total humiliation comes with our first breath of air, is a condition of our breathing. We are embarrassed to have a body that can be subjected to such treatment, and whenever it is subjected to such treatment again—in a first slap from a mother, in a misstep that leaves us astonished on our noses in the playpen—we are freshly outraged. The news that an erect creature should so easily fall down, or that a pretty dinner should make such a mess on the floor, at first appalls us. Then it fascinates us. For a while we want to knock everything down, throw all dinners on the floor, to prove to ourselves that this wild accident of nature is so. We explore our astonishment obsessively, repeating first principles to see if they will repeat themselves.

The duration of our obsession, and the particular thing it repeats, can easily be measured by an experience of the comic source we have had in our own time. We happen to live in a century which saw comedy come leaping, bawling and bandy-legged, from the womb once again. A new entertainment medium, the motion-picture film, had been handed us. But what had been handed us was a blank check, or, more exactly, a blank frame of celluloid. Nothing was known of its possible properties. The rules of the stage, for instance, guaranteed it nothing. The people who were close to its invention had not the least idea of its nature, of the laws that might ultimately govern its use. Film had to find itself from scratch. It also had to find comedy—its comedy, all comedy—from scratch.

It found comedy in a tumble and a bump, in the subjec-
tion of a body to the ghastly embarrassment of being a body,
nothing more. The discovery was so stunning in its newness—
though slapstick is an ancient term and though a vast library
of prior comedy existed to be examined at will—that for some
years the world could scarcely contain its astonishment at the
simple information offered. Because the medium itself was
new, the past, with all its knowledge of complex comedy, was
in effect swept away. We, like film itself, began at the beginning. What we saw at the beginning so transfixed us that we
could not put it away, or imagine refining it, for quite a long
time.

To look back at the earliest film comedy today, including
at least the first two years of Chaplin's work, is—and let the
adjective be ironic—a sobering experience. A man falls down.
Another man falls over him. The two, getting up, knock each
other down again. Chaplin, a cave man in a bearskin, clouts
one man over the head with a spiked club, then another man,
then another, then another. There is no sly relationship
between the cause of the clout and the clout, no point to the
fall other than that it *is* a fall. The act is absolute, self-
contained, gratuitous. It is not funny as we look at it now. It
is merely physical.

We marvel that so mindless, so noncommittal a demonstration of the body's tendency to drop when tripped or clubbed
could have provoked such instantaneous and passionate delight that at once there were millions of theatergoers paying
millions of dollars—in nickels and dimes—to see the demonstration repeated. Chaplin's popularity, for instance, was not
a gradual thing, growing as his films grew in subtlety; it was
immediate and vast, the indestructible result of two years in
which the comedian fell without cause backward into ash-
cans. One wonders how his audience could have seen in this
flailing, brash, sado-masochistic Charlie-one-note the potentialities that were actually there. One wonders even more
how the lesser acrobats who fell around him could ever have

been loved. They were not loved, as it happens, by minds sensitively attuned to the rich complexities of the earlier comic library, by eyes that could no longer be opened in raw innocence. "The comic film," Agnes Repplier wrote, "does not reach the dead level of imbecility which distinguishes the comic strips in our daily press; that would be impossible; but it is without acuteness, and without intelligible purpose." For a mind attuned to *The Way of the World,* just so. Yet the comic film, in its crudeness, was crudely right. It was on its way to its own kind of sensitivity, to what would become and be recognized as art.

It was somehow right to spend a number of years investigating little more than the spectacle of Ben Turpin, cross-eyed, catching his foot in a rope attached to an automobile so that when the automobile roared down the road at fifty miles an hour Mr. Turpin was forced to hop on one foot at fifty miles an hour after it. Indeed, the very fact of the body's vulnerability seemed so inexhaustible a source of surprise that no one was in much of a hurry to take slapstick comedy's obvious second step: the step in which the club is swung and misses, only to land more forcefully later; the step in which what is surely going to happen is devilishly delayed. The comedian Larry Semon eventually developed a piece of business which came to serve him as a trademark. Mr. Semon was bent on rescuing a girl. He battered with his fists on a locked door behind which the villain held the girl. Finally, summoning up all his energies, he retreated eight or ten paces, squared his shoulders heroically, and ran at full gallop toward the door. Just as he reached the door, the villain opened it. Mr. Semon flew across the room, out a window in the opposite wall, and dived three stories to the street, where he landed on his head.

But that is already a refinement: the locked door has opened to make matters worse. The simple proposition that the human body *is* a locked door, that two bodies meeting cannot pass through one another but are forced to rebound, was a proposition sufficient to engage the energies of clowns through some thousands of short, unbelievably successful films, and it was sufficient because it was the base on which comedy rests. In the background—even in these films—there is a faint aspiration: someone is running to rescue a girl, though the footage given to any relationship with the girl is as nothing compared to the footage given to tripped feet. In the foreground, coming at us with express-train speed, is the clumsy contrivance in which man's spirit is housed.

Man, free man, is the prisoner of his body. If his foot is caught, he is not free to leave it; his mind, together with all of its aspirations, must go along with it. That was the vision upon which film comedy founded itself, and it was eminently suitable that the prisoner it showed us should eternally have been chased by Keystone Kops.

To see Chaplin, prisoner of all the itches that flesh is heir to, flip his cane behind him and flex it into position to scratch his backbone where his backbone demanded scratching was to return to the first comic image in Aristophanes' first extant play:

> Alone in the morning, here I take my place,
> Here I contemplate, here I stretch my legs;
> I think and think—I don't know what to think.
> I draw conclusions and comparisons,
> I ponder, I reflect, I pick my nose,
> I make a stink—I make a metaphor,
> I fidget about, and yawn and scratch myself . . .

It is dawn, the body is stiff and must be stretched, the body must relieve itself, there are lice about, thinking will do nothing to banish the crust within which man's knowledge of himself is contained. The crust, the vulnerable and demanding and embarrassing casing of the body, is the first comic fact because it is the improbability that is closest to man: it is *he*. When Bergson, in offering his theory of comedy, speaks of the *process* of encrustation, he is centering his attention—too narrowly, I think—upon the binding force of habit; man acquires habits and the habits tend to freeze him in an unfree posture, making a virtual automaton of him. But the crust is there from the beginning, indissoluble, insistent, the Siamese twin of our hopes. And from the beginning of comedy as we know it, with Dicaepolis picking his nose in Athens, all the way to Chaplin cleaning the wax out of his ears—with his cane—in Hollywood, the properties of the crust are chanted as in a litany, repeated as helplessly as hiccups.

If Dicaepolis itches, Sir Toby belches. Dionysus defecates for our pleasure in plain view, and captious members of the audience are warned by Aristophanes that they had better like his play *The Birds* or prepare to suffer the consequences:

> . . . if we lose the Prize,
> Take portable canopies with you on your strolls,
> Or your new white robes will suffer
> Avine criticism dropping from the skies.

Most post-Athenian theaters have preferred to send their physically distressed characters offstage, though they have all been willing to delay them onstage long enough to indicate the degree of distress involved. In the 1920's the subject proved so freshly fascinating and so irresistible a source of merriment that a comedian, Chic Sale, was able to sustain a long vaudeville career and then cap it with a best-selling book, *The Specialist*, by doing no more than hint at what Aristophanes had been blunt about. The specialist specialized in building outhouses. In the 1960's Italy arrived at its longest-running musical comedy, *Rugantino*, in which the biggest—and the best—laugh had to do with a fellow forced to hide for some time in an empty wine vat; when an interloper refused to believe that the vat was empty he naturally tried the spigot, and, lo and behold, a flow of bright amber fluid rewarded him.

In the *commedia dell' arte* Harlequin appears in a thousand roles, including that of Mercury, though a Mercury whose winged heels have gone limp. As he explains to Jupiter, he is no longer able to fly, because, as he was soaring down a street just now, a servant wench emptied a chamber pot upon him and so thoroughly soaked his wings that if he hadn't had the good luck to fall on a dung heap he'd surely have broken his neck.

"There are no lavatories in tragic palaces," George Steiner remarks, "but from its very dawn, comedy has had use for chamber pots." It does seem unlikely that we shall ever exhaust our astonishment at the body's simplest, if rather peremptory, commands, or that we shall ever cease feeling that they are in some way improprieties.

Toothaches, headaches, bellyaches are all plain insults to a spirit which should be permitted to go about its important work freely and without having to attend to the impertinences of a mere vehicle. The fact that these things are painful is not the main point comedy makes, though all of the blind demands of the body—when they are not rather quickly attended to—do become painful. What comedy insists upon is the irresistibility of the demand, the fact that man cannot shake himself loose of such irrelevant and sore distraction. A man with an ice pack on his head, or with an obviously blackened eye, or with a cheek the size of a balloon is automatically funny because the imprisoning role of the body has been sketched in a single swift line. For the moment matter is undeniably master, as it is when a man is the temporary captive of hiccups. Hiccups are uncontrollable. So are sneezes, and the longer an impending sneeze can be delayed—paralyzing the man about to sneeze and also the conversation around it—the funnier it becomes. In a silent film, *The Strong Man,* Harry Langdon succeeded in extending a very few sneezes into some five minutes of playing time, calling it quits only when his nose threatened to retire into his head like a rabbit's.

When a man can't help what his body is doing to him he

has begun to be a clown. All reflexes are funny, including the familiar and endlessly surprising knee reflex. We still find it hard to suppress a giggle when a doctor taps our knee, or as we watch him tap someone else's; legs are supposed to do our bidding, but here we are, helplessly kicking, powerless to assert control. And if a professional comedian can toy with the reflex, failing to produce it until the hovering doctor is exasperated and then finally producing it in such a way that the doctor is both satisfied and kicked, our delight is doubled. For if what cannot be helped is funny, a kick in the pants that cannot be helped is heaven-sent: *both* parties are powerless in the situation.

But of course there are far greater urgencies than finishing a sneeze or soothing a hangover. According to a fragment left us by the Greek comic playwright Alexis, there are only three "genuine factors in life: drinking, eating, sexual indulgence. All the rest must be called appendages."

Actually, the list needs a bit of tidying up. There is one so-called "appendage" which really ought to be moved into the roster of indispensables: shelter, clothing, the necessary effort man makes to defend his nakedness against heat, cold and bumblebees. But if we count eating and drinking as a single factor, and add the constant need for some sort of cover to keep the rain off, we are still left with a basic trio of aching wants; and the three supply us with what are probably our most familiar comic images. There is the hungry man staring at food; there is the shabbily dressed man shivering in the doorway; there is the sexually deprived man howling at the moon.

"Comedy rolled in shouting under the divine protection of the Son of the Wine-jar," George Meredith says, and Plutarch gives us some sense of the procession as a whole: "One carried an amphora of wine and a bough; another dragged along a goat; a third followed carrying a basket of dried figs; and, to crown all, the phallus."

The craving for food has given us all of our comedy cooks,

our potbellied gluttons, our parasites who are invited for dinner at eight and arrive promptly at eight in the morning, as well as our stingy hosts who keep their larders locked; and the craving for drink has given us our Falstaffs.

Greek gods could be made to drool. When the enterprising humans of *The Birds* decide to starve the gods out of heaven by refusing to sacrifice them any more oxen, Prometheus becomes completely unstrung:

> There's not been so much as a sniff of sacred smoke
> coming up to us from a single human altar.
> I swear, we're hungrier
> than a Thesmophoria fast-day; and, what's worse,
> the damndest lot of starving yowling gods
> from the back country are talking about revolt
> if Zeus doesn't manage to get a decent consignment
> of sacrificial cuts to keep us going.

What the gods and the men of comedy have in mind is handsomely indicated in a pre-Aristophanic fragment Gilbert Norwood calls to our attention. Clowns, it would seem, have always daydreamed of a lost world in which

necessaries came spontaneously. Wine flowed down all the gullies; cakes fought with loaves at people's mouths, crying "Please swallow us, if you like the best quality." Fish came into the house, frying themselves and lying down ready on the tables. A river of soup flowed beside the dining-couches in eddies of stewed meat, and runlets of sauce were at the disposal of those so inclined: there was plenty of choice where to soak your morsel before swallowing it. On plates were cakes sprinkled with seasoning. Roast thrushes with their pastry flew into your mouth, and the buns made an uproar as they jostled round your teeth.

But that is a dream. It is, alas, nothing like the actual world our clowns have wandered into. They have been invited to dinner—when they are invited at all—by Harpagon, who takes the precaution of telling his servants to bring wine "only when the people are thirsty, and not in the manner of these impertinent lackeys who come and provoke them, and put drinking into their heads when they have no thought of such a thing." Food? "We shall be eight or ten; but you must not count upon more than eight. If there is enough for eight, there is enough for ten."

Small wonder that men count their mouthfuls as carefully as one of Plautus' starvelings does:

The other day a buzzard made off with his helping of dinner. He bawled like a baby, went to the judge, and, crying his heart out, asked whether he couldn't have the bird subpoenaed.

Small wonder that Massinger's Justice Greedy, who longs to be "arch-president of the boiled, the roast, the baked," cannot keep from whimpering and stamping his foot when he thinks of a careless cook's oversight:

The cook, sir, is self-willed, and will not learn
From my experience. There's a fawn brought in, sir,
And, for my life, I cannot make him roast it
With a Norfolk dumpling in the belly of it;
And, sir, we wise men know, without the dumpling
'Tis not worth three-pence.

Some things do bring a man to tears, and who could expect the good Justice to silence his cry? "It must ring out, sir, when my belly rings noon," he says.

In comedy bellies are always ringing noon, then one, then two, then accepting boiled shoe if nothing else is at hand. Kate would eat anything Petruchio strikes out of her hand, burnt or not.

The body does not need clothing or shelter quite so desperately as it needs meat and drink, nor will the desire for a cozy fire drive it to the heights of rationalization reached by Demosthenes in *The Knights:*

It's a very presumptuous thing to speak of liquor
As an obstacle to people's understanding;
It's the only thing for business and dispatch.
D'ye observe how individuals thrive and flourish
By dint of drink: they prosper in proportion;
They improve their properties; they get promotion;
Make speeches, and make interest, and make friends.
Come, quick now—bring me a lusty stoup of wine,
To moisten my understanding and inspire me.

But that there is a degree of desperation involved in man's having no fur of his own to warm him is indicated by the standard low-comedy costume. The most noticeable thing about a low-comedy costume is that it doesn't fit. The shoes are too big. The trousers are too big or too small. The hat may be any shape at all so long as it is an odd shape for the head on which it sits. The sleeves of the jacket may cover the hands entirely, as Jimmy Savo's always seemed to do, or they may be working themselves up to the elbow, Stan Laurel- or Lloyd Hamilton-fashion. In any case they are out of fashion, unmatched, and patently never destined for the frame that carries them.

That is to say, *something* must cover the human form and in desperation anything will do. The low comedian has no tailor. He must content himself with what the Salvation Army has thrown away.

The costume serves a double function. It calls attention to man's need and therefore to his nakedness. The need revels and runs riot in coattails that trail along the floor, in starched collars that rise above the nose, in trousers that must be held together by rope. But the nakedness is in constant danger of showing through. Someone will step on the dragged coattails, or on Katharine Hepburn's long train, and the rip will sever man from his elaborate pretense of being free of his actual and undefended body; he is not free now, he will have to run away and hide until the pretense can be restored. The great collar will pop off, right over the astounded creature's head, and the scrawny vulnerability of a neck, scarcely better than a chicken's, will make the man seem more naked than if he were actually stripped. The cord that holds together the trousers will become caught on something, or be inadvertently tied to a dog that is about to spy a cat, and down the trousers will come. Dropped trousers are *de rigueur* in low comedy, as are lost toupees and the appearance of Stan Laurel in his long woolen underwear. The stripping may be piecemeal and prolonged: in his film *The Freshman* Harold Lloyd dashed off to a college dance in a tuxedo that had been hastily basted together and, on the dance floor, lost a pocket, then a sleeve, then everything. Like the basic Harlequin costume, clothing is something patched together to conceal a truth: not the truth of sexuality but the truth of vulnerability. But it can never be more than a temporary defense, and the ultimate image it is straining toward is that of the naked man in a rain barrel.

"For the rain it raineth every day," Feste sings, reminding comic man that he had best carry an umbrella, which will no doubt be blown inside out, and that he must, by nightfall, find a shelter he can crawl into, even if it is only the cradled arms of a canvased statue that is about to be unveiled in the morning.

Having fed and sheltered himself, in however improvised a way, the low comedian will find that he has merely nursed his body to the point where it is ready to make fresh demands. The body is an ingrate: satisfy it in two ways and it immediately acquires the vigor to behave insatiably in a third. It is now ready for sex, whosoever sayeth no.

The "no" of the mind does not keep the phallus from popping up on unsought provocation, as the Greek theater graphically and tirelessly liked to demonstrate. For a considerable period of time Greek comedians wore oversize phalluses strapped about them—the oversize is right, not simply to trade upon the eternally made jokes about the proud length of a good man's penis, but to display the degree of dominance exercised by a physical instrument over a psyche which would often like to be free of it—and it is easy to imagine the laughter of an audience watching a man turning toward a woman and betraying his needs on the instant, helplessly, prisoner of a jack-in-the-box. We are forced to imagine this situation now, because we are less candid about the matter; we hide the absolute imperative and convey its power by a squirm, if that; when Alfred Lunt paused during a love scene in *Amphitryon 38* and uncomfortably straightened his leg, he was thought to be doing something rather daring.

But no matter. Sex, that "cruel and insane master" Sophocles was so relieved to be rid of at the age of eighty, is still very much with us, as it has been through Falstaff's lechery, Tartuffe's lust, Horner's eagerness to spread word that he is impotent so that women will feel safer in his altogether-unsafe company. Though we often degrade ourselves by the tortured evasions of our burlesque shows, and though we tend to go along with the Hollywood formula of displaying sex *in absentia* by showing the groom inadvertently but endlessly locked out of the bridal chamber, we remain aware that sex is more a tyrant than a tease. We suppress most of our urges, for good reason; we suppress a good bit of the conversation that might be made about them, in part to help us forget; but the suppression does not conceal the extent of our bondage, it reveals it. "We might find it difficult," Max Eastman suggests, "to acknowledge, or even to know, that there exists in our bodies a rather indiscriminate yearning to commit adultery. But if we were earnestly advising some young man to take a wife, and he should earnestly reply 'Whose?' that would give us a pleasure out of all proportion to the proper value of such nonsense." The secret is out in our snort of laughter, and when a moviemaker making films with a lingering Mediterranean candor urges actor Marcello Mastroianni to display his frustrated ardor for Sophia Loren by leaping up and down on the bedsprings like a child on a trampoline, while irrational sounds bubble up from the strangled fountain of his throat, the hilarity that sweeps through the audience is not necessarily a hilarity grounded in identical experience; but it is grounded in certain knowledge. Sex makes a man a helpless child again, a bouncing boy as it were, and it is strange that it should be for adults only.

Sex as sex is always a comic subject, never a serious one. Serious as a sexual problem may become for us in our lives, it can never be discussed without becoming in some way funny. The moment we open our mouths to speak, injured and exhausted as we are, we represent ourselves as faintly ludicrous. Friends may listen sympathetically, trying to keep their faces straight; but there is a goatish grin waiting to break out behind the close attention and the sympathy, and because we know that there is—because we understand the situation as fundamentally preposterous—we generally relieve the false sobriety by making the first joke ourselves. It may hurt to make the joke; but it would be terribly humorless of us not to do so. Even husbands and wives who are forced to thrash out the issue verbally cannot do it without wanting to laugh; in the end the discussion probably gains them something by exposing their common helplessness, their common comicality.

Sex must always be funny, because no man is free to be or not to be sexual. A man may choose to be celibate, as many have done; but he cannot choose to be sexless, to be indifferent to or independent of the responses which announce his captivity. As it happens, Molière's most lustful figure wears a clerical gown; and Machiavelli's crafty confessor, Fra Timoteo, is well able to find his way around the problem of who should lie with a wife after the wife has taken a dangerous potion that will help make her pregnant:

. . . when it is a question of a certain good and a doubtful evil, one must never forgo the good from fear of the evil. . . . The

uncertain evil is that whoever lies with you after you've taken
the potion will die. In some cases the man does not die. But,
since there's an element of doubt, it is best that [your husband]
should not run the risk. As to the act itself, to call it a sin is mere
moonshine, for it is not the body that sins, it is the will. The real
sin would be to act contrary to your husband's wishes, and you
will be acting in accordance with them. It would be a sin to take
pleasure in the act, but you *won't* be taking pleasure in it.
Besides, what one should always think of is the end in view.
What are your proper aims? To fill a seat in Paradise and to
make your husband happy.

So, off to bed with an eager—though perhaps soon deceased—
stranger.

But it is not really comedy's purpose to be cynical about
celibacy or to retail the gossip of infidelity. In dealing with
sex, comedy does not mean to be gratuitously leering any
more than it means to reform the habits of the world. Sex as
comedy is not a matter of morals; it is a matter of fact. What
it describes is an amplitude of appetite that cannot be satisfied within reason because reason was not consulted when the
appetite was being formed. Comedy looks at the sexual urge
and notices that it has very little to do with the desire for
procreation, very little to do with any one rationally desirable person, very little to do with the science of eugenics or
with intelligent social planning. As Mr. Eastman says, it is
indiscriminate, and because it is indiscriminate it begins to
be funny. Man is by nature a planner, and here is nature
making an ardent anarchist of him. The urge becomes funnier, objectively speaking, as we see that it is not only
indiscriminate but insatiable, as incapable of satisfying itself
in an intelligent fashion as Pandarus says it is in his song:
"Love, love, nothing but love, still love, still more!"

A man may have a wife, and may have had her many times,
but when Lysistrata persuades the wife to withdraw her
consolations temporarily it is as though the poor husband had
never had sex at all:

> She's left you in a sorry state:
> You have my sympathy.
> What upright citizen could bear
> Your pain? I swear, not I!
> Just the look of you, with never a woman
> To come to your aid! It isn't human!

Thus a member of the chorus sympathizes with a deprived soldier named Kinesias, who decides, with a long sigh, that "There's nothing for it, I guess, but an expedition to old Dog-fox's bordello." And off he trudges, sad slave that he is.

Luckily for alarmed moralists, the lively energies of comic sex are all released in laughter. Moralists do not necessarily understand their luck in this case, and some were very much concerned in the 1930's when Mae West descended a staircase as though she were snuggling into it, put one hand on a newel-post and the other on an unmoored hip, rolled her lower lip clockwise while her eyes were rolling counterclockwise, and invited a Salvation Army officer to come up and see her sometime. What escaped the wary were certain simple facts that any one of millions of delighted moviegoers could have ticked off at the time: that Miss West was fortyish, that she was overweight, that she was no one's current dream of a sex-object, that she was—as she had to be—kidding. A joke is always passionless, in the sexual sense, because the joke is *on* passion and annihilates it. Nothing that is truly funny can ever be titillating, because the very fact of titillation is being rendered absurd. So far from worshiping sex, comedy declares it insane and is happy to be so honest about the matter.

The essential mindlessness of sex as such forever halts it short of the tragic frontier. The tragic aspiration is toward a changed state of being; the aspiration of sex is for much more of the same. "The district is wrong for tragedy," a character in Graham Greene's sex comedy, *The Complaisant Lover*, remarks. Sorry as we may feel for a betrayed husband, there is no being serious about furtive forays into hotel bedrooms where bellboys enter at all the wrong moments, as they always have. It is only when sex itself begins to give way to the passions of permanent relationships, of psychological preferences, of love as a fierce activity of the intelligence as well as the body—and perhaps with some indifference to the body—that the inflections of tragedy make themselves heard. Phèdre has never slept with Hippolytus; her passion is in her head. Romeo is no longer interested in sex, he is interested in Juliet; if he were interested in sex, he would not kill himself.

Dynamene doesn't kill herself, though she has planned to. Dynamene is the deeply distressed heroine of Christopher Fry's short and delightful *A Phoenix Too Frequent* and she has come to the tomb of her recently deceased husband prepared to join him in the afterworld. A soldier of the world happens by. He is handsome, but he is in some distress, too. He is responsible for the corpses of six hanged men, and one of the corpses has been stolen. He will be court-martialed, perhaps executed. Before too long Dynamene has worked out a solution. She will have the soldier, and the soldier can have her husband's body to hang.

The soldier is very briefly shocked.

> Hang your husband?
> Dynamene, it's terrible, horrible.

But Dynamene is a woman of great wisdom.

> How little you can understand. I loved
> His life not his death. And now we can give his death
> The power of life. Not horrible: wonderful!
> Isn't it so? That I should be able to feel
> He moves again in the world, accomplishing
> Our welfare? It's more than my grief could do.

Practically speaking, Dynamene is of course right. Comedy is always practical. Certainly Dynamene would be foolish to fall into Huncamunca's situation, so touchingly set forth in Fielding's *Tom Thumb the Great*. Huncamunca has just this morning rejected one suitor in favor of another and now her intended is apt to be slaughtered in the streets by Grizzle:

> Oh! fatal rashness should his fury slay
> My hapless bridegroom on his wedding day;
> I, who this morn of two chose which to wed,
> May go again this night alone to bed;
> So have I seen some wild unsettled fool,
> Who had her choice of this and that joint-stool;
> To give the preference to either loath,
> And fondly coveting to sit on both:
> While the two stools her sitting-part confound,
> Between 'em both fall squat upon the ground.

In a sober footnote, Fielding calls particular attention to the beauty of the concluding image, putting a bold, bald face upon the double burlesque. Romeo is thinking of infinity, where he will be reunited with his Juliet. Huncamunca is thinking of tonight. Two lines after Dyanemene has decided to trade in her husband, she is looking eagerly about the tomb:

> Let's celebrate your safety then.
> Where's the bottle? There's some wine unfinished in this bowl.
> I'll share it with you.

And we are back to the wine, where we began.

9
COMIC DESPAIR
AND COMIC SOLACE

THE LIST of physical pressures from which man is never free could be extended considerably, could be pursued to the grave if we cared to do so, because the grave is where man's body is going. Low comedy—the kind Stephen Leacock called "the archeocomical or paleoridiculous"—has always very much cared to pursue the matter and has therefore devoted itself fervently to such things as the symptoms of nausea, seasickness above all, or the overpowering need to fall asleep. Even in Chekhov, where comedy is at its most delicate, characters are constantly dozing off while other characters make what they consider their profoundest speeches, and in something as broad as the *commedia dell' arte* it is often difficult to get a Harlequin—or a Scapin—awake. Harlequins and Scapins are essentially as self-indulgent as cats, eager to curl up in a corner once they have had the day's bread and bologna, reluctant even to do mischief until they are prodded into life.

And comedy has always been extraordinarily fond of twins. Twinness invites comedy because identity—which is a spiritual thing—is denied by the body. The two Dromios are actually two different persons, but their bodies say they are not. This accident of nature is a considerable nuisance to a Dromio. He is not only imprisoned by his own body but also, in a harassing way, by his brother's. The absurdity of being human is uncomfortably doubled: the spiritual has now been twice limited by the physical.

Low comedy does not balk at freaks of nature; it takes delight in them, even when they hurt. Any kind of deformity —natural or acquired—will bring the paleoridiculous running, shouting its joy at having discovered one more bit of evidence for its basic proposition: that the free spirit is yoked to a donkey and like Pinocchio may sprout long ears. Ben Turpin's crossed eyes *were* his comic talent; there was nothing else about him that was ever very funny. Bowlegs are funny, and so is Cyrano's nose. Everybody's fat, from Falstaff's to Zero Mostel's, is funny. And when the deformity is functional rather than organic it continues to be funny. Stuttering and lisping are two of the swiftest, most indestructible sources of laughter in the entire low-comedy canon; occasionally we think ourselves above such devices, and reformers are apt to scorn them as antisocial and cruel; the fact remains that there is scarcely a high-school comedy produced in the land that does not lean on them, while the sophisticated professional theater simply translates lisping into effeminacy and continues to go its merry, utterly standardized way.

Today we show some distaste for history's earlier habit of laughing at hunchbacks and making them court fools. We choose to be more humane about the deformed, which means in general that we simply refuse to notice them. I have often wondered whether a hunchback mightn't prefer to be looked at, even if he is laughed at, than to be so discreetly ignored as he is now. How does it feel to watch an eye flick away in studious pretense that nothing has been seen? I don't know, and I have no wish to seem brutal. But there are brutalities and brutalities. The truth, in this case, is that there is something to be seen and the something to be seen is by definition comic: soaring man, and a hunchback may soar as high as any, has been clapped into a vise. That the vise may be in some instances tighter, or strangely varied from the norm, does not alter its character as a vise; indeed it calls attention to that character. It is possible that history's earlier habits were more honest than ours; they may even have been more humane. The position of the hunchback as king's fool may have been good for the hunchback and good for the king. The hunchback was given employment, a defined place in society, and an extraordinary freedom to talk back. The king was given an ever-present reminder of the clay of which his own body was made.

Agnes Repplier has called attention to the gradual bowdlerization and sentimentalizing that overtook the old "fool" legends, which had originally been candid to the point of near-cruelty but had been earthy and clear-eyed and direct. And she quotes a passage from Andrew Lang which may bear repeating:

How singular has been the history of the decline of humour. Is there any profound psychological truth to be gathered from consideration of the fact that it has gone out with cruelty? A hundred years ago—nay fifty years ago—we were a cruel but also a humorous people. We had bull-baitings, and badger-drawings, and hustings, and prize-fights, and cock-fights; we went to see men hanged. With all this we had a broad-blown comic sense. We had Hogarth, and Bunbury, and George Cruikshank, and Gillray. We had the Shepherd of the 'Noctes,' and we had Dickens.

In any case, comedy is habitually indifferent to any pain that may be caused by the display of pain. It is a noncommittal form, simply saying what is so. It is willing to catalogue headache, toothache, and gout, dogbites, bee-stings, and burned fingers, obesity, homeliness, and humps on the back, and then to add—because the necessary catalogue is not yet complete—palsy, senility, and madness. Sir Andrew Aguecheek and Justice Shallow are utterly stock comic figures; so is the fellow who thinks he is Napoleon.

"We went to see men hanged," Andrew Lang says. Comedy

likes to see men hanged, because it refuses to be reticent about anything that may happen to the body. An effigy is generally surrounded by roisterers: who can look at that sacklike shape and not laugh? When it is remembered how imperious that sack once was, with its sexual demands and its fondness for stuffing itself, the laughter can only increase, grow hysterical.

To think of suicide is, perhaps, to think of tragedy: Romeo and Othello and Antony come so quickly to mind. But suicide has often seemed to clowns the only way out of their imprisonment. Certainly they think about it, sometimes they try it. During the first half of our own century, Lloyd, Chaplin, and Langdon made substantial comedy out of the business of leaping from bridges and putting pistols to their heads. A stage comedy of the 1960's, *The Owl and the Pussycat,* fabricated its funniest sequence out of the effort of two suicide-bent lovers to put their heads into a gas oven simultaneously. In Aristophanes' time the matter was earnestly discussed:

". . . Tell me the best route . . . to the Houses of the Dead."
"The best route, hey? Take a rope and hang yourself!"
"No. Delicate throat."
"How about hemlock?"
"No. Feet get cold, legs swell up."
"I'll tell you the quickest way."
"Good. I hate walking."
"Go out to Potterville—"
"Yes?"
"Climb the tallest tower—"
"Yes?"
"And wait for the start of the torch-race.
When the fans shout 'Throw down the torch!'
then you just throw yourself—"
"Where?"
"Down."
"Oh. But that might scramble my brains!"

It will quickly be noticed that there is a slight difference between tragic and comic thoughts of suicide. Even when the clown most ardently wishes to kill himself, he shies not from the deed but from the discomfort of doing it. The rope around his neck itches, the water is wet. In general the clown subscribes to Dorothy Parker's resigned creed:

> Guns aren't lawful;
> Nooses give;
> Gas smells awful;
> You might as well live.

And when the comedian succeeds in nerving himself to the task, when he screws his eyes shut and leaps from the bridge, he lands ankle-deep in the gentle waters below. Or perhaps, as in Murray Schisgal's contemporary comedy *Luv,* he is saved from the drop by a passionate friend who promptly goes over the side himself.

In short, the comic suicide doesn't bring it off. This does not make him a happier, more successful figure than his tragic brother. The tragic hero succeeds at what he means to do. The comic hero is not only enough of a failure at living to want to kill himself, he is also a failure at killing himself. He is doubly frustrated. And, ironically, his frustration is brought about by the persistent nagging of those limitations whose nagging he is trying to escape. As a rule, when he thinks of killing himself he is trying to rid himself of the demands his maddening body makes: he is hungry or homeless or sexually defeated. But to rid himself of that body he must do something uncomfortable to that body, and here he balks. He is its prisoner both ways.

Death, whether inadvertent or intended, is a constant theme of comedy. At the opening of a Billy Wilder film thirteen gangsters are lined up against the wall of a garage and shot down efficiently. Chaplin, in *Shoulder Arms,* makes a hasty little chalk mark for every German he dispatches with a rifle, only to realize he has been too hasty when a bullet comes singing back at him from the direction of his last victim; honorably, he erases one of the chalk marks. Beatrice Lillie drinks a lethal potion and topples backward like a dropped plank. Bob Newhart, told that one must be casual in attempting to lure potential suicides from the tops of buildings, strolls out onto a ledge, glances in surprise at the fellow who has been threatening to jump, and says "Oh . . . hi, there!" The simplest Punch-and-Judy show any one of us saw as children probably included Punch's murder of his wife, his infant child, his doctor, his executioner, and the devil who came to claim him.

Baudelaire remembered what had happened to Pierrot, condemned to the guillotine:

After first struggling and bellowing like a bullock that smells the slaughter-house, Pierrot at length submitted to his fate. His head was separated from his body. The great red and white face rolled noisily down to the prompter's box, exhibiting to the audience the bleeding circle of the neck, the severed vertebra, and all the gory details of a joint of butcher's meat, carved up for display in a shopwindow. But, suddenly, the decapitated trunk, revived by the force of the creature's irresistible thievish monomania, got to its feet, and triumphantly made off with its head, which, like a ham or a bottle of wine, and far more sagaciously than Saint Denis, it stuffed into its pocket!

All of this in the name of laughter. Why? Because to contemplate any true ending for a comedy is to contemplate death. Only death will end the joke. Man cannot ever be free of the matter that impedes, annoys, and limits him until he is in fact severed from that matter, until his consciousness is cut free of the machinery that clogs it. Only then may his soul, like John Brown's, go marching on, utterly uninhibited. Tragedy does often conceive of a future for the immaterial spirit. Comedy, finding its anchor in matter, discovering humor in the humbling of the free spirit by a sore toe, must end its days—if it is to end them at all—in the dissolution of the toe, of the hide, of the phallus, of the bowel. As we have seen, comedy most often avoids its only possible conclusion by the adroit device of coming to no conclusion at all: before an actual ending can be arrived at, an artificial one is trumped up. But the bleak breath of the actual, unstated ending is often felt in the play like a subtle draft in a warm house. There is a song in the fourth act of *Cymbeline* that lets the draft into that play, and it may be taken as the song that comedy, because of its nature, cannot stop whispering:

> Fear no more the heat o' th' sun
> > Nor the furious winter's rages;
> Thou thy worldly task hast done,
> > Home art gone, and ta'en thy wages;
> Golden lads and girls all must,
> As chimney-sweepers, come to dust.

With so much of dust in mind, how is it that we continue to regard comedy as a warm house? We see that its rooms are filled with the malcontent and the maimed, we hear the rumor of death in all the corridors, we know what Jean Anouilh means when he says that "Molière was the blackest of playwrights, blacker than Shakespeare." Yet we are very much at home in comedy. It seems a snug form.

It is. There are several reasons why comedy warms us, and the first of these is that we are deeply enamored of our limitations. Though we spend a great part of our lives trying to free ourselves of the comic imperatives—we force ourselves to eat less, we struggle to suppress sexual clamor—and though we are aware that we are truly free to be about what most concerns us only when we are out of bondage to the impertinently physical, we carry one piece of knowledge about with us always: surrender is sweet.

We may hate our hunger; but we cannot really hate satisfying it. We may find ourselves exasperated by the insistent need for sex, especially when we should like to show ourselves above it; somehow we can find it in our hearts to endure our exasperation, provided we get the sex. Constipation can be a confounded nuisance; but apparently everyone present understood Alexander Woollcott's enthusiasm the bright summer morning he walked onto the lawn at Bomoseen, stretched his arms wide, and exclaimed "I have just had the most magnificent bowel movement!" Comedy shows man shivering; but the shiver itself instantly suggests how nice it is to come in out of the cold.

What plagues man promises also to please him. Each of the nuisances that retards man's free movement, that calls him back imperiously to attend to an around-the-clock need, repays him somewhat for his trouble. If man is put to considerable inconvenience in dealing with all of the impedimenta he drags about with him, he does not precisely feel cheated by it. Physical necessity summons him, deflecting him from his free course; it then hands out cookies. A filled gullet and an emptied bladder are equally rewarding; and when the body becomes so demanding that all free activity must stop, sleep is as pleasant as can be.

The fact of the matter is that in one part of his mind man likes being helpless. It is his only form of hooky, the only holiday he gets. If he had a choice between needing to eat and not needing to eat, he would undoubtedly behave like a Spartan and choose not to need to eat. It would take one more worry off his mind, remove one more brake from his activity and his aspirations, which are always spurring him, sacrificially, toward a freer future. If he were offered some simpler and less bothersome means of reproducing himself, he would probably feel conscience-bound to accept it. His basic bent is toward an ever greater flexibility, toward easier movement with fewer encumbrances, toward mutation. Men work themselves to death now; they would shed themselves to death—or to a new kind of life—if they could. They know this. And they consider themselves lucky, they are delighted, not yet to have been given the choice. Food and sex and sleep and a warm bath have all been imposed upon them. And they look at their helplessness in the matter and laugh. They laugh because the imposition is ridiculous. And they laugh because they like it.

The laughter of comedy, then, is always a compound, even a contradiction: it is half a snort, half a sigh of gratitude. The man laughing is doubly aware: he sees that he is a prisoner and he knows that he enjoys the jail. We have not been concerned in our discussion with the nature of laughter prior to the appearance of formal comedy and are not going to be. Comedy itself is quite enough to try to deal with. But when psychologists and philosophers do probe back into the dim beginnings of laughter—dim, because they are the properties of infants who cannot tell us what amuses them so when they look at us—they generally wind up talking about the sensation of tickling. That children—or adults, for that matter—should laugh when tickled is odd. Being tickled is not pleasurable in the sense that eating a good meal, or getting closer to the fire, is pleasurable; it has something painful, or at least nerve-jangling, in it. But the problem is odder still. Human beings also laugh when they are *not* tickled. When they successfully dodge the determined tickler, they shy away in glee, laughing though nothing has happened. The very thought of being tickled, the *possibility* of it, arouses laughter. But this, I think, is our delight in being helpless asserting itself again. We see that we are vulnerable. But we are also amused and happy to be vulnerable, because our vulnerability has brought us, even as infants, so many warm comforts. We are exposed, and our exposure may prove humiliating. But our awareness that we may be ravaged coincides with our awareness that the ravaging may very well be pleasant. Dependence so often ends in delight.

There is thus a passive element present in comedy that never appears in tragedy. Our limitations are forced upon us. But the gratifications they demand are forced upon us, too. We have no choice but to please ourselves in certain ways.

The laughing man is the man who submits, gives in for the moment, openly admits that he is the captive of sensation and that he can be tickled, or teased by the aroma of dinner cooking, or stirred by the sight of a shapely thigh. The tragic man is an ascetic who will have none of this. Sensation, gratification, all comfort must be sacrificed as limitation is brushed aside in the free thrust forward, however that thrust may end. Tragic man is humorless, or, if he has humor, as Hamlet does, it is humor out of joint, displaced, half-mad with exasperation. The wholly humorless man is a man who is unaware that he *has* any limitations; he is smug, and often something of a Puritan.

However the psychologists may settle their own debate on the trigger that releases laughter in children, the laughter that greets deliberate comedy—comedy meant to be looked at rather than lived—is an informed laughter. The intelligence is able to *see* the disparity between a flexible instrument and the monstrously inflexible appendages from which it can never wholly sever itself and to make a judgment upon the curious mismatch. It can understand, with Bergson, that "the living body ought to be the perfection of suppleness," but that it is kept forever short of its goal by "a kind of irksome ballast which holds down to earth a soul eager to rise aloft." The ballast is "inert matter dumped down upon living energy," and "the impression of the comic will be produced as soon as we have a clear apprehension of this putting the one on the other."

But thus far Bergson confines us to quite a cool judgment, to a critical response that is wry enough but something less than merry. After all, the sight of so much irksome ballast might very well prove irksome, and the effect of comedy might be wholly—rather than only partly—abrasive. Something else that we know must be added to do the joke justice. We have our own experience of the irksome ballast, we have been there. And we know *why* Marcello Mastroianni wants to get into bed with Sophia Loren so badly, *why* Bert Lahr feels such ecstasy at getting his shoes off, *why* Carol Channing devours dumpling after dumpling as the plot goes on without her. Ballast is bothersome, but ballast is grand. Now we are able to laugh wholeheartedly, not simply with a seeing eye but with a remembered appetite. We confess to ourselves that, for all that is irksome in it and for all that it does to keep us from rising aloft, limitation itself is a pleasure. Only freedom produces absolute pain.

We strike a balance, then: we say that it is absurd to be so limited and it is lovely to be unable to resist the temptation to be limited. We groan and give thanks in the same breath. Even so, the image we see would not strike us as all that funny if we thought it an entirely personal reflection upon ourselves, if each of us thought that he alone was the fool snuggling contentedly beneath blankets when he might be up and about making spiritual history. Not one of us could endure the humiliation of being the sole slacker, the only tosspot in a town full of supermen. If all responsibility for advance were ours, and we found ourselves unable to advance because we couldn't give up smoking or wenching, we should simply and wholly detest ourselves. Who would have the heart to laugh? Luckily, comedy makes its accusations by incriminating absolutely everybody, and that is the second of its salves.

Comedy insists not upon the uniqueness of its hero's qualities but upon their commonness. It is tragedy that attends to the unique man, to the self-assertive plunger who isolates himself from his fellows in order to rise above them. Comedy constantly suggests that we join the rest of the boys at the back of the bar. Comedy loves company, because it is miserable and because everybody else is, too. While swapping complaints at the back of the bar, the boys will quickly discover that they all have the same complaints. With the discovery they will burst out laughing.

The sense of companionship that is essential to comedy if the despair inside comedy is to be endured at all is a sense felt on both sides of the footlights. The clowns onstage need fellow clowns. A lone clown in a play soon languishes: the Fool in *Lear* sickens from being so knowing and so isolated, and he vanishes; the Clown in *Othello* cannot remain in the play beyond a moment. More often than not comedians come two by two from the ark, one tall and one short, one fat and one thin. A comedy team is more easily arrived at than a comedy star working solo, because the double image instantly suggests the prevalence of what is deplorable in the human condition: Oliver Hardy is not the only incompetent in this world, Stan Laurel is his proud equal. Even when one member of the team is little more than a "straight man," rapidly setting up loaded questions for his zanier companion to answer witlessly, he is sorely missed when he is gone: Jerry Lewis has always seemed a little *too* peculiar, too estranged from the species, since Dean Martin left him. A clown too much on his own comes to seem merely mad. The sign of the ampersand always suggests comedy: we do not have to be told in advance the nature of the work that is to be done by Harrigan & Hart or Weber & Fields or Clark & McCullough or Wheeler & Woolsey or Olsen & Johnson. Furthermore, there is a tendency for the team to increase and multiply, so that we continue to expect comedy as we go to see the Three Stooges or the Four Marx Brothers or the Five Little Foys. Seriousness produces no such gatherings of the clan.

The business of working in tandem is, of course, as ancient as Aristophanes, and the expectation of comedy's first audiences was very much like ours: Pithetaerus would not arrive in Cloud-Cuckoo-Land alone, he would have Euelpides at his heels, bumbling and querulous; Dionysus would go to Hades with Xanthias comfortingly close. These tag-along friends are not simply confidants, as they might be in tragedy; they are counterclowns, boobs of a feather, living proof that human ineptitude is not exceptional but universal. In tragedy, Phèdre does need an Oenone simply to listen to her; in comedy, a Dromio needs another Dromio to be *like* him, as

Sir Toby needs Sir Andrew, and Sir John needs his lustful Doll. Whenever a comic figure has no companions, he is apt to be hurt in the play, hurt by his vulnerability; Malvolio is such a figure, and we are sometimes so sorry for him in his isolation that we flatly refuse to laugh. The general tendency of comedy is gregarious, in self-defense. Ben Jonson arrives at a universe in which all men are deceivers ever. Unable to choose among them, we are at liberty to enjoy them all.

There are exceptions, to be sure, to this rough-and-ready rule of two's comedy and three better still. Single clowns exist and thrive: Beatrice Lillie is at her best when no one is bothering her. But the need for companionship has not ceased. Single clowns, when they are great clowns, almost never play out their tricks surrounded by straight performers to whom they must address themselves. That would make them loners. Instead they dispense with other performers altogether and commune directly with the audience. A different kind of commonness is being established, however uncommon the clown may seem to be.

A question that once stumped me when I was discussing comedy with a group of students was this: Why do people laugh at Beatrice Lillie before she has done anything? The question contained a hidden conclusion: if people will laugh before anything funny has been done, isn't humor largely a matter of expectation, of rumor or reputation, of a predetermined state of mind? I couldn't contest the fact at hand; I have seen Miss Lillie bring off the trick too many times. The curtain rises, without music or other fanfare. Miss Lillie enters, perfectly groomed, from the upstage portals and makes her way toward us with great simplicity. At the footlights, with her hands clasped, she smiles a tentative but sweet smile of welcome—not too sweet; not sweet enough to constitute a comment on sweetness—and then she waits. With her eyes fixed directly upon us, and with neither mockery nor roguishness in them, she continues to wait. She waits until the audience laughs. It always does.

Why? I would be rash to say, but I don't think it has much to do with preconditioning. I suspect it works this way. We who are in the auditorium are respectable people. We have dressed decently for the occasion. We have come quietly into the theater, been polite to those near us, sat straight in our seats as we waited for the curtain to rise. We have probably applauded Miss Lillie on her entrance and returned her first smile. But now our smile has quieted down again, as smiles do until they are further encouraged. Our faces have fallen into composure, which means that they have fallen, momentarily. We are ourselves, our sober selves. We sit attentively, and with some dignity, waiting.

Miss Lillie waits right back at us. She is *exactly* as sober, *exactly* as dignified, *exactly* as tolerant, as we are. No more and no less. A serious actor would be more dignified than we, and we should not laugh at him, at least not yet. A vulgar comedian might at once be less dignified than we, and we should feel pushed; we might try to laugh, somewhat feebly, over our innate resistance. But there is one thing we cannot resist, one thing that never has to be explained to us as a source of comedy, and that is a literal duplication of ourselves as we seem just now. There is no glossing over the appearance of two women at the same party in the same dress; they must scream on sight. Children engage in face-making contests, one duplicating as precisely as he can the changing expressions—the changing *serious* expressions—of the other for the sole purpose of seeing which can go on longest *without* laughing; laughter is the norm.

And no consciously sober person who meets another person he recognizes as sober in just the way he is can possibly help having the foundations of his sobriety undermined. The structure collapses on recognition, because some part of it is an artifice, and in the mirror-image the artifice is the thing most clearly seen. We know that we are not really the persons we are pretending to be just now. We are not nearly so sober, or so dignified, or for that matter so well-dressed—what had to be pinned together, and then concealed, at the last minute before we came?—as our adopted image claims, and all that is needed to reduce us to helplessness is to see the image immaculately repeated in a void. Nothing is added, no comment is made, we are simply looked at with our own eyes. The relationship of Miss Lillie with her audience is always an unspoken conspiracy. *"We know, don't we?"* is the essence of it.

Later on, Miss Lillie will do highly improbable things, such as lowering herself demurely to a bench and, at the moment of contact, sliding clear across it as though it had been inexplicably greased. But she begins with what is both a simpler and subtler intimation: there are two of us exactly alike, and one of us ought to be ashamed.

Comedy spares us shame by pairing us off. "Recognition comedy" is a commonplace term and is generally used to describe comic situations in which virtually all members of the audience will at one time or another have found themselves. The children of the household are beginning to feel superior to their parents, the bride's first dinner turns out badly, husband and wife never seem to want sex at the same time. In these instances it is expected that members of the audience will turn to one another with a "Just like John!" look and take half their pleasure in comparing the activity on stage with the familiar behavior of themselves and their neighbors. The sense of companionship has been increased in two ways. Companionship with the performers has become the next thing to identity. And companionship in the auditorium has been heightened by the urge to exchange glances; the members of the audience do not forget one another in their absorption with the play but are encouraged to remember one another. If this sort of "recognition" is sometimes dismissed as too easy and too cozy, and too ready to trade upon an audience's predispositions, it is because it is so basic a comic maneuver that it often succeeds without the support of either talent or invention. Whole comedies go by without fresh penetration of the material and survive nonetheless; the material is so fundamental, and produces so predictable a response, that it can be handled by hacks without injury. But the fact that a hack finds reliable what another man might wish to refine infinitely does nothing to invalidate the substance of the jest; it simply proves that it remains valid in the clumsiest of hands.

I suspect that all comedy contains an element of direct recognition, however subtly the I–thee relationship may be intimated, and that the solo performer who does not have some sort of double on the stage is carrying the mirror-image over into the auditorium itself, in effect making the audience the other half of the comedy team. It is the essence of true humor, Louis Kronenberger has remarked, "for the humorist to ally himself with the joke; to be, as it were, a fellow-victim or culprit, a me-too in presumption or folly . . . humor is a form of honest admission, and shows a willingness to go naked."

To have *no* counterpart in the universe, to be unable to see at least one other body stripped naked and one other face strained, is to be Oedipus, or Prometheus. Uniqueness, aloneness, is unbearable in comedy and shatters it, as Bert Lahr showed us when, in *Waiting for Godot,* he stopped making us laugh long enough to become aware of his own solitude. He had made us laugh while he fussed with his aching feet. He had made us laugh while he talked at endless cross-purposes with a comrade-in-waiting. But there came a moment when he seemed to sense that the cross-purposes were truly endless, that they were a permanent condition of life, that the wall between two men could never be breached and that all men—even men doing the same things—were sealed-off rooms to one another. Not only was Godot not coming. His comrade was not a comrade. The universe housed Mr. Lahr, but it housed no echoes of himself. He was one and one only, untouched, unjoined, unknown. On this intuition he turned his great bulbous face toward us wrenched all awry, a convulsion of the cold and silent moon.

His spasm was a spasm of separateness, and it lanced comedy to the heart.

If, on the other hand, the ruined Oedipus, on the point of leaving Thebes, were to meet at the city gate another man who had *also* killed his father and married his mother, tragedy would be as swiftly dead. Let the two men compare notes, become cronies in corruption, and laughter must break loose no matter what has gone before. To be the precise duplicate of another man, even in suffering, even in nobility, is to become funny and to see the other man as funny, which is one reason why Schlegel could call comedy "the democracy of poetry."

The companionship of comedy is prismatic, throwing off its shafts of friendliness in every direction: the clowns on stage tend to join forces with other clowns; when they do not, they swiftly join forces with the audience in the auditorium; and the audience in the auditorium is constantly reminded of its own solidarity. This last point, I think, is a little bit misunderstood. Almost everyone realizes that laughter increases as the size of the audience increases, and not in simple proportion to the added numbers. Show a film in a small and half-empty projection room and the laughs it generates will be scattered, feeble, without momentum. Show the same film in an ample, well-filled auditorium and the laughs will link arms, overlap, mushroom. Hollywood legend is filled with instances of comedies that were judged failures and even abandoned until, by one accident or another, they were exposed to a single crowded house and proved themselves irresistible—to a crowd.

Most often we think of this swelling volume as a mere matter of sound. More people make more noise. We realize, too, that people laughing trigger one another to some degree: some sounds in the auditorium are infectious and stimulate others. But the matter goes somewhat deeper than that. It is not only sound waves that are being multiplied. Life histories are being multiplied. Looking at a film in a projection room with a few other people inhibits laughter because we are intensely conscious that, should we laugh, our laugh may give something away. It may give away more than our possibly defective taste; it may give away our secrets. To respond to something done on the screen, and to run the risk of being the *only* one to respond, places us in the exposed position of having identified ourselves with a character trait which is shameful because it is shared by a very few people, perhaps by no more than the figure on the screen and ourselves. We are nervous that laughter may betray us as departures from the norm. Laughter is an open sound and hence a confessional sound, and while we are well aware of our weaknesses we do not care to announce them publicly unless we are reasonably certain that they are universal weaknesses.

Courage comes with numbers. So does candor. The more people there are present the more likely we are to think that *some* other pariah will laugh and that we shall not be left wholly alone with a response that identifies us as culpable. We give ourselves more leeway, become a little more honest. And having heard our confession echoed, even if only by a beginning handful of those present in the auditorium, we drop our guards further, perhaps altogether. When an audience finally hears itself, as a whole, admitting in a burst of laughter that it recognizes, as a whole, a pattern of behavior it had hitherto thought singular, private, idiosyncratic, and just a bit shocking, the power of comedy to deal with despair by simply multiplying the despairing is fully at work. "The universal dissolvent" Hegel called it.

Each of us has probably had the experience of reading something funny when alone on the beach or on a subway train or in a restaurant, and of suddenly laughing aloud in these isolated circumstances. Immediately we are embarrassed. We feel ourselves fools, something close to hysteria creeps into the laughter if it is at all prolonged. There is a wrongness in laughing aloud on a deserted beach, a curious humiliation that prompts us to close the funny book on a subway train or leave a restaurant quickly before we feel too helplessly exposed. Even at home, where we do laugh more freely in private, the urge to interrupt the reading and find a wife or child in whom to confide the joke is all but irresistible. Private laughter is in some deep sense improper. Comedy was meant for company; it is too degrading to be endured alone.

There is a third way in which comedy compensates for the bleakness of its vision. It acknowledges that limitations are pleasant and it insists that they are suffered en masse. It also places man midway up the mountain, where he can look below him and look above him and see that he is halfway home. If he is not an unimpeded creature, neither is he one on which the books have finally been closed.

Comedy's commonest method of doing this is to give man hooves and tails and donkey's ears. The method is one of illumination by inversion, and it has been in use from the form's beginnings. If, as Hazlitt says, Aesop "saw in man a talking, absurd, obstinate, proud, angry animal; and clothed these abstractions with wings, or a beak, or tail, or claws," the earliest writers of comedy for the theater were by no means blind to the likeness. Crates wrote a play filled with talking animals whose principal request to the hungry men about them was to "fry fish and kippers, and keep your hands off us," and even the gods were tutored in animal behavior. In a fragment of Cratinus, Leda is advised "to assume all the habits of a graceful hen, brooding on this egg." Whether the characters of a play might be men, gods, animals proper, or all three, the habit of naming plays to suggest a certain correspondence of kingdoms—*The Wasps, The Birds, The Frogs* —was as natural to Aristophanes as naming men after foxes and vultures and crows would be to Ben Jonson. No one knows when two men first made up the fore and hind parts of a dancing horse, but the image of Bottom wearing an ass's head remains for us a central image of comedy, and the *Cucurucu* of the *commedia dell' arte* is only one in a parade of roosters leading to Rostand's *Chantecler*. All men have noticed how animals resemble them, or how they resemble animals, and perhaps some have envied Epops' success in exchanging human fuss for heavenly feathers. Epops, once a man and now a bird, finds his new life not at all bad. "No money, of course," he says, but life is a pleasant diet of poppy seed and myrtle, white sesame and mint, with a bird's-eye view "of all lands under the sun, of every sea" thrown in—not to mention marriage to a rather sweet nightingale. "It's a non-stop honeymoon!" cries one of his admiring visitors from the trying world below. Whether man's fantastically envisioned return to a less complex animal status is regarded with envy or with disapproval—in Ionesco's *Rhinoceros* the growth of horns on the forehead is made a symbol of barbarous retrogression—the evolutionary link between two kinds of ass is a thing much on comedy's mind.

At first sight this would seem a device for demeaning man, for reminding him that in his slavery to the senses and to all natural functions he is not far removed from the sheep that can so easily be substituted for a baby or from the piglets that can be equated with sexually desirable young girls. If Aristotle thought that comedy dealt with creatures beneath us, here, surely, are the creatures—ourselves seen as lower animals.

But that is not the point of the device. Epops may indeed have been willing to swap life on earth for life with a nightingale, and he does now wear feathers, moulting from time to time. But he has not become wholly a bird. He speaks and thinks and commands as a man. He possesses, simultaneously, "a bird's-eye view of things and a man's knowledge." He is a double image: he is a man who has become a bird and a bird who has become a man.

On a coarser, funnier level, the piglets bought by Dicaeopolis in *The Acharnians* are double, too, and the comedy comes of the shuttling back and forth of identities. A greedy Megarian wishes to sell his nubile daughters under the pretense that they are sows. Dicaepolis is by no means averse to the purchase, but he is certainly not taken in. He has pinched over the merchandise too thoroughly for that. When the Megarian declares the first of his daughters to be "a natural proper pig," Dicaepolis replies, "Perhaps it may, but it's a human pig." And Dicaepolis makes the purchase not because he wants pigs to sleep with, but because he wants girls.

That is to say, in "animal" comedy the joke always depends upon the knowledge that, although the human being may indeed resemble an animal, he isn't one. Man is another creature altogether, and comedy begins with his otherness. Animals are not funny as such. As Bergson says, "the comic does not exist outside the pale of what is strictly *human*. A landscape may be beautiful, charming and sublime, or insignificant and ugly; it will never be laughable. You may laugh at an animal, but only because you have detected in it some human attitude or expression."

Nor do we laugh at an animal because, in occasionally resembling a man, it seems something less than a man. We laugh at it because it seems, for the moment, something *more* than an animal. It seems like us. What we are doing is pointing to our own relatively advanced state in the evolutionary order of things, to our "moreness." Here we stand, seemingly at the center of things, or at least part way up the natural ladder, very much like the lower animals but not so much like them that we can really be confused with them. To pretend to confusion, or to make a forced equation between man and beast, is to make a joke.

Comedy stands squarely upon this "moreness" and spends so much time dipping back into the ways of the animal kingdom in order to emphasize it. Calling attention to resemblances is the surest way of isolating differences. The distinction between man and beast is best seen when the man has been given horns and hooves and a tail and *still* isn't acceptable as a beast.

Comedy does, of course, satirize man when it puts donkey's

ears upon him. The ears are not meant as a compliment. But if satire is a form of criticism, and if the donkey's ears are a kind of scolding, we must be careful to know why the criticism is imperative, what the scolding is all about. Obviously man is not being scolded simply for resembling the donkey or the dog or the crow. Mere resemblances are no more than part of man's evolutionary heritage and as such no subject for scolding. What the fellow in the ass's head is being blamed for is behaving like a donkey when he doesn't happen to be a donkey. He is ridiculed for being too much the donkey and not enough *himself*.

Satire implies a defined self which is presently being betrayed. It does not say "all men are animals," it says "all men are men and deserve whipping when they so far forget themselves as to behave like animals." There is nothing prejudicial in this, be it noted, toward animals. Whatever prejudice is going is directed against men—men who, in an excessive surrender to the limitations they love, are in danger of slipping back down the ladder.

Comedy looks at man, then, at eye level, measuring him for who he is and what he is. It does not uselessly denigrate him or kick him about. It understands that he has climbed a notch or two out of the valley. "If Man were absent from creation, there would no longer be any such thing as the comic," Baudelaire said, "for animals do not regard themselves as being superior to vegetables, nor vegetables as superior to minerals." Comedy begins with man's knowledge that he is superior to minerals, vegetables, *and* animals, and he indulges himself in so much animal play both to show where he has come from and how far he has come.

This third of comedy's consolations is not to be obscured by the spectacle man makes of himself when he wears his hair as shaggily as a dog's or wrinkles his itching nose as nervously as a rabbit does. It is a consolation precisely because it places man in an evolving scheme of things *and not at the bottom,* because it displays man's limitations as being less severe than those of creatures beneath him, because it lets something of the tragic landscape—the long climb toward freedom—on which it has been superimposed shine through. Man is a joke but not literally a jackass.

At the same time, he hasn't moved much lately, and the rung of the ladder just above him is slippery. He notices tragic man passing him on the way up the ladder, overleaping the next rung, perhaps the next three or four rungs in a bound, and then either destroying himself in his too-quick ascent or safely vanishing into the clouds above. When he, comic man, tries to emulate this ascent, he rarely so much as gets a foothold one notch up; even to lean an elbow on the nearest rung is to skid and lose balance, and maybe to wind up head downward while his locked knees struggle to stay locked in a saving grip.

But, trapped though he is in a highly tentative midway position, he knows that a full scale exists and that somebody up there looks down on him, just as he looks down on creatures who have not come as far as he. Laughter, according to Baudelaire, "is the expression both of man's sense of superiority to the beasts and of his anguished sense of inferiority in relation to the Absolute." Whatever there is of anguish in this laughter, there is solace in it, too. The solace comes from knowing tragedy, from knowing that the spirit does move and that even the poor clown has gained an inch. Without such knowledge, without tragedy's having made the first statement and laid out the master plan, comedy would be hopeless through and through, and no fun.

Comedy, even at its lowest, is utterly dependent upon the existence, and the sometime success, of the tragic aspiration.

10
THE CLOWN
GOES ROUNDABOUT

COMEDY is a tolerable form, then, and is even thought to be a "happy" form, because man is able to accept his limitations philosophically. The knowledge that these limitations are often pleasant, that they are exceedingly common, and that they are not so severe in his case as they are in the lower orders of being, all help him to endure the pressures that his material envelope places upon him and that so clearly foretell his death. The characteristic comic ending is a shrug. This is the way things are: bad, and not so bad. Even the Rajah of Rukh, in William Archer's *The Green Goddess,* is able to adapt himself casually to what is actually a crashing failure. Having pursued a desirable woman the whole night long only to have her snatched from his mountain fastness by the bothersome arrival of the R.A.F., he surrenders the wench, lights a cigarette, and murmurs the last line of the play: "Well, well—she'd probably have been a deuce of a nuisance."

Laurel and Hardy went further. In the face of impending disaster, they stood still and did nothing at all. The long career of this comedy team was founded on less than a shrug. Was a pie coming through the air? Was a fiendish fellow about to seize Stan Laurel's derby and pull it forcibly down over Mr. Laurel's eyes and ears? Very well. The comedian saw the pie coming, knew what his enemy was about to do to his derby. With his eyes open, he waited with infinite patience for the foreseen worst. When the worst came he did not attempt to evade it. He did not even flinch. He accepted. Then, without either haste or hope, he slowly removed the creamy meringue from his face, slowly tested the derby rim to see whether or not it could be pried loose again.

Occasionally he cried a little. More often he pressed his lips together as if to say "Just what I expected!" and resumed his methodical effort to restore himself to normal vulnerability. To be sure, he could—and would—strike back. But the striking back would be as slow, considered, essentially indifferent as the receiving.

It seemed never to occur to Mr. Laurel or Mr. Hardy that any other sort of response was possible. They were clay, and clay was coming at them. That was that. Laurel would lift his wrists limply and let them drop again; Hardy would weave his shoulders this way and that as though he were about to do something violent and then, with a shudder, let them collapse without having done it. If either of them had been named Prometheus and tied to a rock he would have looked directly into the camera with disgust and stayed there.

But we have already added a new note to our score. The clown has looked beyond himself and seen an avalanche coming.

As we advance a little bit beyond the very lowest of low-comic gestures, without yet leaving slapstick behind, we do not abandon our concentration on the dragging feet of matter. Instead we confront matter head on, as it exists in the world outside ourselves. Comedy's first aching thought is about the personal ballast everyman carries with him. Its second thought is about the barrier to freedom thrown up by the rest of the tangible world. Everything from a mud puddle to a mountain is hostile.

No, hostile is too strong a word. Such things become truly hostile only in the plays of a Harold Pinter, dark comedies at their lightest and more often agreeably clammy melodramas, where man's inability to identify the secret presences that do make him shudder tends to invest the most ordinary inanimate objects with potential danger. If I do not know what disturbs me, may it not be the aspidistra, the tablecloth, the vacuum cleaner? In effect, inanimate objects are made hostile by being personified, and the vacuum cleaner comes at me across the room like a large bumblebee with teeth.

T. S. Eliot has recorded both the helplessness of material man and the assertiveness of the matter that surrounds him in *The Cocktail Party:*

> You're suddenly reduced to the status of an object—
> A living object, but no longer a person.
> It's always happening, because one is an object
> As well as a person. But we forget about it
> As quickly as we can. When you've dressed for a party
> And are going downstairs, with everything about you
> Arranged to support you in the role you have chosen,
> Then sometimes, when you come to the bottom step
> There is one step more than your feet expected
> And you come down with a jolt. Just for a moment
> You have the experience of being an object
> At the mercy of a malevolent staircase.

Most second-stage slapstick, however, is quite impersonal, emotionally neutral. The deck chair that I cannot fold up does not hate me; it merely has laws of its own I cannot fathom. When I spread my cloak over a puddle so that a woman will not get her feet wet and the woman who steps on my cloak vanishes from sight into the bottomless mire, the accident is not the work of an enemy; it is the end product of a material world put together in such a way that I cannot anticipate or circumvent all its properties. Matter is unconquerable; even an atom that is split behaves in an uncontrollable way and I will do well to get well out of its way.

This sort of comedy turns its attention away from the noisy commands of the body and centers upon the silences of the

house in which the body lives. There are, it seems, two limiting envelopes: even when I have regained my strength by
feeding my body I cannot walk through board fences. One
prison meets another, and though my own private prison is
quite mobile, the one it meets is fixed, stolid, impermeable.
The material universe outside me can be kicked, and beaten
upon, and even—to a degree—budged. But it cannot be dissolved. It will be there to confront me again when I come
back.

The blunt clash of inviolable envelopes is obvious, of
course, in the most rudimentary comedy. The man who is
desperate to relieve himself must find a place in which to do
so; and the door of the outhouse may be locked. The man
who is hungry enough to boil a shoe may have more than his
hunger to contend with; he may burn his fingers on the pot
before he has done with the boiling.

But the focus may shift from what is inescapable about
one's appetite to what is inescapable about the tablecloth on
which dinner is eaten. If the hungry man inadvertently tucks
a corner of the tablecloth into his vest along with his napkin,
he is going to take the entire dinner setting, silverware and
all, with him when he rises; the tablecloth has its own logic of
weight and texture and tensile strength, a logic that cannot
successfully be defied.

Comedy often plays with the attempt to defy, or to ignore,
the properties of matter. It makes material puns, as it were.
Ed Wynn is a spy. Lucille Ball is a counterspy. They are having a drink together in the obligatory café. She is having a
liqueur, in a glass Tinker Bell could lift. He is having brandy
in a snifter big enough to take a bath in. He suspects she has
poisoned his drink. Craftily, while she is looking away, he
switches glasses.

The joke is visually delectable because the substitution is
impossible, and Miss Ball won't be deceived for a minute.
Matter just does happen to have shape and size, as it has
density and a habit of staying in motion once it has been set

in motion, and when it intrudes upon the best-laid plans of mice and men the plans had better be flexible. Beatrice Lillie, wearing a smart black coat with a white muff over one elbow, plans to smack her fist into the palm of her hand in order to emphasize a strong point properly. Raising a fist, however, entails movement of the elbow, and the muff slides downward to land in her palm one split second before her fist does. The fist produces, quite naturally, no more sound than that of snow falling.

Matter intervenes simply by being there. W. C. Fields means to walk up a staircase. He is talking at the time, but his hand has a good grip on the staircase railing. Up, up, and up he goes until he discovers, just short of disaster, that he has mounted successive pieces of ordinary furniture which happen to have been placed on the room side of the stairway.

And all of that silverware comes tumbling out of Harpo Marx's coat sleeve, astounding us that so much that is both heavy and slippery could have been retained and concealed for so long. As it happens, this familiar bit of business was always more effective on the stage than in motion pictures, I think because we know that films are pieced together and that the property man might have supplied them only a moment before the tumble was photographed; on the stage, Harpo had to deal with the bulky materiality for some time without suggesting that he was secretly burdened down. The weight was weightier, the bulk seemed bulkier, when it fell.

These are miniature examples of tangibles that obtrude upon our intentions and must be dealt with for the realities they are: muffs, drinking glasses, secreted silverware. Actually, comic man is faced with a behemoth of a material universe, a titanic arrangement of solidities that hem him in as effectively as a maze of mirrors in a Fun House. Wherever he walks he bumps his nose.

We are not accustomed to seeing this passive resistance on the part of matter developed on any very large scale in the theater. Euelpides can kick a rock and hurt his foot because it was always perfectly possible to provide the orchestra of a Greek theater with a few rocks; Eddie Foy, Jr., can wear so much padding in his shoulders that it is impossible for him to get through a doorway because Broadway can build doorways of the right size to halt him.

But it required the invention of film to let us see matter, the juggernaut, bearing down on comic man at full speed or to let us see man, the unsteady colossus, wrestling with physical masses on the most precarious of perches; we shall have to rely upon film to help us grasp the full impact of the encounter. Two comedians, Harold Lloyd and Buster Keaton, quickly perceived the relationship that could be established between man and the more monstrous physical laws that control his movement through an environment. Lloyd concentrated on gravity and hoisted himself hand over foot until he'd reached the tops of tall buildings—the top of the world, in effect—where the faces of giant clocks refused to support his weight and where unsecured steel girders eased themselves out over the void the moment he'd clung to them. The stunt finish of a Lloyd thriller became an abstract dance of equations: so much pressure equals so much displacement equals so much downdraft equals so much scramble. The articulation of man's bones contended with the articulation of the physical universe in a naked place, high and dizzy.

Keaton, cooler, subtler, more thoughtful, played with a wider range of toys, all of them massive. What would happen if a man and a girl who knew nothing of ships were set adrift on an ocean liner without fuel or compass, anchor or map? The intended scale is made explicit: when Buster sees another ship which might have rescued them steaming indifferently away across the horizon, he plunges into the sea, ties a small rowboat to the prow of his ship, and proceeds to row with all his might—tugging the big ship with him—after the vanishing vessel. He is a minnow dragging the Leviathan. Physical laws and limitations make the comedy everywhere. When a ship tilts to a certain angle every cabin door on the deck swings open at the same lazy rhythm. When a girl starts at point A on B deck, and a man starts at point B on A deck, their hurried journeys in search of each other must overlap with such mathematical regularity that we, looking at both decks, can read their running as though it were a musical score. Undersea, there are new pressures, and newly absent pressures. Buster, in diver's helmet, has descended to the ocean floor in order to repair a leak in the ship's lower hull. Having finished his work, he wishes to wash his greasy hands immediately. He approaches, in slow motion, a pailful of water he has brought to the bottom with him, rinses his hands thoroughly, and then empties the water into the surrounding water. $0 = 0$, and we see it happen.

Keaton repeated the experiment in scale with railway trains and with hurricanes. If a lone man must manage a runaway locomotive and at the same time attempt to halt and to steal a long string of cars manipulated by enemy forces, what fundamental physical laws is he up against? Will a burning bridge take the weight of a train? For how long? If, during a hurricane, an entire building drops down from the sky over a man, dare he open the door of the building without unsettling the delicate balance that still holds the house together over his head? Matters must be thought through, and tested carefully. Tons of lumber, or tons of steel, are about to fall. Comic man lives inside, and beneath, a contention of weights and pressures that may come together with a thundering clap at any moment.

Now as our attention, in this kind of comedy, is directed away from the clumsiness of man's own equipment to the intractability of the environment in which man must live and may at any moment die, several interesting shifts of emphasis take place. At the moment when the clash of man with other matter is most intense, at the very moment when man's body is most vulnerably exposed to physical forces greater than itself, man's body suddenly becomes superbly flexible, almost as supple as man wants it to be, as Bergson suggested it *ought* to be.

Forgotten for the moment is the body's deplorable tendency to skid on waxed floors and to lose consciousness at great heights. With the time of crisis at hand, and survival the issue, every sort of magical maneuver comes to seem possible. Adroitness asserts itself and the body rides matter bareback with the finesse of a drunken angel. The clown walks over roof tops, hitches rides on a passing chandelier, negotiates city traffic from the handlebars of a driverless motorcycle, leaps from silo top to haystack with consummate skill. The body knows a trick or two, and is nearly equal to the contest.

None of this denies man's personal limitations. It simply places them in a new relationship, pits them against inexorable forces that are more limited still. A house that has begun to fall cannot stop falling. But a man can step out of the way. Gravity cannot reverse itself. But a man can jump *up*. The tables are turned for the moment, because our eye, for the moment, is fastened upon physical realities which function even more rigidly than man does. Looking at a plane spinning wildly out of control, utterly at the mercy of the stresses playing upon it, we see that it is even more helpless than the incompetent man inside it is. The plane must go where it is going. The man may yet—just possibly—grab the knees of a passing parachutist as he bails out, and have a fine comic chat on the way down. The flexibility is a flexibility by contrast, by inversion: a heaviness comes to seem a lightness alongside the avalanche absolute. Nevertheless it suggests a kind of victory.

The nature of this temporary, if delicious, victory is curious and needs to be examined. It is always temporary, by the way: when the whirlwinds have hurled half the universe at a man, and he has dodged or outwitted every force that has come his way, there is invariably one brick left to fall. It does fall and it does hit him—not hard, just as a forget-me-not.

How does a man badgered by intense personal limitations

ever succeed—even temporarily—in getting the better of a vast blind cosmos that is limited in itself and additionally limiting to him? The universe is limited in itself because it cannot behave other than it does. It is additionally limiting to man, because it is a jail built over a jail: if a sleepy clown manages to get himself out of bed in the morning, he has accomplished nothing more than the right to go dig ditches; he has fought himself only to fight something tougher. It is unthinkable that two drags should end in a gallop.

Generally speaking, the clown-against-the-universe goes about his work in two ways. He first, and most naturally, takes evasive action. He does not suppose that he is going to be able to alter matter. He has looked the situation over, it is clear to him that a cop's nightstick is hard, that men twice as big as he are probably twice as strong as he, that the unmoored piano that is now rolling down the driveway at him will have an unfair advantage at contact, that when pressed he is never going to be able to flee straight through a wall the way cats in animated cartoons do. He has observed the structure of the universe and decided to go round it.

He is a circler, an outsider, an artful dodger, a vagabond by choice. He knows that certain simple needs of his body require attention, but he would very much like to satisfy these with a minimum involvement in the battle against the elements. The elements make him wary. He does not think he is going to win in that league. Better not to lift a finger than to have the finger smashed with a hammer, better not to challenge a machine that may at any time swallow him whole. It puzzled me very much, when I was younger, that Chaplin should have become a universal figure in becoming a tramp. As a child visiting my grandmother's house in Illinois I did see an occasional real tramp coming along the alley to beg for food at the back door. But that is a very dim, and not at all typically American, memory. By the time I was seven or eight and going to Chaplin films, there were no longer any neighborhood tramps to be seen. At the height of his fame and

powers Chaplin acted out a way of life that was unrepresenta-
tive of the age and country he lived in, making his greatest
films in the 1920's when everyone seemed to be growing
richer and the ramble along the alleyways was in general
quite unnecessary. The fact that the alleyways were obviously
British alleyways puzzled me further. *Why* had America—and
then the rest of the world, rich or poor—seized with such
passion upon an image of which it had so little direct knowledge? Chaplin not only played an outsider, going round; his
behavior and environment were actually outside the ordinary
experience of the people who so completely believed in him.

The answer, I should guess, is that Chaplin touched not at
all upon any national characteristic or upon any representative experience of an age—indeed, it was strange and slightly
alien to see him suddenly doing so in *Modern Times*—but
instead had stumbled upon a comic response to life so fundamental that it needed no local or immediate context. The
very absence of such a context permitted him to leap all
national boundaries as it now permits his films to survive the
radical changes in the social structure that have taken place
since the films were made. He had rediscovered the evasive-
ness of Harlequin, who never did an honest day's work in his
life. He had unearthed one root response we make, or would
like to make, to the material pressures that command us to
build social fortresses against them by hard labor. He copped
out. To be a tramp may be humiliating. It is not half so
humiliating as putting one's shoulder to the wheel and having the shoulder broken. There is a canny comic wisdom in
avoiding a confrontation that is only going to prove one's
equipment inadequate. Bergson defines the caricaturist as
someone who has perceived "the deep-seated recalcitrance of
matter." The tramp has perceived it too, and has washed his
hands of it. Tip one's hat to what is recalcitrant and shuffle
off the other way.

It is of this deliberate disengagement that the clown's
marvelous suppleness is born. The clown becomes adroit at

dodging, rather than winning, encounters. His first ingenuity is given over to making certain that there will be no contest. Harlequin is catlike, supple as can be, in slipping around corners when his name is called. No errands for him, at least not until he is caught. Chaplin runs from the hands of the law or the employer, feels the hand close on his neck, drops to his knees so that the pursuer passes over him, and reverses his field to scramble off the other way. The agility is almost greater than anything that would have been required for work. The skill of refusal is the first skill of the clown.

It strikes me that this infinite grace in going roundabout may account for the circuitousness of much comedy construction and may very well justify what is often thought of as an improvisational looseness. Aristophanes' comedies, as we've said, have often been under fire for failing to grow organically in their second halves; they circle and recircle the subject instead. The criticism has been echoed in a thousand cases since, and no complaint is commoner than that a comedy has, after establishing its initial situation, run itself ragged inventing variations upon a single theme. But this repetitive action, in which the clowns run from door to door looking for easier access into the same building, may be inherent in comedy, a part of its premise. Matter is hard, resistant. The fool isn't so much of a fool that he doesn't know this. Rather than pit himself directly against what he knows will defy him, the wise fool sneaks around it, lopes around it, dances an untiring ballet of delay around it, looking for a loophole, a tent flap under which he can crawl. The easy way in is for him, if he can find it; and because there is no easy way in, he dances his sly search forever. The structure of comedy may participate in this "forever," uncoiling itself like so many laps around a track instead of penetrating the center as tragedy tries to do. It is conceivable that circuitous plotting is the proper plotting for comedy, or at least that it is one of comedy's most natural designs.

Another design finds the clown willing to engage in the

struggle. But he does not engage in it as a tragic hero does. To begin with, he *assumes* that matter cannot be altered to suit him and he wastes no time trying to dominate it by spiritual force. He knows that *he*, being so limited, cannot hope to change the greater limitations that press in upon him. But, in the course of his generally frustrating experiences, he has noticed something. He has noticed that while he can never defeat matter, matter can be made to defeat matter. Matter can be used against itself to further, however temporarily, the clown's own ends.

And so he tricks the universe by obeying its laws. In his film *The General* Buster Keaton is pursuing a stolen train, though he has nothing but his own Civil War locomotive and one snub-nosed cannon, hooked on behind, to work with. The men in the stolen train ahead have scattered railroad ties all over the tracks to slow Keaton down. Keaton crawls onto the cow-catcher of his moving locomotive and succeeds in picking up the first tie without losing his balance. As he approaches the second tie, which straddles one rail at an inward tilt, he raises the one in his hands, holds it poised in the air for a measured fraction of time, then sails it forward to catch the oncoming tie at its outward tip. The leverage is perfect, the two ties fold together like a fan, both tumble away from the miraculously cleared rails. One resisting piece of matter has been used to resist another resisting piece of matter so that the two become equal, neutralizing and removing themselves from the immediate human path. Later, Keaton aims his cannon at the rear end of the train ahead. Just as he fires, a bend in the track swerves the target car out of range. The same bend, however, has brought the front end of the pursued train into view. The cannonball follows its natural trajectory and, missing what has been aimed at, hits something better. A curve can be played against a straight line.

For some years Joe Cook delighted audiences with an elaborate construction designed to enable a sleepy musician to strike a triangle on beat. Mr. Cook was, at the moment, playing "Three O'Clock in the Morning" as a cornet solo, and he wished to embellish his solo with the tinkle of a struck triangle on the very last note of each phrase. In order to accomplish this difficult feat of precision timing—especially as his accompanist was constantly dozing off—on his own first note he slapped a stooge with a slapstick, the stooge used a slingshot to spur a monkey into action, the monkey climbed up a scaffold to drop a coconut on a chess player, the chess player immediately struck his partner in the face, his partner kicked an Indian who was bending over nearby, the Indian drew his bow and shot an arrow at a construction engineer astride a large crane, and the construction engineer swung his crane into position to dump a cabbage upon the head of the chap with the triangle, alerting him in the nick of time to achieve harmony with Mr. Cook.

A kind of success can always be had when the properties of matter are respected and employed, though the journey is apt to be a long one and still roundabout. One must accept an imminent landslide and then see whether it can be used to budge a reluctant mule. There is no direct challenge in this, to landslide or to mule. One simply takes unfair advantage of the internal harmony of the enemy.

The clown, in his sly opportunism, can take advantage of another natural enemy: accident. In general the use of co-incidence in a play is held against the dramatist, though it is surely clear that many of the comedies we admire most—Molière's *School for Wives* above all—rest their cases upon coincidence as though they were filing a legal brief against the universe. Actually, coincidence is suspect only in tragedy, where man must assume full responsibility for his free acts; in comedy it is nothing more than the acknowledgment of one more natural limitation, the fact that chance interferes with the closest calculations. Tell your boss that you are going to your grandmother's funeral and the chances are that he will go to the ball game. Chance is a fact of life, a limiting rather than a liberating one—even when chance frees a man from something he has wished to be rid of, it cannot be said that he has exercised any freedom, only that ineluctable weights have inadvertently tipped in his favor—and comedy could not be complete without a worried nod in its direction.

In *The School for Wives* Horace meets Arnolphe and confides to the older man that he is in love. Arnolphe is delighted, being a believer in love, until he realizes that Horace is talking about the girl he has earmarked, and imprisoned, for himself. Horace asks Arnolphe's help in outwitting the man who has imprisoned the girl. Arnolphe promises help and goes home to lock the doors. Thereafter the two meet and miss, at windows, in gardens, at gates, until they have spied and counterspied themselves into exhaustion over a world run by luck, good and bad. Blind chance blinds men, who grope after one another in the dark, stumbling, cursing, grappling with the wrong objects until the lights suddenly come on to reveal that the world has won, inexorably, indifferently, mathematically.

The laws of permutation and combination come into play, and so an unmarried father who has hoped to keep the birth of a child secret has quintuplets. It was time for quintuplets in the calculus we move through. The man who knows that he *must* lose a poker game if he is not to be shot dead by the suspicious sheriff who is dealing will, by the comic probabilities, draw four aces.

The improbable probabilities are intensified in comedy so that we shall be able to catch the universe in the act of shaking the dice and throwing snake-eyes ten times running, which is perfectly possible. But a clown can turn accident to his advantage, if he keeps his eyes open and estimates the odds correctly. The seventh time a blow falls he can see to it that his opponent is standing in his place.

Comic man, then, has two practical responses ready for the resistance he meets in matter: he can tip his hat and walk the other way, testing its resistance as little as possible; and he can wait, watchfully, until it outmaneuvers itself, slyly taking advantage of its regularity. He also has ready an impractical response, one in which he indulges himself frequently. He can fantasize. He can dream. It is the third and last course open to him.

When he is tired of running away, when he is tired of tricking a system by playing the system against itself, he permits himself the luxury of imagining that there is nothing to run away from and no inflexible system to fear. He transforms himself into a bird or a god or a Puck or a magician—the magician may be as thoughtful as Prospero or as carefree as the Harlequin Sorcerer of eighteenth-century pantomime—and, for the moment, all things yield to him. He can circle the globe or quiet the seas or stuff his belly or seduce Alcmene as his fancy requires, without effort or fear of rebuff. The obstacles that constitute the real world, and that provoke by their impermeability most of the comic ricochets he dances out for us, simply vanish; he dreams himself free of them, lord and master of matter, king of bed and banquet table, hero supreme. Fantasy is comedy's escape hatch, its private passageway to felicity.

There is no such thing as tragic fantasy, for the freedom of tragedy must be real, an actual exercise of the will for which man is willing to pay. Tragedy takes its gains seriously, whereas comedy merely pretends to them. And fantasy must always, even within its comic homeland, be a secondary form. *The Tempest,* much as we admire it, is not quite so robust or vigorous a play as *Twelfth Night,* Molière's *Don Juan* is no real companion for *The Misanthrope* or *The School for Wives.* Undiluted fantasy is at its most brilliant in Aristophanes, yet when we are looking about for something to revive we are more apt to seize upon *Lysistrata* than upon *The Birds,* and not merely because *Lysistrata*'s sex-play seems so marketable; the play itself feels sturdier to us.

For all of its undeniable charms, pure fantasy occupies a secondary throne in the comic pantheon, because it makes less of the world than the world actually is. It removes obstacles that are there. Perhaps we most often think of fantasy as offering us something more than life. A winged horse, after all, is a horse with wings *added* to him.

But in point of fact a winged horse is less a horse than one without wings is. The horse has lost his own identity without acquiring a new one that is real. As he is not a true horse, he is not a true bird; he is not really a true anything. And the blithe dismissal of truth, pretty and playful though it may be, ends in a defect of truth. The fantasist enjoys himself, and entertains the rest of us, by being less than candid.

In a way, fantasy constitutes the clown's ultimate evasion of a universe he cannot best. For a moment, the clown denies that the universe as he knows it exists. Suddenly the rivers run gravy, all girls are pliant, Ariel will do the errands while Harlequin stretches out for a catnap.

> There is nothing more practical or more enjoyable
> Than a pair of wings. Suppose you go to the theatre
> And find it's some Tragedy or other: well, of course
> You're bored, and hungry, so off you fly home,
> Take care of your belly, and get back for the last act.
> Or say you develop a sudden case of the runs.
> Do you sit there and spoil your suit? No. You simply
> Zoom up into the air, do your job, fart twice,
> Catch your breath, and coast back to your seat again.
> Or maybe you're an Adulterer, of all things, and there's
> Your girl's husband in the front row gawking at
>   the Chorus.
> A flap of the wings, and you're off you know where;
>   and when
> You've laid the lady—a flap of the wings, and you're back.
> Wings? There's nothing like them!

As the chorus of *The Birds* has already pointed out, anyone who's interested in the pleasant life should come promptly to Cloud-Cuckoo-Land, where "we practice what your laws forbid." All laws—God-made, nature-made, man-made—dissolve here.

The Birds is fantasy unlimited, as *The Tempest* is. Not all fantasy goes all the way, however. A comic writer who wishes to relieve his clowns of their bothersome limitations may do so temporarily, by a blow on the head or a magic potion or any other means he has at hand of helping them to drop off. He can give them surcease, letting them smile in their dreams and letting us see what splendid images of themselves they are smiling at, and then return them, no doubt with another blow, to the sorry circumstances they left behind them.

A writer may also compose a play which is one tenth, or one eighth, or one third fantasy throughout its course. The unreal is woven directly together with the real. The trick calls for no more than the suppression of one—any one—of life's binding conditions. Take something away from the clogging complexity of man's daily journey, remove any single thread from the multicolored strait jacket man wears, and the consequent freedom of movement—however narrow or particular its channel may be—instantly opens the door to fantasy. There is now one cord that cannot coil about the clown's neck.

For instance, it was always easier to deal with fantasy, or to have the clowns behave fantastically, in silent-film comedy than it ever has been on sound film. A dimension of the actual universe had been conveniently removed: the dimension that defines and limits things by speech and telltale noise. Larry Semon could dive from a second-story window, land on his head, get up and walk away. Watching him do what was patently impossible, but not hearing him do it, we laughed. The same sequence in a sound film is not tolerable. If a clown's head hits the street, we hear the crunch. The crunch reminds us of the truth, the whole truth. The sound itself, realistically recorded, is unbearable; we do not believe the fantastic resurrection that follows; and we do not laugh. *Too* much of the world is now with us.

The same piece of business can still be used in an animated sound cartoon, because the victim is plainly a stylized drawing to begin with and because the sound, when it comes, will be the sound of a *bong!* or a bell or a deliberately inadequate flute note. Physical dimensions have here been removed and so has the reality of sound. That the project is virtually hopeless in realistic sound comedy has been more than amply demonstrated by Stanley Kramer's attempt to return to the fantasy world of the Keystone Kops, *It's a Mad, Mad, Mad, Mad World.* Here cars crashed down cliffsides and men toppled from tall ladders to land on hard marble, but the cars and the men produced approximately the noises that would have signaled their respective demises in life. Anything more monstrously unfunny would be difficult to conceive.

Realistic sound can, of course, be used to comic effect in realistically organized films, films which have acknowledged the maddening solidity of the menacing universe. When Laurel and Hardy, burglarizing an unfamiliar household at midnight, turn the knob of what they suppose to be a safe only to have the radio blare forth deafeningly, the telltale blast is immediately funny. But for a clown to indulge himself in the light fantastic, ridding himself for the moment of all troublesome impedimenta, one or another of life's constricting laws must be formally relaxed.

The peculiar advantage which silent film possessed in this one respect may seem to have been the result of mere accident—the fact that at that time the screen *could* not speak or produce sound. But comic playwrights have often deliberately relaxed laws in much the same way, to much the same purpose. Amoral comedy, for instance, is a form of fantasy. It removes morals from the world. The Restoration theater thrived upon a kind of comedy in which it was assumed that every man and woman would gobble up all the sex he or she could get without a moment's qualm of conscience or without a thought for any possibly unpleasant aftermath. Conscience simply did not come into play; neither did consequences. Clowns were free to lust as much as they liked, provided they did so with wit, grace, forthrightness, and the energy that comes of unruffled confidence. We were free to look at sex-play, and particularly at the dexterities—verbal and psychological—which prepare for, accompany, and follow upon, sex-play, in the abstract. Here was the thing itself, divorced from lifelike considerations, offered us as pure choreography—ingenious, absurd, brilliant, cold. The figures on stage, being other than moral, were of course less than real. But by absolving them of the need to think twice, or to fear ever, we had given them the full rein of their rakishness, invited them to do brilliantly the one thing they did, agreed with them to fantasticate for a while for the sake of the spectacle. "The great art of Congreve," Charles Lamb once said, is best revealed in the fact that "he has entirely banished from his scenes . . . any pretensions to goodness or good feeling whatsoever. Whether he did this designedly or instinctively, the effect is as happy as the design (if design) is bold."

In *The Importance of Being Earnest* Oscar Wilde did not concern himself with banishing goodness. He banished emotion instead. In his kind of fantasy—and this play is again a kind of fantasy—several pairs of young lovers are permitted to go about their love-making without hearts. These young lovers make love rationally:

"We must get married at once. There is no time to be lost."
"Married, Mr. Worthing?"
"Well . . . surely. You know that I love you, and you led me to believe, Miss Fairfax, that you were not absolutely indifferent to me."
"I adore you. But you haven't proposed to me yet. Nothing has been said at all about marriage. The subject has not even been touched on."

"Well . . . may I propose to you now?"

"I think it would be an admirable opportunity. And to spare you any possible disappointment, Mr. Worthing, I think it only fair to tell you quite frankly beforehand that I am fully determined to accept you."

If life were made of common sense, love would be as it is in Wilde's play. The play does, after all, speak certain truths, omitting perhaps only one: the human heart becomes entangled in what might very well be accomplished by intelligence and generally ends by making a mess of things, especially the things it desires most. There are no messy misunderstandings here between Gwendolen and Ernest. Gwendolen's vision could not be more sublimely unclouded. The people of the play are free to say what is on their minds, because their minds are utterly clear; no unseemly emotion roils them. Again, the spectacle is delightful. Again, the spectacle is delightfully unreal.

In each of these cases we have been imagining something: a universe without morality, a universe without emotion, a universe without obstacle or penalty of any kind. Some fantastic comedies take away a single inhibition and leave the rest in lifelike view; others buckle the walls in all directions; all are, fundamentally, forms of escape for harried clowns.

Devious to the end, the harried clown sinks back, exhausted by his long labor of avoiding labor, and rests his head upon that downiest of pillows, the pillow of pretending. Snug and smiling now, he projects himself as master of the world by the simple expedient of suspending the world's structure, and his quite literal flight of fancy, whether it is a brief dream sequence in a Chaplin film or the whole of *A Midsummer Night's Dream,* whether it envisions a world without sound or a world without sentiment, is the last trick our poor clown can play—the trick he plays on himself in his sleep. He has had a feeling all along that the world should be more reasonable; surrendering reason, he makes it so.

The flight from reality in which the clown indulges is of course a joke too and contains its own inverted honesty. It is the same joke that has been made from the beginning, seen now in its absence. Restoration comedy does not banish morality outside its own boundaries; if anything, it reminds us of how powerfully present the pressure of morality is. Emotion does not dry up in London because an Oscar Wilde play is being performed in London; Londoners laugh precisely because they see what Oscar Wilde has left out.

It is funnier, really, to watch a notorious brute being exquisitely polite to his wife than it is to watch him beating her; we recognize instantly that his conduct is improper to his character and a mockery of the marriage that exists. When there is so much food available that our sated fool is willing to wave away the last grape offered to him, or when W. C. Fields, as Brigham Young in a nightshirt, enters the stage to count off a whole bedful of chorus girls, we understand that the sublime circumstances before us are simple reversals.

And we know that all fools must wake up again.

11

THE CLOWN INVADES
THE TRAGIC LANDSCAPE

Hₑᵣₑ is a thing that long disturbed me. Going back to
the films that I loved in my youth, I could see two contraries
emerging, and they seemed to defy any rational principle.
Buster Keaton produced one kind of comedy, Chaplin quite
another. And Keaton's was the purer use of the form. That
is to say, there was no admixture of sentiment, no bid for
pathos, no confusing of the comic and tragic modes.

Keaton was cool, detached, and very strictly funny, never
suggesting for a moment that we need worry ourselves about
what might happen to him. If a building fell over on him
during a cyclone, we were not to be apprehensive; when the
dust had cleared he would be standing—to our confident
delight—in the small space made safe for him by an open
second-story window. If Keaton built a boat in his garage and
discovered, once it was finished, that it was a good bit larger
than the garage door and that he would have to yank the boat
out by main force, we were not to be distressed as portions of
the house broke loose during the tugging; we were not even
to feel for his wife and children as the entire house collapsed
behind them due to Buster's mismanagement. We were to see
limitation functioning as humor *without emotion,* just as
Keaton himself never displayed any emotion. Keaton, known
as the man who never smiled, was in fact less expressive still;
he never seemed to *feel.* He personified, as sparely and

cleanly as a comedian could, that "absence of feeling" which Bergson associated with the comic: "It seems as though the comic could not produce its disturbing effect unless it fell, so to say, on the surface of a soul that is thoroughly calm and unruffled. Indifference is its natural environment, for laughter has no greater foe than emotion." Keaton was indifferent to oceans, cyclones, Indians, and his heroines. He was always formally in love, and formally dedicated to preserving his leading ladies from destruction. But he treated them as *things*, stuffing them into bags, hurling them into boxcars, stepping on them in the process of helping them, shaking the living daylights out of them when they behaved less than intelligently, which they generally did. Keaton's comedy was Euclidean.

Chaplin's, by comparison, was formally blurred. If laughter has no greater foe than emotion, Chaplin constantly made bargains with the foe. Once he had discovered his true bent, he forced the same situation to house both pathos and broad comedy. He did not alternate them; he fused them. When he had managed to steal a breakfast for himself in *The Circus*, he paused to show sympathy for the forlorn bareback rider, horsewhipped by her father and starved into the bargain, who came from her wagon prison to sit beside him. He was in love with the girl, and gentleness itself. Until she snatched a bit of his food. Then he hit her. But there is none of Keaton's detachment or objectivity in the quick slap. It is a momentary assertion of self-interest, of the impulse to survival, within a context of continuing affection. You know that a moment later he will sigh and share anything he has with this girl. In *The Kid* he clings to a child as though he were its mother; in *City Lights* his heart is open to the illness of a blind girl; in *The Gold Rush* the choicest sequence depends upon his sorrow at having been made a fool of by a girl he adores.

As comedy, Chaplin's work is hopelessly impure. Yet no one has ever questioned—no one questions now—Chaplin's superiority to Keaton. Even those who love Keaton without reserve, as I do, acknowledge it. Nor does the superiority rest on any distinction of kind between them. No one suggests, say, that Chaplin was an actor whereas Keaton was a clown. Both are comedians, unmistakably. Yet the impure comedian is greater than the pure comedian. Surely we have stumbled upon a contradiction in terms, come up against a formal impasse.

But, in truth, we have not. For if tragedy is the mother form, and the source of comedy's being, then the nearer a comedian comes to embracing the form that gave him birth— *without losing his own identity*—the richer and more complex will his personality be. He shows us *more* than the clown who has cut apron strings altogether and gone to live in isolation. He shows us who he is, and also how he got that way. We see the interplay of similarity and variation in a dizzying double exposure, a dance of light and shade in which the shade, comedy, is more pronounced for the light it gives dimension to.

The pure clown, on the other hand, has moved away from his origins to set up housekeeping for himself. He is tidier, controlling his own world wholly as he does. The line of his work is more severe, its tone unconfounded by overtones. We see, in a way, a cold perfection, a reduced essence as clear as one of Plato's. Our view is aesthetically exhilarating, for we admire things which are true to themselves alone.

But our satisfaction is a little bit diminished because comedy, moved away from tragedy, must of necessity be approaching zero. Maintaining too strict an identity must, we sense, in the end come to loss of identity, for the family name is Tragedy and when the family name is altogether rejected or lost there will no longer be a home to return to or a provenance to be charted. Comedy wholly loosed from tragedy is, perversely, comedy bastardized. The word is harsh, but because comedy comes into existence as a comment, as a footnote, as a blemish on something greater than itself, it paradoxically loses caste as it turns purer. Comedy and tragedy are not equally independent impulses best developed in contrary directions. The primacy of tragedy permits it to assert itself separately, taking no notice of comedy when it chooses to go unaccompanied. But comedy, being in essence a shadow, requires a body to stand between it and the sun; it can dance only while that other body is dancing.

Because the tragic impulse is comedy's indispensable alter ego, it must ultimately play a large and ambiguous part in comedy's life. Comedy, being so dependent upon it, does more than develop saucy attitudes toward it; it becomes emotionally involved in its activities. Robert Warshow pointed out that Chaplin's tramp, "despite his ultimate frigidity, at least maintained an active flirtation with the world, always escaping in the end but keeping up the excitement of the chase and even hinting strongly that he might like to be caught if only he did not like more to get away."

Flirtation is an excellent word to describe comedy's behavior as it begins to abandon slapstick and deal more directly with tragedy's proud pretensions to intellect. Comedy means to mock mind and spirit now. But once it has put foot into this landscape, and is in effect *inhabiting* tragedy, it cannot help but take on some of tragedy's qualities.

Aspiration is the most obvious of these, and the mixed feelings of the clown as he wraps this particular quality about him can readily be seen in Chaplin's work. Heroic aspiration is about to be derided. The tramp is going to swagger manfully and snap his fingers beneath the nose of a brute who has been manhandling the girl—only to quail and disappear like a blown feather the moment the brute raises his arm inadvertently. The tramp will enter the lion's cage fearlessly—only to scurry away, squirrel-like, and shinny up a pole the moment the sleepy lion yawns.

Yet in the act of parodying aspiration something of real aspiration begins to attach itself to this clown. Chaplin reduces dignity to candid, quivering terror. But more and more he comes to possess dignity. Cornered by a policeman, he does not begin to run from him until he has first tipped his hat. Finding himself running alongside another culprit who is also being chased by a policeman he tips his hat to the culprit without slowing his pace. In an alley, with trash raining down on him from the windows above, he meticulously removes gloves which have no finger tips before he selects, with a connoisseur's judgment, the cigarette butt he means to smoke from a case that was once a sardine can. There is some mockery of manners in this. There is also a genuine fastidiousness. In the process of satirizing aspiration, the comedian has acquired it. His aspiration may not extend much beyond good form—certainly it does not extend to labor—and it will not, in a crisis, keep him from kicking an intolerable child in the stomach. But what there is of it is increasingly innate, actual, realized. The clown has come so close to the thing he is parodying that a degree of it has rubbed off on him. And he is proud of what he has absorbed.

As comedy toys more and more with tragedy's playthings it becomes increasingly committed to them, in however foolish a way. Monsieur Jourdain is no gentleman, but he would truly like to be one. "I am crazy to be a scholar," Molière's impetuous hero assures his tutors, "It makes me furious that my father and mother didn't make me study all the branches of knowledge when I was young." Monsieur Jourdain's fury is mitigated, as everyone knows, by his delighted discovery that for the full forty years of his life he has successfully been speaking prose. That pleases him. He is happy with consonants and vowels, too, though you won't find in Molière's text one of the nicest lines Bobby Clark spoke when he played *The Bourgeois Gentleman*. When it was explained to Mr. Clark that the letters of the alphabet were divided into vowels and consonants, he gave thought to the news for a moment and then volunteered, "That's only fair."

Having ventured into the realm of intellect for the purpose of belittling man's prospects for self-improvement, the clown—even when he is quite a low clown—very often develops a passion for self-improvement. Sometimes he assumes, rather disastrously, that the improvement has already taken place. Dogberry, for instance, cannot bear being thought an ass. "I am a wise fellow," he wants his detractors to know, "and, which is more, as pretty a piece of flesh as any is in Messina; and one that knows the law, go to; and a rich fellow enough, go to; and a fellow that hath had losses; and one that hath two gowns, and everything handsome about him." Mangling his words nicely, he begs of his listeners that they "suspect" his years and his place.

One reason there is so much injured dignity in comedy is that dignity is genuinely sought for, or touchingly laid claim to. The Chaplins, the Monsieur Jourdains, and the Dogberrys of this world are all creatures leading a double life. They have been created to ridicule pretension; they do it by earnestly believing in the qualities they have been created to ridicule. Caught in their own webs, so to speak, they are fools we feel for. Here they are, intended as shafts fired at a target. And they are so enamored of the target that they insist upon standing in front of it.

This irony is, of course, a deliberately arranged comic effect. But it is an effect that depends upon granting to tragedy the power and persuasiveness of certain of its claims. Tragedy claims that man may aspire. Comedy seems to nod thoughtfully and, though still stumbling over its own feet, aspire, too. It aspires not only to gentility—or to being as pretty a piece of flesh as any in Messina—but to the tragic hero's courage. If the clown is by nature a coward, knowing full well that his situation is hopeless, he is nevertheless an admirer of brave men and wistfully envious of the boldness of Achilles. He has been known to make a mighty effort to turn himself into an Achilles.

Plautus' *Miles Gloriosus*—The Braggart Captain—is the archetype here, later better known as one or another variant of the *commedia dell' arte's* Capitano. "When I was born in this great theater of the world my birth was different from all other births," a Capitano bellows, making himself as godlike as possible. "Observe! When other children are born they are born nude and puling: I, when I was born, was already clad in a suit of armor, roaring like an impatient lion and hissing like an enraged serpent!"

The Capitano always has a skeptical companion, who at this juncture generally makes a remark on the order of "I guess your mother's womb suffered mightily from such a strange conception," though making it aside to himself. Not that the Capitano would deign to notice if he heard. A Capitano has already inflated himself to full tragic dimension and has no time for the conversation of ordinary mortals. Like many tragic heroes he has assaulted heaven, and unlike some tragic heroes he has won:

"And when I beheld the army of the courts of heaven drawn up to make desperate attack upon me, what did I do? I took aim and discharged a pyramid into the face of Jove. Jove, seizing that same pyramid and changing it into a white-hot thunderbolt flung it back at my head. Taking it with my right I sent it again to the heavens and made after it with a leap so dexterous that I alighted in the middle of the heavenly squadrons. Arrived there I drew my sharp and flaming sword, put the whole army to flight, and taking prisoner the Lord of the Air I bound him to the axle of the Hemisphere and began to address him with bitter words."

Thus the Capitano has, by his own account, done rather better than Prometheus. Or he would have if, on this particular occasion, Venus hadn't strolled by and distracted him from his ultimate triumph over Jove. As it happens, there never is any triumph for a Braggart. Something always intervenes. Given an opportunity to slaughter five hundred men with a single stroke of his sword, as is his reported custom, the Braggart declines. "They were worthless infantrymen," he explains, keeping his sword well sheathed, "I let them live." He does not take full advantage of the romantic conquests that might be his, either. When his companion reports that the women along the streets keep asking "Is this fellow Achilles?" he waves both the comparison and the women away. "It's such a nuisance for a man to be so handsome," he sighs, no doubt glancing at himself in his highly polished shield. His shield is so highly polished because it has never seen any sort of action.

This is all stolen thunder, stolen from tragedy and carefully pocketed. The Braggart is careful to see to it that his courage is never put to the test. I think my favorite variation of the type is one that turned up rather late in the *commedia dell' arte's* history. He was called Scaramouche and, as Callot drew him, he was notoriously small in stature. He looked and he buzzed like a bumblebee. In addition, he *would* fight. With his sword flashing in the wind like a rain of daggered ribbons, he fought furiously—though always with his back to his opponent. Indeed Scaramouche fought with such fury that he invariably lost track of his opponent.

Most pretenders to such courage do not exert themselves to this degree. They have, perhaps, reliable friends who will leap forward in the nick of time to pin their arms and hold them back from the threatened fray. Or then again, they may select their fights. W. C. Fields, in *The Bank Dick*, tended to turn to pale aspic whenever actual bank robbers invaded the building he was sworn to protect. But, seeing a child with a toy pistol, he was action personified, leaping upon the infant, wrestling with him, disarming him, ousting him with fierce command.

The ferocity in each of these instances is fraudulent, and the clown is a cardboard Achilles. But as comedy probes beyond its first faint acknowledgment of tragic aspiration and its counterfeit adoption of the tragic posture of courage, it can no longer make such incompetents of its clowns. Once it has ventured past mere manners and bluster into the actual activity of the intellect, it is forced to make its fools truly intelligent. This is, in a way, a beginning surrender to tragedy, for it constitutes an admission that the intellect exists and is in many ways an able instrument. But comedy can take no other course. Intellect cannot be thoroughly belittled unless it is actively present, and comedy must grant to its own heroes some part of the power normally reserved to, and so much prized by, the tragic hero if it is to discover any flaw in that power. Comedy must allow for a degree of real achievement, handing over to the clown intellectual energies which are altogether genuine, providing him with a suppleness of mind and a force of cerebral invention that no longer have to be pretended to. The gift is real. The clown is delighted to have it. Tragedy, being borrowed from on an ever-increasing scale, is slowly folding its arms about the zany who has ventured so close.

Mosca and Volpone, for instance, are extraordinarily intelligent men, lightning-quick in their calculations, subtle in their methods, able, able, able. Challenges are nothing to them; or, rather, they are everything to them—meat and drink, mother's milk, energizers. A challenge is a spur to fresh improvisation—and off a flexible mind goes on its self-appointed rounds, dodging and devising, estimating the enemy exactly, triumphing time after time. Even Horner is a remarkably shrewd man to have thought of rumoring himself impotent in order to make his lady-victims feel safe with him. Sir Giles Overreach is clever; it takes a clever head to turn a profit by prostituting one's own daughter. Comedy is finally full of these mentally agile, mentally accomplished fellows, and—temporarily, at least, and under one binding condition—they sometimes achieve their goals.

Cedric H. Whitman, in his study of the Aristophanic comic hero, uses the Greek term *poneria* to gather together, in capsule, all of the powers such clowns have been granted, or have seized.

Poneria in modern Greek indicates not wickedness, but the ability to get the advantage of somebody or some situation by virtue of an unscrupulous, but thoroughly enjoyable exercise of craft. Its aim is simple—to come out on top; its methods are devious, and the more intricate, the more delightful. Moralists might disapprove of them, but the true *poneros* knows that they are justified by that heroic end so dear to every Greek—the joy of victory, "even for an eggshell." *Poneria* is wonderfully useful in politics, business, love-making, and family fights. Far from concealing its triumphs, one boasts of them; for though the word may be translated simply "cleverness," it also connotes high skill in handling those challenging aspects of life in which the agonistic tendencies of Greek psychology find a field of enterprise. It connotes further the qualities of protean resourcefulness and tenacity of purpose, and with all the world to gain, it can afford to dispense with any superfluous high-mindedness. Yet it has its own kind of transcendence, if one recalls that the isolated, helpless individual of the prologue to the *Acharnians* [our old friend who scratched himself in the morning and knowingly bought pretty girls offered as pigs] finishes by sweeping all resistance before him.

Here we are well into tragic country: protean resourcefulness and tenacity of purpose end in a kind of transcendence. Such heroes do often best the gods, raiding Hell, starving Heaven, catching Zeus's thunderbolts and hurling them back as the Capitano only boasted of doing. They are mighty, mighty men, and they win their victories with their minds.

There is just one catch, one limiting condition. Everything that their minds do is done for the satisfaction of their bodies. An immense spiritual activity is unleashed in the interests of matter. Spirit, fantastically active, does not seek spiritual advance; it seeks material comfort, and finds it. Volpone wants money in his treasure chest and women in his bed. Those are the things to which his splendid intelligence is dedicated. Mosca wants what Volpone has got and, having an even better mind, no doubt will get them. Pithetaerus rids himself of men, wins an argument with the birds, and goes on to conquer the gods for one reason only: his personal, private, uncomplicated comfort. These are creatures who intend to fill their bellies, stretch out on down, wave a wench in beside them, and afterward snooze. They are willing to think endlessly, and brilliantly, to bring such a state of affairs about. They even enjoy the thinking because it has such a low end. A contented intellectual is one who knows what he is looking for, not one who is trying to find something.

And when it appears, from time to time, as though some clown had the general good in mind, when the comedian seems to be seeking a universal panacea that would constitute a spiritual advance, the chap is putting you on. Dicaepolis, the hero of *The Acharnians*, wants peace in the world, as Dionysus, in *The Frogs*, wishes contemporary playwriting to be better. But these gentlemen do not really perform their labors out of ardor for the common weal; they do what they do for their own pleasure. The whole joke of *The Acharnians* is that Dicaepolis is perfectly willing to work out a private peace between himself and the enemies of Greece. Let the absurd nation do what it likes; let him alone. Perhaps we should say that that is only half the joke. The other half consists in what Dicaepolis wants to be let alone for. "Caress me," he cries when all has been concluded, "strip off incumbrances, my pretty dear, and take me off to bed." And off the two go, happy that "We've won to-day, wineskin and all!" We know what the night will be like, and why peace was wanted. We don't for a moment criticize Dicaepolis' purposes, mind you; but we aren't confused about them, either.

Behind all of this the playwright may possibly have purposes of his own: he may even have the common weal in mind. But that is not the light in which he presents his comic hero. There would be no comedy if all of the urgent intellectual and spiritual activity weren't subordinated to blissfully gross ends. Here are the powers, and here is what they are put to, comedy says, laughing—and remembering its sorrow at the same time. Our original incongruity—that of infinitely flexible talents harnessed to a fixed, inferior appetite—still stands, shaking its sides and also shaking its head.

The loftiness of the talents employed may be nowhere better seen than in Restoration comedy, where much more than craft is at work. We have mentioned Horner's craftiness in rumoring himself impotent, but that is the least—and in a way the crudest—of the skills employed by the rakes and country wives who make their tongues do such sly work for them. Even lying is not the greatest intellectual achievement of the rogues of the Restoration. The ultimate roguery is to deceive with candor, to tell the complete truth about oneself in order to accomplish one's quite selfish ends. The method is all over *The Way of the World:*

". . . I believe I gave you some pain."
"Does that please you?"
"Infinitely; I love to give pain."
"You would affect a cruelty which is not in your nature; your true vanity is in the power of pleasing."
"Oh I ask you pardon for that—one's cruelty is one's power; and when one parts with one's cruelty, one parts with one's power; and when one has parted with that, I fancy one's old and ugly."

Or in the celebrated proposal scene, as Millamant sighs in deep honesty over Mirabell's offer of marriage:

". . . My dear liberty, shall I leave thee?. . . I can't do't, 'tis more than impossible—positively, Mirabell, I'll lie abed in a morning as long as I please."
"Then I'll get up in a morning as early as I please."
"Ah! Idle creature, get up when you will—and d'ye hear, I won't be called names after I'm married; positively I won't be called names."
"Names!"
"Ay, as wife, spouse, my dear, joy, jewel, love, sweetheart, and the rest of that nauseous cant, in which men and their wives are so fulsomely familiar—I shall never bear that—good Mirabell, don't let us be familiar or fond, nor kiss before folks. . . . Let us never visit together, nor go to a play together; but let us be very

strange and well-bred: let us be as strange as if we had been married a great while; and as well-bred as if we were not married at all."

When all of Millamant's conditions for marriage are met— there are a great many—she may, just possibly and by degrees, "dwindle into a wife." A wife is what she intends to be, of course. She beguiles her suitor by being blunt with him.

Candor, high intelligence, genuine grace and true wit are the properties on display here. "The point is," Louis Kronenberger says of Millamant and her behavior, "that she is the very best product of a certain world, a certain kind of life: the point is, equally, that she does not rise above it." As with the comedy of manners generally, and Restoration comedy in particular, the aim of minds honed to the greatest keenness and delicacy is, in the end, preposterously low. Bed. And if not bed, then high tea and the playhouse, where the lowness of others may be rumored or observed with undiminished elegance.

Shaw sent such people to Hell, not because they had done wicked things but because they were only interested in doing comfortable things. Heaven he reserved, really, for participants in the tragic struggle upward, for those who possessed brains and were willing to use them unequivocally. "In Heaven, as I picture it, dear lady, you live and work instead of playing and pretending. You face things as they are; you escape nothing but glamor; and your steadfastness and your peril are your glory." If you can just show a man "a piece of what he now calls God's work to do, and what he will later on call by many new names, you can make him entirely reckless of the consequences to himself personally." Such a man will forget all that pursuit of pleasure, health, and fortune that has produced comfort but no advance. He will know for dull dogs the folk who have won their contentment, and settled for it: "They are not beautiful: they are only decorated. They are not clean: they are only shaved and starched. They are not dignified: they are only fashionably dressed. . . . They are not artistic: they are only lascivious. They are not prosperous: they are only rich . . . and not truthful at all: liars every one of them, to the very backbone of their souls." And they will be most happy in Hell, which is "a place where you have nothing to do but amuse yourself."

For a writer of comedy, Shaw is hard on all that makes for comedy. But he is not unrealistic. Comedy knows that glory is where the peril is—in tragedy—and that its own lot, even when its appetites are satisfied, is a sorry one. It does understand what *Man and Superman* is all about. And so it continues its exploration of the tragic heartland, quick to mock, cut to the quick. It has granted aspiration and shown it ill equipped. It has then granted the equipment, a real power of thought, and shown it thoughtlessly subordinated to gross ends. It still has one more question to contend with.

Is the mind, when it is not subordinated to gross ends and when it is free to take itself seriously, so good as all that? Or is intellectual activity itself limited, overrated, unreliable? When the mind is not held in bondage to the body, does it suffer from constricting pressures of its own, failures inherent in its natural functioning? In short, are the very best heads boneheads?

Having been given some qualities of mind, the clown is now ready to attack all qualities of mind. The effect is scandalous.

12
THE CLOWN
GIVES SCANDAL

Comedy has often been thought to give scandal, even to do damage to the species it insults. Perhaps the form's most notorious breach of manners occurred very early in its history, on the day it did patent injustice to Socrates.

Socrates, however his fellow Athenians may finally have dealt with him, was—and still is—regarded as the perfect type of intellectual man. Uncommitted to prearranged positions, daring enough to question every other man's last article of faith, Socrates opened his mind to unobstructed play, made Liberty Hall of it. Eternally testing for flaws, teasing his colleagues' minds along the path of cool-headed inquiry, Socrates symbolized, in his lifetime and forever after, the unlimited potentialities of the flexible psyche. He did not argue; he asked. He did not prove propositions; he pared away false premises until truth—or something like it—could assert itself. As best he could, he kept the machinery of his mind free and supple, docile before experience, attentive to fact.

Whereupon Aristophanes clapped him into a basket and sent him packing toward the heavens, where, with his feet well off the ground and his head thoroughly in the clouds, he behaved most peculiarly. He did not ask his students questions. He clouted them with ready answers:

SOCRATES (*loftily*).   Mortal, what do you want with me?

STREPSIADES.   First, what are you doing up there? Tell me, I beseech you.

SOCRATES (*pompously*).   I am traversing the air and contemplating the sun. . . . I have to suspend my brain and mingle the subtle essence of my mind with this air, which is of the like nature, in order clearly to penetrate the things of heaven. I should have discovered nothing, had I remained on the ground to consider from below the things that are above; for the earth by its force attracts the sap of the mind to itself. It's just the same with the water-cress.

Socrates' student would like to know who or what causes the rain to fall. Socrates answers, serenely, that rain is caused by his friends, the clouds, who are true goddesses superior to Zeus as well as the font of all his inspiration:

. . . and I will prove it. Have you ever seen it raining without clouds? Let Zeus then cause rain with a clear sky and without their presence!

STREPSIADES.   By Apollo! that is powerfully argued! For my own part, I always thought it was Zeus pissing into a sieve. But tell me, who is it makes the thunder, which I so much dread?

Socrates gestures, no doubt with sublime confidence, toward the chorus of Clouds:

SOCRATES.   'Tis these, when they roll one over the other.

STREPSIADES.   But how can that be? you most daring among men!

SOCRATES.   Being full of water, and forced to move along, they are of necessity precipitated in rain, being fully distended with moisture from the regions where they have been floating; hence they bump each other heavily and burst with great noise.

STREPSIADES.   . . . How can you make me credit that?

SOCRATES.   Take yourself as an example. When you have heartily gorged on stew at the Panathenaea, you get throes of stomach-ache and then suddenly your belly resounds with prolonged growling.

STREPSIADES.   Yes, yes, by Apollo! I suffer, I get colic, and then the stew sets a-growling like thunder and finally bursts forth with a terrific noise . . . and when I seek relief, why, 'tis thunder indeed. . . .

SOCRATES.   Well then, reflect what a noise is produced by your belly, which is but small. Shall not the air, which is boundless, produce these mighty claps of thunder?

Socrates is blissfully sure of himself. The fact that, even so parodied, he is more nearly right than Strepsiades, who has always assumed that Zeus did the work with the equivalent of a watering can, does not conceal the facile and false analogy by which he has arrived at his dogmatic conclusion. This Socrates is a fellow who uses his mind to produce, with great pride, "thoughts, speeches, trickery, roguery, boasting, lies, sagacity." These values are all morally equal; the mind can be made to do just about anything, and to do it gloriously. Furthermore, the student Strepsiades catches the hang of things quickly. After very little tutoring, he feels that his mind has "spread out its wings," and that he is now sufficiently educated to "babble about trifles, to maintain worthless arguments" and to employ his new fund of "petty reasons" to outmaneuver and confuse all opponents. The intellect has become a delightfully valuable weapon for overriding, rather than discovering, truth.

There are those who are still appalled that Aristophanes should have misrepresented Socrates in this way—and the portrait *is* a misrepresentation of the man. Along the way there have been critics who charged Aristophanes with having played a part in the real Socrates' downfall; spreading this sort of nonsense through the Greek body politic may have strengthened the hand of those reactionary forces that succeeded in bringing Socrates to trial. Scandal created by a great playwright may have helped bring a great thinker to his death.

Few authorities are any longer willing to view Aristophanes—and comedy—as accomplices to a murder. At is happens, twenty-four years elapsed between the appearance of the play and the death of Socrates. Audiences understand that all satire involves exaggeration. Besides, the play was unsuccessful. We do not have the original version, which failed. The revised version was not presented at the major festivals. However irreverent Aristophanes may have been, the case for the prosecution is weak.

Yet the play is disturbing. It should be; it was intended to be. The real scandal of the play lies not in what it said about the living Socrates but in what it said—and continues to say—about the human mind. As a form, comedy has moved into new and apparently forbidden territory. It is all very well for comedy to display the awkwardnesses of the body and the difficulties of dealing with the material universe as sorry burdens *imposed* upon the flexible mind, as bothersome companions which the mind must make allowance for as it goes about its free activity. But to step beyond this, to dismiss the body and the material universe as mere secondary impediments and to show the free mind itself as treacherously unfree is a far more unsettling thing, creating in the viewer—at first sight and even long afterward—a degree of psychic shock.

For the intellect is the instrument upon which man depends for a future. It is sacred to tragedy, the source of tragedy's freedom and the guarantor of its forward movement. Prometheus may be physically bound to a rock, but he is intellectually free enough to call Zeus to account and to compel the very heavens to make an accommodation with him. The tragic chorus, eternally singing of "clear intelligence, force beyond all measure," knows very well indeed where power and flexibility lie. In calling intelligence into question, comedy strikes "high."

In passing, we have had occasion to mention a handful of "high" comedies—*The Way of the World, The Importance of Being Earnest, The School for Wives*—though we have not bothered to call them that or to say what the descriptive term means. We have, at the back of our heads, a rough-and-ready notion of what the term means: a preoccupation with conscious style, a display of elegant manners, an emphasis upon verbal dexterity. A recent *Reader's Guide to Literary Terms* gathers together our loose impressions this way:

HIGH COMEDY: A term broadly applied to satiric comedy whose appeal is primarily intellectual. There are no precise criteria for distinguishing high from low comedy, but where the latter achieves its effect with jokes and buffoonery, high comedy works with intellect and wit. In general, it is graceful, witty, and urbane. . . .

There is no mention of the fact that it is savage. Yet high comedy is a far more venomous form than low comedy, in the end a more deeply despairing form. Low comedy is cheerful, in its vulgar way, about what cannot be helped. But high comedy takes aim at what *can* be helped, at accidents and errors that ideally should never take place at all. To say that high comedy's "appeal is primarily intellectual" or that "high comedy works with intellect and wit" is to suggest that the form makes intellect attractive, that it exists almost to praise intellectuality and to deify man's wondrous wit.

That is not its thrust at all. High comedy invades intellect in order to expose its pretensions, to display its ghastly interior contradictions. It makes use of mind to mock the value of mind. It employs wit, genuine wit, to call attention to the essential shallowness of its activity. High comedy might be said to waste wit on what is worthless, to summon up all of the powers of the human intelligence in order to defeat the purposes of the human intelligence. High comedy is "high" because it invades tragic territory and makes free of its tools;

but it has propelled itself high in order to bring the intellect low.

As a result there is often a certain edginess, a degree of uncertainty and a pinch of resentment, in our experience of high comedy. I do not know that anyone has ever made a study of the unconscious hostility that high comedy has so often had to contend with, particularly among intellectuals. The results of such a study might surprise us, and I am no longer thinking of so blatant a case as the near-libel Aristophanes directed against Socrates. *The Clouds* is not the only celebrated high comedy ever to have failed. *The Way of the World,* for all that we call it a masterpiece, failed in performance, too; indeed, the hostility of its first audiences drove Congreve from the theater. *The School for Wives* drew the fiercest criticism from literary sources that Molière ever had to contend with; only *Tartuffe* gave him greater trouble, and that for slightly different, though related, reasons. We still squint at *The Misanthrope,* ostensibly troubled by its curious form, but perhaps more deeply troubled by what it is saying. Bernard Shaw did not like *The Importance of Being Earnest.* Though Oscar Wilde's play went on to become highly successful and though Shaw's disapproval has been explained away—Shaw saw the second performance, which was said to be faulty—there are sound enough reasons for Shaw's standoffish attitude. Shaw was an intensely rational man. He might mock reason in his own comedies, but only to a rational purpose—which he carefully explained in his prefaces. *The Importance of Being Earnest* is without rational purpose. It makes light of the workings of the mind simply to make light of them. Thus it is an irreverent play; to Shaw it may well have seemed an irresponsible one. There is something gleefully malicious about it.

In many cases high comedy makes us so nervous that we flatly refuse to believe what it is doing. *Much Ado About Nothing* is one of Shakespeare's high comedies. It contains all of the "graceful" appurtenances we like to attribute to the form: a civilized atmosphere, a high degree of artifice, a hero and heroine who live by wit alone. So long as Beatrice and Benedick are exchanging felicitiously phrased insults, or playing overhearing games in the garden, we quite understand that they are comic figures. What else should they be? Then, suddenly, we are precipitated into a scene over which actors, directors, and critics are quarreling to this day.

The scene is simple enough, and its tone, so far as I am concerned, is unmistakably plain. It is comedy through and through. Beatrice and Benedick have been tricked into recognizing their love for one another. They are both on the point of acknowledging it openly, though this presents a wee bit of difficulty since they have specialized so long in insulting one another. Furthermore, as bad luck generally arranges these things, Beatrice has just learned that her cousin and dear friend Hero has been spurned at the altar by Benedick's dear friend Claudio. This is not precisely the propitious moment for Benedick to make his avowal of love.

And so, naturally, it is the moment when the two are thrown together. Beatrice is in a fine, feminine fury over what has happened to her friend; high-spirited to begin with, she is a bundle of explosives now. Benedick is utterly out of his element, hopelessly inexperienced in his role as suitor, baffled by close exposure to the feline temperament at bay, clumsily tentative in his gestures of comfort. Beatrice is ready for him, and he is in for it.

BENEDICK. Lady Beatrice, have you wept all this while?
BEATRICE. Yea, and I will weep a while longer.
BENEDICK. I will not desire that.
BEATRICE. You have no reason: I do it freely.
BENEDICK. Surely I do believe your fair cousin is wronged.
BEATRICE. Ah, how much might the man deserve of me that would right her!
BENEDICK. Is there any way to show such friendship?
BEATRICE. A very even way, but no such friend.

BENEDICK.   May a man do it?

BEATRICE.   It is a man's office, but not yours.

BENEDICK.   I do love nothing in the world so well as you: is not that strange?

BEATRICE.   As strange as the thing I know not. It were as possible for me to say I loved nothing so well as you: but believe me not; and yet I lie not. I confess nothing, nor I deny nothing. I am sorry for my cousin.

BENEDICK.   By my sword, Beatrice, thou lovest me.

BEATRICE.   Do not swear, and eat it.

BENEDICK.   I will swear by it that you love me; and I will make him eat it that says I love not you.

BEATRICE.   Will you not eat your word?

BENEDICK.   With no sauce that can be devised to it. I protest I love thee.

BEATRICE.   Why, then, God forgive me!

BENEDICK.   What offence, sweet Beatrice?

BEATRICE.   You have stayed me in a happy hour. I was about to protest I loved you.

BENEDICK.   And do it with all thy heart.

BEATRICE.   I love you with so much of my heart, that none is left to protest.

BENEDICK.   Come, bid me do anything for thee.

BEATRICE.   Kill Claudio.

BENEDICK.   Ha! not for the wide world.

BEATRICE.   You kill me to deny it. Farewell.

BENEDICK.   Tarry, sweet Beatrice.

BEATRICE.   I am gone, though I am here: there is no love in you. Nay, I pray you, let me go.

And so on, until she has trapped him into doing the unreasonable thing she wants him to do. The scene continues with further false farewells from Beatrice, calculated to bring Benedick to a sufficiently rash state of mind to promise the unthinkable, and with characteristically vixenish insults to his manhood designed to persuade him that he will be behaving nobly in executing the lady's idiotic command. The sequence as a whole is a little marvel of man-baiting, of adopted postures. I have cut it off here because we have already passed the point of contention.

"Kill Claudio" is the crucial phrase, and our understanding of how it is to be read determines the tone in which all the rest of the passage will be played. Is "Kill Claudio" a melodramatic command, almost a tragic one? Or is it a laugh line, the very crest of the wave of nonsense that has been building up? Do we take Beatrice's request as emotionally sincere or as intellectually outrageous?

Most productions of the play that I have seen have opted, strangely, for the former. Beatrice is awash with tears; her very heart is breaking; she can see no other course to take. And Benedick is thereby placed in a sort of love-versus-honor conflict that is not much removed from the torment of soul sometimes visited upon the heroes of Racine and Corneille. The situation is earnest, not foolish. It sounds rather as though centuries other than our own had often chosen this course, too, as nearly as one can gather from the pauses and sighs that mark that promptbook of Charles Kemble or from the image of Ada Rehan, as reconstructed by Arthur Colby Sprague, opening the scene by prostrating herself at the altar, weeping.

But it is a very hard choice to bring off. Nothing in any of the earlier passages between Beatrice and Benedick prepares us for this sort of sentimentality or for the personal agonies of melodrama. We have become accustomed to two delightful artifices who seem all perverse head and no heart. Suddenly we must wrench our whole experience awry, begin to treat Beatrice and Benedick not only as entirely different kinds of people but as people inhabiting an entirely different kind of play. True, the play has a streak of unmotivated melodrama in it elsewhere, notably in the taken-for-granted villainy of that dark Don John who slanders Hero and misleads Claudio. But until now Beatrice and Benedick have kept their own house in order, and it has been the true house of the play, the dominant stylistic architecture. And it is going to become that again quickly in the last scene they play together, when the sparring wits will continue to bait one another playfully even on the brink of marriage. Furthermore, the structural under-pinnings of the sequence are not serious. Rumor has gone out that the rejected Hero is dead of grief, but she is not, and we know it; so do Beatrice and Benedick. A trick is at work beneath the situation proper and beneath any emotion it engenders or contains; for Benedick to kill Claudio in order to avenge the death of a girl who is not dead is preposterous. Everything before the sequence, everything after the se-quence, and everything under the sequence, tells us that the sequence must be comedy. Therefore to play it soberly or sentimentally is simply "startling," to use Mr. Sprague's word as he enters the area.

When the scene is played as comedy throughout, it plays magnificently. Beatrice's rage is funny, being in excess of the facts to begin with. Benedick's flounderings are funny. The deviousness with which Beatrice lures Benedick through pro-testations of love and a declared willingness to do anything to prove that love into a commitment to kill his best friend is wiliness at its most wicked and at its most amusing. Bene-dick's final, helpless, love-blinded and courage-challenged decision to take on the absurd task becomes a new and noble rationalization that closely echoes the extremely funny, fatu-ous and self-deceiving rationalizations by which he has earlier arrived at his determination to marry Beatrice. Even his subsequent challenge to Claudio, played as the posture of a man who has had to nerve himself to the tasks of a shining knight, continues to be essentially comic in effect. After all, the whole rigadoon of comings and goings and challenges and declarations is going to be exploded in a moment anyway— and by means of still another playful trick.

Yet there are critics who cannot abide the thought that "Kill Claudio" is funny, just as there are actresses who are unwilling to make Beatrice foolish enough to say it in sheer temper. And there are reasons for this resistance. For the high comedy has reached its high point, and at its high point the intelligence of its witty central figures, which has been crumbling steadily for several acts, collapses into virtual insanity. Temper and spite have got the better of mind: all reasonableness flies out the window as love and hate twist the intellect in the direction of highly unintelligent work; two cultivated people whose minds have displayed the dexterity and sting of wasps are rendered mindless by their emotions, overwhelmed by the instant's passion. Urbanity is dissolved; sophistication is turned to naïveté; control is lost. And since such control as we have is intellectual, we do not much like to see it lost. We may laugh. We *will* laugh, because we cannot help ourselves. But the spectacle is so unnerving that actors, directors, and audiences have connived together for years to evade its implications by forcing upon it a gentler, less disturbing, interpretation.

The case of Chekhov is much worse. Chekhov called his principal plays comedies. He battled with directors, with critics, with audiences to stage them, to discuss them, to *see* them as comedies. No one would listen to him, as he often and bitterly complained. "Why is it that my play is persistently called a drama in posters and newspaper advertisements?" he cried out at the time of *The Cherry Orchard*. "Nemirovich-Danchenko and Stanislavsky see in my play something absolutely different from what I have written, and I'm willing to stake my word on it that neither of them has once read my play through attentively. Forgive me, but I assure you it is so."

The director Stanislavsky chose to see *The Cherry Orchard* as a tragedy, and he staged it that way. "Stanislavsky has ruined my play," Chekhov mourned. "Is this really my *Cherry Orchard?* Are these my types? With the exception of two or three roles, none of this is mine. I describe life. It is a dull, philistine life. But it is not a tedious, whimpering life. First they turn me into a weeper and then into a simply boring writer."

That Chekhov's major plays have gone on being performed as tragedies, or near-tragedies, is well known. The
stamp of the original productions has become so firm that
Chekhov's influence on other writers has not really been his,
but Stanislavsky's; most imitations of the Chekhovian form
contain very little comedy and insist upon sustaining a mood
of twilit regret, frustration, languor. When Chekhov
heard that a certain actor was to play the title role in his early
Ivanov, he was appalled. Chekhov felt that Ivanov's two long
monologues were decisive for the play, and he knew that the
actor would "deliver both monologues 'intelligently,' i.e.,
with overwhelming languor."

What has caused all the trouble? Precisely the issue of
"intelligence." Apart from his occasional vaudevilles, Chekhov did not write low comedy. He wrote comedies of the
mind, comedies in which the most serious issues were reduced
to absurdity by the malfunctioning of the instrument that
ought to have been able to resolve the issues effectively. The
failure of intelligence is his perpetual theme, the strait-
jacketing of the intelligence by preconceived attitudes his
principal comic image.

If we read him wrong it is because we are reluctant to see
our own seriousness—our own intellectuality—parodied.
Comedy cuts too close to the bone here, touching us in our
pride, affronting our freedom, whipping out from under us
the dignity that makes us tragic.

Just how close comedy may cut to the tragic bone can be
seen in the following passage from *The Cherry Orchard*—but
read it warily. The student Trofimov, the eternal intellectual, is addressing the members of the household:

Humanity goes forward, perfecting its powers. Everything that's
unattainable now will some day become familiar, understand-
able; it is only that one must work and must help with all one's
might those who seek the truth. With us in Russia so far only a
very few work. The great majority of the intelligentsia that I

know are looking for nothing, doing nothing, and as yet have no capacity for work. They call themselves intelligentsia, are free and easy with the servants, treat the peasants like animals, educate themselves poorly, read nothing seriously, do absolutely nothing; about science they just talk and about art they understand very little. Every one of them is serious, all have stern faces; they all talk of nothing but important things, philosophize, and all the time everybody can see that the workmen eat abominably, sleep without any pillows, thirty or forty to a room, and everywhere there are bedbugs, stench, dampness, moral uncleanness— And apparently with us, all the fine talk is only to divert the attention of ourselves and of others. Show me where we have the day nurseries they are always talking so much about, where are the reading rooms? They only write of these in novels, for the truth is there are not any at all. There is only filth, vulgarity, orientalism—I am afraid of very serious faces and dislike them. I'm afraid of serious conversations. Rather than that let's just keep still.

What kind of passage is that? On the face of things, we are almost certain to take it seriously, as actors almost invariably play it seriously. Surely nearly everything that Trofimov says is true. Surely our own liberalism must make us feel an earnest, even urgent, sympathy for Trofimov's concerns: the poor, the uneducated, the filthy and unhoused. Because a Russian revolution later erupted with the intention of correcting just these injustices, the passage must now seem prophetic: Chekhov was in the vanguard. And when Trofimov speaks of humanity moving forward, "perfecting its powers," he is adopting the fundamental tragic stance, echoing its evolutionary voice. Who can dispute his contention that "one must work"?

There is just one hitch. Trofimov himself does no work. He is marching nowhere, except in his words, except in his self-deluded head. Trofimov is a perpetual student, the student who never leaves the library for any field of action, a rousing talker with no capacity whatever for realizing the objectives he talks about. He is the same fellow who, a little later on, will not even enter into a relationship with so much as one other person. He will not marry, because he is "above love." Immediately after this last high-minded assertion, Chekhov carefully instructs us as to what our attitude toward Trofimov should be. Trofimov leaves the room and promptly tumbles down the stairs, causing a great clatter. The intellectual clown's incompetence is underscored. But that is a relatively rare stress in Chekhov's work. For the most part we are to listen and discover the irony for ourselves—in Konstantine's enthusiasm for "unconventional" theater, in Ranevskaya's determination to preserve her beautiful trees, in everyone's infinite, much-talked-about, self-romanticizing "boredom."

That is to say, we enter the realm of seriousness, of intellectuality, of something very like tragedy in order to display the terrible, and inevitably funny, limitations that exist *within* seriousness, *within* intellect, *within* the tragic landscape. We are not throwing stones from a great distance; we are breaking the windows from inside the house.

Of course the task is a delicate one. Comedy has penetrated so deeply into what is most vital in our lives, into what is sober about our condition, into the resources we possess for saving ourselves, that humor is no longer a sledge hammer, it is an almost invisible knife blade, scarcely more than a giveaway glint on the underside of things. Anyone who prefers not to see what is comic—which is to say, limited—in the behavior of Chekhov's characters can easily give all of his attention to the unhappy eventualities of the play and none of it to the self-delusion that has brought such things about. How sad it is that the appealing Ranevskaya must be driven from her ancient home! The fact that an ounce of common sense, exercised in time, would have prevented the disaster is comfortably ignored. The appealing lady has no common sense; we prefer not to notice. The man who comes from Chekhov without having acknowledged the comedy that

Chekhov insisted was there comes away rather humorless himself. But he does, in a way, save face.

For we seem to dislike being told that the intelligent, the sensitive, the endearing or the put-upon may lack common sense. In 1966 John Gielgud, as accomplished an actor as the contemporary theater knows, brought to New York a revival of *Ivanov*. In it the peripheral figures who waste their time on cards, gossip, and unworkable schemes for improving their lives were permitted to be seen as funny. But in the center of this crowded field of social satire the three principals—Ivanov himself, his tubercular wife, and the younger girl who offers herself to him—appeared, puzzlingly, as straightforward, near-tragic icons. Mr. Gielgud played Ivanov exactly as Chekhov feared his first actor would: intelligently, "with overwhelming languor." The mixture of comic secondary characters and "straight" principals was unassimilable.

What had happened? Once more Chekhov's intentions in writing the play had been almost scrupulously ignored. As biographer Ernest Simmons says, "in the character of Ivanov he attempted to expose a type that had been much written about but inadequately understood. . . . Ivanov was intended to symbolize those people among the educated class who . . . had fallen into dejection and despair. Chekhov wished to debunk this type, to unmask the futility of the intellectual who dreams pleasantly about his past accomplishments but quails before the abuses of the present, then experiences a vague sense of guilt over them, and ends with unstrung nerves among the 'shattered' and 'misunderstood' people of society." Ivanov is as much a satirical figure as any of the nonentities around him, although, since he is a man of intellect, the satire must be discovered within his intellectuality.

Chekhov's letters explain his subtle comic intentions clearly. The younger woman, Sasha, who is apparently deeply in love with Ivanov and courageously willing to marry him after the death of his wife, is by no means so open, so virtuous, so self-sacrificing as all that. "She is the type of female," Chekhov says, "whom males do not conquer with the brilliance of their plumage, nor with their suppleness, nor with their courage, but with their laments, whimpers and recitals of failure. This is a woman who loves men in the period of their decline. Ivanov hardly had time to become disheartened before the young lady was Johnny-on-the-spot. She was only waiting for this moment. Goodness, she has such a noble, sacred problem! She will raise the fallen, get him up onto his feet, give him happiness. . . . It is not Ivanov she loves, but his problem."

And even Ivanov's relationship with his tubercular Jewish wife is not altogether the bid for pathos it seems. The wife indeed is pathetic, though she is able to summon up enough energy to tell her self-dramatizing husband a home truth or two. But what sort of marriage has this been? How did it come about? It would at first seem that Ivanov has been a man of principle in marrying a Jewess in a society that probably would look askance at him for doing so. But Chekhov is not balancing the uncorrupted liberal conscience against anti-Semitism at all; he is not even talking about these two things seriously. He is, by indirection and in retrospect, drawing a portrait of an excitable, overly romantic young intellectual, "a man who has hardly clambered off the school bench, rashly takes on a burden beyond his powers, simultaneously takes up schools, peasants, scientific farming, . . . makes speeches, writes to the minister, struggles with evil, applauds the good, does not fall in love simply and any old way, but inevitably with either bluestockings or psychopaths . . . or even prostitutes whom he tries to save from their fate, and so on and so forth." Anna need not have been a Jewess. She might have been a Gypsy, an Oriental, a cripple—*anything* sufficiently out of the ordinary for Ivanov to have prided himself on bravely embracing. Love had no part in this; a posture of idealism did.

Everywhere Chekhov uses his intellectual and emotional

misfits not to tug at our heartstrings, but to open our eyes to
the fact that what they did and thought and felt has been
improperly grounded from the beginning. Chekhov's characters see themselves as tragic. But Chekhov's point is precisely
that they are not. They are poor, dear fools—well meaning,
but constantly and ruinously entangling themselves in their
own misapprehensions.

Intellectual comedy—which is comedy raising questions
about the intellect—does not bother or baffle us quite so
much when we are able to reduce the degree of intelligence
displayed by a character to a coarser, and therefore safer,
level. Perhaps the ruling stock figure in this sort of comedy is
the pedant, an overblown and fantastical clown who has been
with us for hundreds of years. The Dottore of the *commedia
dell' arte* is a pedant. That is to say, he is a learned man, with
a degree from the University of Bologna, and his principal
activity is to display his learning so relentlessly that we come
to see it as the obsession of a fundamentally not very good
mind. Intelligence is reduced to an acquired trait; it is not
something innate, but something that can be bought by
paying tuition and paid out in uninterrupted sententious-
ness. The original Dottore was a doctor of philosophy; he
later became a doctor of medicine, which is in itself a comforting reduction.

"The good doctor," Duchartre tells us, "is a member of
every academy, known and unknown. . . . It is a curious fact
that, although he spends his entire time with his nose in a
book, it is always painfully difficult for him to give a Greek
or Latin quotation without murdering it alive. . . . But,
luckily enough, he is endowed with prodigious aplomb,
which usually intimidates even the best instructed of his listeners until, unable to endure any more, they rise up and
give him a sound beating. But even then the flow of his elo-
quence rarely ceases."

Pinpointing the intellectual level of the Dottore, however,
has not always been easy. Actors playing the role and audi-

ences enjoying the performance seem to have preferred pushing him down a bit, so that the learning being satirized would not quite seem real learning. Allardyce Nicoll quotes a commentator who lived at the end of the seventeenth century as saying that "the part of the Dottore has not to be so dignified [as that of Pantalone] . . . but, through the liveliness of spirit and the redundancy of words, it may be carried somewhat out of the serious sphere—not so much, however, as to drag it down to the level of the second Zanni." That is to say, the cartoon is most welcome when its content is not too "high." At the same time it must not be permitted to become altogether "low," lest its point be missed:

". . . the actor playing the part must be learned enough to be able to illustrate his ideas, in fitting time and scene, with some Latin sentence, some text or pronouncement of authority. . . . A number of years ago there was introduced a special style in the playing of the part, whereby the Dottore mutilated his words, saying, for example, "terrible urinal" for tribunal . . . but, since it was realized that this rendered him far too stupid and clumsy, it has been abandoned."

In short, we tend to prefer our intellectual comedy to occupy a sort of middle ground, where the flexible mind is shown to be in some fairly obvious ways inflexible but where its ultimate suppleness is not too severely challenged. The level at which Molière used the Dottore—in this case a quack doctor—is just about right for us, considering our sensitivities. The quack doctor has succeeded in locating a patient's liver on his left side and his heart on his right. A bystander is puzzled, though deferential:

"It seems to me that you place them wrongly; and the heart is on the left side, and the liver on the right."
"Yes, that is the way it used to be. But we have changed all that; now we use an entirely new method in medicine."
"Oh, I didn't know that. I ask your pardon for my ignorance."

"No harm done. You aren't obliged to be as well informed as we are."

We are also readily comfortable with the comedy of the Fixed Idea, no matter what it is the mind is fixed on. Sheridan's Doctor Rosy, for instance, did dearly love his dead wife. But, being so thoroughly a doctor, he cannot possibly remember her except in medical terms:

Oh, poor Dolly! I shall never see her like again; such an arm for a bandage—veins that seemed to invite the lancet . . . and then her teeth—none of your sturdy fixtures—ache as they would, it was but a small pull, and out they came. I believe I have drawn half a score of her poor dear pearls. . . .

Doctor Rosy is weeping by this time over the loss of a good woman who was so perfectly a patient. And I suppose there is no more celebrated instance of the arrow-shaft mind—the mind that knows its direction and pursues it in all weathers— than one Molière wrote for himself to play. Orgon is so obsessed with Tartuffe, and with Tartuffe's patently fraudulent piety, that he simply cannot hear anything other than the monomaniac rattle inside his own head:

ORGON.   Has all been well, these two days I've been gone?
How are the family? What's been going on?
DORINE.   Your wife, two days ago, had a bad fever,
And a fierce headache which refused to leave her.
ORGON.   Ah. And Tartuffe?
DORINE.   Tartuffe? Why, he's round and red,
Bursting with health, and excellently fed.
ORGON.   Poor fellow!

The scene goes on, of course, to report that while the mistress of the house was unable to eat, Tartuffe gorged himself; that while the mistress of the house spent a feverishly sleepless night, Tartuffe snored gloriously. "Poor fellow!" is Orgon's response to each piece of information.

We do not squirm at, or try to tame, this sort of comedy, because it is clear to us how the near-paralysis of mind has come about. It is, fundamentally, the result of habit. A good enough mind has occupied itself too exclusively with a single channel of activity. Naturally, the channel has narrowed and deepened from such overuse until it has finally become a rut. Trudging along in an unconsciously created ditch, eyes fixed forward in what must now be called tunnel vision, the man who is obsessed with medicine or piety or the mathematics of playing cards permits himself to be ruled by his obsession. But this does not suggest that there is anything unreliable about the intellect as such. The intellect has merely been abused.

Much of Bergson's theory of comedy depends upon the encrusting force of habit. Speaking of mind and body both, Bergson noted that "a flexible vice may not be so easy to ridicule as a rigid virtue." Rigidity is what begets comedy; any *"mechanical inelasticity"* which leads a man to behave in an automatic way, looking neither to the left nor to the right, but absent-mindedly treading familiar tracks, will make us laugh quite quickly. "The comic is that side of a person which reveals his likeness to a thing, that aspect of human events which, through its peculiar inelasticity, conveys the impression of pure mechanism, of automatism, of movement without life."

Mind-blindness comes of letting too persistently indulged interests and too regularly pursued attitudes accrue like barnacles on the fundamentally supple intellect, forming a hard shell about it and confining its free activity. Bergson had a favorite jest that pretty well summarized the situation:

"It was suggested to a contemporary philosopher, an out-and-out arguer, that his arguments, though irreproachable in their deductions, had experience against them. He put an end to the discussion by merely remarking, 'Experience is in the wrong.' "

Thus far can man's willfulness take him. But it is the will, really, that is doing the damage. The mind, as mind, remains more or less blameless. If Bergson's theory, obviously true so far as it goes, has never seemed quite ample enough to account for all of comedy, it is—I think—because comedy at its most impertinent behaves just a bit more daringly than Bergson would wish it to. It goes beyond saying that the intellect can be rendered inflexible by habit. It wants to hint that the intellect in its original and purest state is an unreliable instrument for man's most vital purposes.

That is a bold charge, but comedy, rightly or wrongly, is inclined to make it, and sometimes to make it stick. For instance, the tools which the intellect has devised for carrying out its operations come constantly under comedy's scrutiny. Logic is one of those tools. In his play *Rhinoceros,* Eugene Ionesco is eager to display the absurdity of thinking that the tool as such has any value:

LOGICIAN. Here is an example of a syllogism. The cat has four
paws. . . .
OLD GENTLEMAN. My dog has got four paws.
LOGICIAN. Then it's a cat. . . . Another syllogism. All cats die.
Socrates is dead. Therefore Socrates is a cat.

This sort of thing, by the way, does not strike me as particularly funny. It is too easy, too one-sided. Bergson insisted that the comic effect was achieved by the spectacle of something mechanical encrusted *upon the living.* But the last three words are an indispensable part of the statement. Behind or within the automaton that has come into existence we must see or sense the flexibility that properly belongs to the creature and that has nearly been erased. The automated mind must retain an echo of the free mind that ought to have been; otherwise we shall have no incongruity. Ionesco's satirical figures too often seem to me wholly automated, flattened out beyond the possibility—or even the memory—of free activity.

Yet comedy has had its successes in challenging the tools of the mind. I have sometimes wondered if our lofty contempt for the pun is not perhaps a defense mechanism. Words are a tool of the mind, an essential tool of all our free intercourse, and it is somewhat disturbing to be reminded that they are dreadfully unreliable, that they can change places with one another without warning. Even a good pun is essentially a defeat, as Hazlitt has pointed out. Hazlitt cites, with some pleasure, "the reply of the author of a periodical paper called The World to a lady at church, who seeing him look thoughtful, asked what he was thinking of." His reply, of course, was, "the next World." As puns go, that is a good one, and an apparent intellectual victory for the man who made it. He has used his intelligence to satisfy his questioner without precisely lying. But he has done so at a price. He has defeated the purpose of words, which is communication. Thus Hazlitt calls his victory "a perversion." A pun invariably registers the collapse of meaning. It does not give us two meanings for one; it gives us neither of the meanings the colliding words were designed to reveal. The mind is delighted by its own deviousness, but its content is blocked.

We are in the habit of calling puns "low," though, since they poke fun at an indispensable tool of the mind, they are actually the lowest form of "high" comedy. I suppose that most people would describe the Marx Brothers as low comedians as well; sometimes they are. But when Groucho and Chico enter into a sequence in which a parcel of Florida real estate is to be auctioned off, the comic problem is not physical or material but intellectual. Groucho is the auctioneer. He wants Chico to help him by bidding up values. Chico, of course, has no money. But Groucho carefully instructs him to increase each bid that is made by two hundred dollars, forcing the sale price higher. Chico agrees. When the auction begins and there is no first offer, Chico bids two hundred dollars. When there is no second offer, he bids another two hundred dollars. In fact, he has learned his lesson so well that when another bidder does try to get into the contest, Chico is too quick for him, upping his own bid by two hundred dollars more. In due time Chico has bought everything, and Groucho is wishing that one of them were dead.

Slapstick of the intellect is perhaps what these confusions may be called; the form embraces malapropisms, verbal misunderstandings, faulty intellectual connections of every sort. When a hostess says, to a departing guest on the doorstep, "I was so nice to have met you," the switchboard of the brain has simply provided a wrong number. When Groucho Marx says, "I would not belong to a club that would have me," he is scrambling the switchboard deliberately.

And we are not inclined to take this sort of comic comment amiss or to mistake it for near-seriousness. One or another critic may see in Groucho Marx an image of "anarchy" and hail him as a forerunner of the drama of negation, but we do not really find Groucho threatening as he shreds the intellectual processes by which we make our hard-won advances. Though what is happening to the poor brain in these instances is difficult to formulate in a philosophical way, we recognize the instances as not much more than lucky-unlucky accidents. Bergson would simply have explained that the immaterial intellect—a force of the soul—was compelled to release itself through matter, literally through gray matter. Whatever a man thinks or wishes to say must work itself out in the physical brain. And because the brain is physical, something of its materiality tends to cling to, and to clog, the otherwise perfectly supple thought. Whether one accepts the concepts of the soul and immateriality or not, we have practical experience to help us grasp what happens to us. One of our commonest sensations is of having a complete, coherent, luminous and delightfully free idea darting about in our heads and of being unable to make our brains do the work of releasing it properly, whether in speech or in writing. We scurry after the thought, hoping to trap it in the right words and proper sequence that will display it perfectly; we reach, grope, retrace our steps, make off in a new direction as though the idea could, like a horse, be corralled. In the end we make a botch of the idea at worst, an unsatisfactory approximation of it at best. We hear, as we express the thought, how much of it we have managed to bring out alive; and we hear, alas, how much of it we have left behind. Our tools are not as good as our intentions. But the idea was there. It is still there, still clear, as we curse ourselves for having given it scars while giving it birth. We sigh; we have not yet evolved sufficiently fluid forms for conveying quickly and without error the fluid thing in our heads; perhaps extrasensory perception will someday do it for us.

Much more difficult to understand and tolerate, however, is that highest form of "high" comedy which ventures to suggest that the fluid thing in our heads, the actual and thus far invisible concept we hold there and wish to release, is itself untrustworthy. Comedy, probing forward, wishes to laugh at our thoughts *as we think them,* wishes to show us that our deepest seriousness is suspect, wishes to challenge that freedom of intellect which alone makes tragedy possible. If tragedy is an account of our continuing evolution, comedy now dares to suggest that the evolutionary state we have arrived at is inadequate to the purposes of further evolution. The possibility of transcendence is being mocked, the hope of an "epiphany" discounted. It is not surprising that we should show nervousness whenever comedy enters directly into the landscape from which it came and from which it at first cut itself off to function as semi-autonomous comment. Comedy itself gives evidence of a considerable uncertainty as it does so.

Even so, it is on the verge of its richest formulation. No matter how uncertain the tone and tentative the footwork displayed, comedy is now about to submit itself to an ultimate test of its own truths. It has advanced all the way into tragic terrain in order to meet and mock the intellect at its freest, feeling fairly certain that the intellect is flawed.

Once there, though, and brushing shoulders so intimately with its opposite, it runs an unexpected risk. In penetrating tragedy so deeply, comedy has come home to its source—for which it must inevitably yearn. A child is drawn to its mother even when its survival depends upon being independent of its mother.

And tragedy, as though sensing the ambiguity of comedy's love-hate attitude toward it, may very well make comedy a tantalizing proposal. It may suggest to all clowns that they are free to be free, that they can, if they wish, throw off their shackles and join in a universal advance.

The proposal is shocking to comedy because accepting it would mean the end of comedy. But, having ventured so close, it is faced with a choice.

13
THE CHOICE

Is it possible that in asserting man's freedom tragedy means to say that man is free to choose whether he will be tragic or comic?

Here is an impossible question, for comedy a potentially suicidal one. And yet comedy must face up to it, must push its own assertion that man is irretrievably limited—limited without choice—all the way. For until it has tested this assertion absolutely, until it has discovered for itself whether man is free *not* to be comic, it will never have defined itself absolutely. It will be maintaining a point of view for which it lacks ultimate proof.

What to do?

Comedy must square off with tragedy, meet it on equal terms: freedom versus limitation, in a battle to the death, or life. Up to now it has enjoyed a certain advantage: anyone whose business it is to look for flies in the ointment is almost certain to find a fly in any ointment. The world is quick to believe scandal, and the fact has always given comedy a comforting edge.

Suppose, though, that comedy, having granted man's high aims—with certain impolite reservations—and having granted man's spiritual equipment for achieving those aims—again with certain impolite reservations—were now to agree, tentatively, to grant one thing more. Suppose it agreed, simply as a working hypothesis, that human limitation was not an absolute, not *necessary*. Suppose it accepted tragedy's insistence that the exercise of freedom was not only man's greatest dream but also his principal realized activity, never mind at what cost. Suppose it were to wrestle with the notion that the powers of freedom were in fact greater than the drags of limitation, that the momentum of the forward thrust was irresistible enough to render relatively impotent, in the long run, the retards upon which comedy capitalizes. If man were to be envisioned not as a being helplessly subject to limitation but rather as a being free enough to decide for himself whether he wished to be limited or not, what kind of comedy could comedy make of that?

It could make two kinds. It could show us a comic hero possessed of a high and free intelligence, possessed of a right to come and go as he pleases, who knowingly and in perfect freedom chooses to be bound. This man knows himself to be better than his bondage; and he holds out his wrists to the cords. Without being compelled to do so, he elects limitation. He is Falstaff.

Comedy could also show us—or, at the risk of its life, try to show us—a comic hero possessed of a high, free intelligence, possessed of a right to come and go as he chooses, who determines to exercise his right to come and go without limitation of any sort. Uncompromising and resolute, he turns his back upon limitation, will have none of it. At whatever cost to himself, or to comedy, he elects freedom. He is Alceste, the so-called misanthrope.

Falstaff and Alceste are the ultimate comic alternatives, the choosers who choose differently.

Falstaff's credentials as a free man cannot very well be questioned. He is *Sir* John Falstaff, and he moves in the company of kings. In a sense, he is king among them—for a time. At the most superficial social level, he owns as much dignity as he cares to exercise. He can be pretty much where and what he likes in the realm; it would seem that we first see him in the Prince's apartments, and we last see him, so sadly, where he belongs—face to face with the King.

But Falstaff's social credentials and aristocratic freedoms are not much to the point; they are only minor guarantees to make us certain of the man's size. His size is neither in his standing nor in his belly. It is in his head. Falstaff is that very rare creature, the man who knows himself. He may bluster and lie upon occasion like a Capitano; but he is no Capitano, for he does not believe in his own bluster or delude himself with his own lies. Neither does he expect others to be deluded, not really. He is happiest, and most quick-witted, when he is being caught out. He likes being caught out. It satisfies him, satisfies his sense of justice. He is fond of God's own truth and will not shy from it. Letting all of it come out makes him twinkle. He sees double always: he sees what he is by right, and he sees what he is by wrong, and he whoops with joy at the compounded knowledge.

"I must give over this life," he says as he clears his fat wits, "and I will give it over. By the Lord, and I do not, I am a villain."

"Where shall we take a purse tomorrow, Jack?" asks Hal, quickly mocking his resolution.

" 'Zounds, where thou wilt, lad" comes the answering roar, without pause for a change of heart.

Now Hal is wry with him. "I see a good amendment of life in thee, from praying to purse-taking," he teases.

"Why, Hal, 'tis my vocation, Hal. 'Tis no sin for a man to labour in his vocation."

Falstaff's vocation is to know how to pray and to prefer snatching purses, just as it is to know what courage is and to much prefer cowardice:

"Can honour set to a leg? No. Or an arm? No. Or take away the grief of a wound? No. Honour hath no skill in surgery, then? No. What is honour? A word . . . Who hath it? He that died o' Wednesday. . . . Therefore I'll none of it."

Is this simple rationalization? Does Falstaff believe in his own logically conceived catechism? Not at all. Does he expect us to believe in it? Never. What we are listening to now is a most subtle thing: the rationalization that mocks the mind's power of rationalizing. Here is what we may arrive at, Falstaff is saying to us, if we *choose* to use our marvelously flexible minds in a certain way. We can get the better of our minds, make our minds do our other bidding, enlist our minds in the cause of comfort and walk from the field pretending that we have done thought justice. But the whole process is a wink, a conspiracy between us. Falstaff knows and we know, and we know that Falstaff knows, the entire catechetical chain is a cunning hoax. The mind might have told us to go forward to honor; and we have taught it not to. We have used our noblest instrument against itself, cheekily, sneakily, with a warm leer of self-satisfaction. Falstaff understands Hal's honor perfectly well, as he does Hotspur's. In full knowledge, and with a wicked twist of the tool that gave him his knowledge, he ardently embraces dishonor.

This is altogether different from, and on the comic scale infinitely more complex than, the rationalization that is wistfully half believed or the pursuit of comfort that is not thought about at all. Benedick rationalizes when, having sworn never to marry, he decides to marry because "the world must be peopled." Benedick is kidding himself, and the spectacle is very funny. Volpone simply does not bother to justify his pursuit of pleasure to himself; dismissing thought, he lunges headlong at his pleasure like an extraordinarily talented animal.

Falstaff soars high above both of them. He is incapable of an unconsidered action; he considers everything carefully and flagrantly chooses the worst. And he never, under any circumstances, pretends to be what he is not. What sort of man is he? "I was as virtuously given as a gentleman need to be; virtuous enough, swore little, diced not above seven times a week, went to a bawdy-house not above once in a quarter—

of an hour,—paid money that I borrowed, three or four times; lived well, and in good compass . . ."

Falstaff's absolute self-knowledge, together with his absolutely accurate estimate of what a king might think of his association with a young prince, is handed to us on the handsomest of platters, upside down. He raffishly assumes, for a moment, the voice of Prince Hal's father, the king:

"If then thou be son to me, here lies the point: why, being son to me, art thou so pointed at? Shall the blessed sun of heaven prove a micher and eat blackberries? A question not to be asked. Shall the son of England prove a thief and take purses? A question to be asked. There is a thing, Harry, which thou hast often heard of, and it is known to many in our land by the name of pitch. This pitch, as ancient writers do report, doth defile; so doth the company thou keepest. For, Harry, now I do not speak to thee in drink but in tears, not in pleasure but in passion, not in words only, but in woes also: and yet there is a virtuous man whom I have often noted in thy company, but I know not his name."

"What manner of man, and it like your Majesty?"

"A goodly portly man, i' faith, and a corpulent; of a cheerful look, a pleasing eye, and a most noble carriage; and, as I think, his age some fifty, or, by'r lady, inclining to three score; and now I remember me, his name is Falstaff. If that man should be lewdly given, he deceiveth me; for, Harry, I see virtue in his looks. If then the tree may be known by the fruit, as the fruit by the tree, then, peremptorily I speak it, there is virtue in that Falstaff. Him keep with, the rest banish."

Falstaff plays the part almost too well. The words he puts into the king's mouth are right words; he could not make sport of them if he did not hear and understand their truth. Truth hovers like a ghost over the playfulness. And when he comes to speak of himself he is dangerously close to the mark again, though he has—poking fun at himself—painted a paragon. Jovially making black white, and lewd chaste, he invites us to invert everything if we would see how matters truly stand. With a little shiver, we realize that we must invert "Him keep with, the rest banish," too.

Falstaff must be banished because he has banished himself, by free choice and in clear light, from the beginning. He has banished himself, that is to say, from the world of responsible action: "I were better to be eaten to death with a rust than to be scoured to nothing with perpetual motion." Motion, the cruel thrust forward, is not for him; men are going to die anyway, and he'd as lief die with Doll on his lap, pint in hand. His is a possible choice. He has made it knowing the alternative, made it again and again and once again. His massive strength as a comic figure lies in the deliberateness of his choice. First "Well, I'll repent. . . . I have not forgotten what the inside of a church is made of." Then, quickly, before he dare persuade himself, "Come sing me a bawdy song: make me merry."

Only once—and that at the very end, when age is upon him and the once merry world has turned toward action—does he falter in his self-assessment. Briefly, he seems to have forgotten the cold implications of his playing at king. Briefly, he seems not to realize that his endlessly repeated commitment to one kind of world has in fact committed him to it. He seems to think that Hal, now king, will be able to accommodate him in that other world of action and honor and tragic aspiration. He listens, unbelieving, to the words his friend now pronounces:

> I know thee not, old man. Fall to thy prayers. . . .
> Make less thy body hence, and more thy grace;
> Leave gormandizing; know the grave doth gape
> For thee thrice wider than for other men.

A cold Hal; and no comfort in old comforts. We do not really like Hal—the new, determined, ascetic Hal—at this moment. Men who elect to take up arms against their comforts, who choose what may become the tragic course, are often unattractive at the moment of choice, for it is the moment at which they separate themselves from their easygoing fellows and from all that delight in bondage in which the rest of us indulge ourselves. We cherish Falstaff more than Hal just now, much more. Falstaff has made a glory of our own weaknesses, has come out foursquare in favor of them, has made us feel warm and well-companioned in our wickedness. A pity the world cannot be what Falstaff, and all the rest of us, would prefer it to be: open abandon to all the drink and all the lechery and all the jolly knavery that ever was.

But, alas, the world must be about its business, which seems to lie elsewhere. We are trying hard to swallow our grief before Hal's speech is done, trying to tighten our belts and to refocus our eyes to see if we cannot stomach and perhaps approve Hal's action. Yes, it must be approved. We see, plainly, that Hal must do what he is doing, not because he is Hal or because he is an ingrate or because he is a king, but because Falstaff is Falstaff. Falstaff is his own creation, not Hal's. He has *made* himself rust. The decision, now, is not Hal's. It is a decision Falstaff made for himself, in perfect freedom and with his sharp eyes open, long before. The rejection is not Hal's. It was Falstaff who rejected the world of honor. There is no new thing to be done here; we simply confirm an old thing done.

Cry for the man who has dug his own grave wider than another man's? Indeed. We cry for him more than we ever shall for Alceste, the comic man who chooses freedom over bondage. The man who chooses freedom cannot be so pathetic: whatever he suffers, he will always have his sense of rectitude to sustain him. But here we must cry the ultimate comic cry—the cry of the willingly captive spirit for whom, in the end, captivity is not enough. A great spirit makes a great choice: limitation. High intelligence plumps for a bellyful. Then, at the last, there is a sensation left over—a sodden, blinking, awareness that the vast joys of limitation were only the joys of *limitation*. There was another thing to be reached for which is now irretrievably lost. The spirit, wiping wine from its mouth, groans. The cry of the clown is the cry of the man who has not become tragic.

When comedy is deliberately adopted as a way of life, when its possibilities are explored and exhausted without equivocation or reservation, when surrender is total and the commitment to limitation exclusive, comedy's ending must be what Falstaff's is: despair. Falstaff has submerged himself in the perishable.

But that ending is something to have been discovered, once and for all, just as getting to it is something to have experienced. For Falstaff's purpose is to put comedy to the test, to see how much delight is in it when it is experienced as an intellectual absolute, to inhale its heady draughts until man's capacity for self-indulgence is fully realized. Along the way, Falstaff, more than any other man, has embraced comedy, clapped it to himself in a bear hug, elected it as soulmate. He is its apostle, it is his creed. Falstaff is the comic figure who makes comedy, knowing what he is doing all the time.

Alceste is the comic figure who despises comedy. Alceste cannot bear human limitation, in himself or in anyone else. He wishes to wipe away all the graffiti, to look through the glass and see the landscape unstained.

The hero of Molière's *The Misanthrope* is not precisely a man hater; certainly he is not a woman hater. He has—or has had—a very close friend in Philinte. And he is passionately in love with Célimène. What he cannot bear is their surrenders. He loves them too much to wish to see them in chains, above all in self-imposed chains.

Alceste lives in a world in which intelligent men and women quite cheerfully compromise themselves in their minds and hearts. His companions neither say what they mean nor mean what they say—they are sustained by gossip, entertained by insincerity; words, glances, embraces are all pawns in a game which does indeed keep life bubbling

brightly but which rigidly excludes from life any direct
acknowledgment of its truths.

Alceste is all out of patience and railing at Philinte in the
very opening moments of the play:

> I've been your friend till now, as you well know;
> But after what I saw a moment ago
> I tell you flatly that our ways must part.
> I wish no place in a dishonest heart. . . .
> I see you almost hug a man to death,
> Exclaim for joy until you're out of breath,
> And supplement these loving demonstrations
> With endless offers, vows, and protestations;
> Then when I ask you "Who was that?," I find
> That you can scarcely bring his name to mind! . . .
> By God, I say it's base and scandalous
> To falsify the heart's affections thus . . .

In bartering truth for an easy accommodation, the men
and women about Alceste are—in Alceste's view—denying
their own best natures. They are using that most magnificent
of tools, the human intellect, to arrive at false equations.
They are corrupters of themselves. Falstaff may delight in
deliberate rationalization because Falstaff is a connoisseur of
limitation. Alceste can only be shocked that human beings
should wish to deceive themselves or others, consciously or
unconsciously, at any time:

> I'd have them be sincere, and never part
> With any word that isn't from the heart.

Scolding and then scalding, reasoning and then reviling,
Alceste buzzes through the play like the bad conscience of
comedy. In effect, he is sternly commanding all of his friends
not to be funny. For if human behavior horrifies him, there is
something that horrifies him much more. What Alceste ab-
hors above all is the comic attitude toward life.

The comic attitude accepts limitation, supposing it to be inevitable, and it has two firm defenders in the play. Philinte of course is one of them and he states the classic comic position clearly:

> Come, let's forget the follies of the times
> And pardon mankind for its petty crimes;
> Let's have an end of rantings and of railings,
> And show some leniency toward human failings. . . .
> The rigid virtues of the ancient days
> Are not for us; they jar with all our ways
> And ask of us too lofty a perfection.
> Wise men accept their times without objection. . . .
> I take men as they are, or let them be,
> And teach my soul to bear their frailty. . . .

That is the shrug with which all genial men resign themselves to imperfection. The voice of reason it is often called, though it does not seem at all *reasonable* to Alceste. It is echoed, alas, by the girl Alceste loves, a girl who is sensible not only about the world as it is but about her own winning ways:

> Is it my fault that all these men pursue me?
> Am I to blame if they're attracted to me?

Célimène *is* to blame, sweet thing that she is, because she encourages adoration. But what should she do? Take sticks to her adorers? Come, come, it can't hurt *much* to have a little fun, you can hear her saying to herself as she goes off to tease a man or two, or taste some scandal, or tell a not terribly important lie. Life would be intolerable if there weren't a bit of giving in now and then.

And so two intolerables confront each other. Alceste's uncompromising sincerity would be intolerable to Célimène; and any insincerity is intolerable to Alceste. We are not necessarily forced to take sides here, only to notice that, because Alceste insists upon acting as a wholly unfettered man, comedy is approaching the point at which it may not be able to tolerate its own content.

Comedy can tolerate Alceste just so far. Alceste is himself funny and therefore can be housed in the play—at least until its abrupt bleak ending—because he too is limited. It is customary to say that he is limited by his intolerance, that his comedy is the comedy of the fanatically fixed idea. But that is what we say when we are defending comedy rather than Alceste. It is a judgment arrived at from a biased point of view. Strictly speaking, Alceste is never inaccurate in his estimate of the people about him; and inaccuracy is one of the earmarks of the comedy of fanaticism. More importantly, the particular intolerance he displays cannot be called, without interior contradiction, a limiting one; it is specifically anti-limitation, and its whole surge is toward freedom. If Alceste in any way limits himself by shutting himself off from a society he despises, he is simply putting a limitation on the limitations he will accept. And that is a freeing action, however painful it may prove to the man performing it. Alceste is not self-deluded; he is as good as his word and therefore free to speak it.

The unambiguous limitation that actually operates in *The Misanthrope* to keep Alceste within the bounds of comedy is his helpless passion for a coquette. Despising coquetry, he adores Célimène. He is bound, by heart and by flesh, and no doubt even by mind, to all that his mind would be rid of. Because he does not delude himself, he understands his situation exactly:

> I know that love's irrational and blind;
> I know the heart's not subject to the mind,
> And can't be reasoned into beating faster. . . .

His own heart beats faster in defiance of his reason. He knew what Célimène was before he submitted himself to her charms or to her treachery. He went into the game with his eyes open, as he has them open now. He is possessed by two passions, really, both of them impossible to satisfy. One is a passion for Célimène and the other is a passion to change Célimène. These would cancel each other out in any case, but his plight is worse than that. Instead of fastening his affections upon an ordinarily playful girl, a girl whose merely feminine pleasure in teasing might have been just enough modified to make some compromise possible, he has put himself into the hands of a superb professional, into the hands of a woman whose natural talents would be wasted if she did not charm the planet, inhabitant by inhabitant. Most men are happy that Célimènes exist even when they are seeing through them: without Célimènes the universe might gain in straight dealing, but it would lose terribly in color. It so happens that Alceste is the one man in the world who asks not for color but for pure white light.

Absolute contraries have bumped head on, with no power in themselves to modify themselves. They are caught in the crunch. So is comedy. Comedy has come to a parting of ways, edgily, mysteriously, fatally. For comedy to go on, Alceste must give in.

But Alceste will not give in, will not agree to limit himself in order to possess the creature he loves. He is comedy's Coriolanus, too certain of where virtue lies to knuckle under, or even bend a knee, to gain his pleasure. He is, by intention, a tragic man and he now backs comedy to the wall, presses it to its breaking point. Insisting upon freedom for himself, he wants Célimène to choose freedom, too:

> Woman, I'm willing to forget your shame,
> And clothe your treacheries in a sweeter name;
> I'll call them youthful errors, instead of crimes,
> And lay the blame on these corrupting times.
> My one condition is that you agree
> To share my chosen fate, and fly with me
> To that wild, trackless, solitary place
> In which I shall forget the human race.

But Célimène, though she loves him, is not going to join him. She knows herself too well for that. She is a born comedienne, master and victim of the revels. She is a creature of limitations who is never really going to rise above, or even learn to dislike, those limitations. She says as much plainly:

> . . . I fear I lack the force
> And depth of soul to take so stern a course.

And so Alceste must turn away from her, she from him. The comic girl and the man who would be tragic must part. The love affair is over.

Comedy is over, too, now, at the very end of the play. One of its principals has refused to be contained by it. The other choice—not Falstaff's—has been made. The form flickers, its lights seem about to go out. Fortunately, it is time for the play's curtain to come down and for the audience to go home remembering what it can of what was funny. No one is asked to stay long enough to see the comic shell crack and fall open, to dwell on its new emptiness. We have had an intimation, a foretaste, of an aridity that might take us beyond comedy, but the issue has not been forced. Comedy's face has been saved by abruptness. The usual "happy" ending, which would have been arbitrary in any case, is not there; but neither is Alceste's next step there, the step into the wilderness.

Where does Alceste go and how does he fare? We cannot say. We know what happens to Falstaff, but not what happens to this man. We have seen him throw up his hands in despair of comedy's despair:

> When I survey the scene of human folly,
> Finding on every hand base flattery,
> Injustice, fraud, self-interest, treachery . . .
> Ah, it's too much. . . .

And we have seen him act on his beliefs. If his beliefs are wrong, and if everywhere he goes he can find only additionally exasperating instances of human limitation, then he is a fool. He has given up his delight for a madman's dream. If, on the other hand, he somewhere meets one person capable of transcending comfort and compromise, or perhaps if he should himself succeed in achieving the intellectual freedom he yearns for without at the same time yearning backward toward Célimène, then participation in the tragic advance will be his reward. Saints are fools who were proved right.

Whatever happens to Alceste, a decisive thing has here happened to comedy. It has returned to its own womb. One comic figure has refused to add to the graffiti that deface, and cover over, the aspiration of tragedy. He has tried hard to erase the graffiti other men, mocking men, shrugging men, have put there. One comic figure has insisted upon shedding all ballast—all of it, even the love for others that binds and impedes. One comic figure has forsworn comedy to walk directly into the tragic landscape from which comedy came.

Returning to its womb, comedy ceases to exist as an independent entity. Comedy and tragedy become one again; by implication, they are tragedy.

14
TRAGEDY NOW

FROM the beginning there have been only two dramatic forms. However whimsical a catalogue Polonius can invent for himself—"pastoral-comical, historical-pastoral, tragical-historical, tragical-comical-historical-pastoral"—the effort is clearly an effort, and it is in the end a joke. Comedy and tragedy have crossbred endlessly; but they have never given birth to a third member of the family.

This is odder then it seems. The novel, for instance, genuinely opens itself to an infinity of Polonius-style variations. While we may speak of a "comic novel," we never speak of a "tragic" one, even though many novels have an obvious affinity with the tragic spirit. Or at least we do not speak as though tragic content constituted the other half of the novelist's world. Nor has the novel produced any other twin terms to make its nature plainly dual. We need a hundred ready modifiers to deal with the adventures of the form. The novelist's world is not polarized; it is open to nearly any imaginative use a man wishes to make of narrative prose.

Drama has always been peculiarly polarized, and its stubbornness in this matter is of some significance. The fact that we have come to a time in the theater when many playwrights are unwilling to avail themselves, or convict themselves, of either clear intention and so choose to label many examples of their work "a play in three acts" does not alter matters; we continue to think "comedy" or "tragedy" as we go to the plays. If we have a present habit of substituting the word "serious" for the word "tragic" in distinguishing between the two kinds of play we go to see, we still know that the word is a substitute and we know what it is a substitute for. A "serious" play is a play that might have been a tragedy if only it had taken one step more. We are a bit vague about what the step ought to have been; but we know that mere seriousness is something short of full commitment. Sobriety alone has something safe about it; it ponders without plunging. We see that we are dealing with earnestness, but we sense a loss of nerve; and we are all careful—whether we are playwrights or playgoers—not to make for our rueful thoughtfulness any more majestic claim. The one thing that bothers us about *Death of a Salesman* is whether or not it is a tragedy. We are not content with calling it a good serious play, or with having it be one. We do not rest in the satisfaction that it has moved us deeply in the theater. Because it has moved us so much, we must nag at it. Is it or is it not something *more* than merely serious? The better the play the more we itch for it to go all the way home, to realize itself absolutely.

For we understand that the "serious" plays we see have their source in the tragic impulse; that their object is indeed to risk a searing; that they stake their claim to importance, dignity, nobility on their echoing a still greater matrix. Playwrights, and some playgoers, are constantly demanding that "serious" plays, as opposed to workable comedies, be given preferential treatment by critics and audiences, be respected simply for their aims, though in fact seriousness as such is not necessarily a more elevated attitude than the comic stance: seriousness as such may be the state of mind of a drudge. What the demand for preferential treatment plainly indicates is a conviction that something not now completed may in time, and with nursing, be completed.

Seriousness, hammered away at, may open to reveal the hard bedrock of tragedy, in which case the theater will be in full possession of its other self again.

The sustained duality of drama, even when one or the other of its forms is in a notoriously weakened state, must suggest something to us. It must suggest that in one way or another the two basic forms, when they are put back to back, together say all that can possibly be said about man upon a stage. Apparently they have needed no true variant, no third voice, ever; they need only to expand to their own due proportions in order to exhaust the space drama can occupy. Drama, at least until our own time, has been thought the imitation of an action. That in itself is a circumscribed arena: drama does not mean to engage itself in lyric modes of feeling, in the penetration of landscape or still-life, in the nounless intuitions of music. It means to confine itself to a thing done.

The physical stage instinctively circumscribes itself to accommodate drama's intention. It does not offer us a limitless field of vision, as the novel does, nor does it seek to relate us to cosmic rhythms by overleaping the materiality of the cosmos, as music does. The stage offers us a bounded open space which men enter, cross, and leave. Between the time that men enter the space and the time they leave it, the crossing changes them. The change is the action.

What can plays say about action? They can say that man is free to act, and that he is not. So much and nothing more. Having said that man is free to act, plays can explore that freedom existentially, displaying its achievements and its costs; the result will be what we have called tragedy. Having said that man is not free to act, not entirely free, plays can insist upon every limitation man has ever complained about; the bill of complaints, the litany of limitations, we have called comedy.

But one of these statements—as statements they are non-committal, being reflections of a condition rather than propositions about a condition—is greater than the other. The tragic statement is the original and fundamental statement, the mother statement, because it coincides exactly with the intention of drama as a whole. If drama's impulse is to display an action, tragedy is the form that sees man free enough to act, to act extensively, even to act absolutely. When the tragic hero says "I *will*," he is doing drama's work without reserve. Comedy, which we feel in our bones to be the lesser form, is indeed the lesser form because it comes into existence as a comment upon tragedy, and in fact upon drama. It is a species of criticism and, hence, parasitical. It does not initiate action; its desires are all passive. Rather it derides action for the inhibited and otherwise oppressed thing it is. "Oh, no, you won't," it says, pointing to the stone wall just ahead. Comedy could not create drama of its own power; its feet are too sore, its burdens too heavy, for it to cross the circle unaided. Comedy will cross the circle when it is kicked across or chased across or carried across; left to its own devices it will simply run in circles forever, or until it is tired enough to lie down. Comedy is a dependent. It requires tragedy to budge it into its characteristic posture of dragging its feet while thumbing its nose. Tragedy is the thought of drama, and comedy the afterthought.

It would not seem, in these circumstances, that comedy could long survive the reported death of tragedy or maintain itself in any very fit condition during one of tragedy's cyclical silences. And so we are, in our own time, confronted with an apparent paradox. "It is a commonplace of modern literary thought that the tragic mode is not available even to the gravest and noblest of our writers," Lionel Trilling has said; and the unavailability of the mode has been a fact of life for some three hundred years. That is a very long time—though it is not the longest that theatrical history has had to reckon with—for a primary energy to have absented itself. Yet we have had, and do have, comedy. While tragedy has been away, we have had Sheridan and Wilde and Synge and Shaw;

and though tragedy is still away, we have Jean Anouilh and any number of writers of successful commerical comedy to keep us company.

There are two questions to be asked. *Has* tragedy ceased to function as the guarantor of drama's life? And what is comedy doing outliving the only energy that moves it?

Uncountable reasons have been given for the absence of anything we are willing to call tragedy since Racine yielded to his conscience and put down his pen. The most generalized reason that might be given—which is that the tragic impulse has asserted itself unmistakably only three times in the long history of the theater and that we may simply be enduring a necessary betweentimes now—is not one that can detain a theater-lover long. It is a vague reason, it does not even ask what circumstances may have provoked the tragic impulse into appearing when it did appear, and, more than that, it is the kind of reason that invites a throwing-up of hands. While it is obviously true enough that if we are ever to have tragedy again we must wait for unpredictable social circumstances to release its energies—the effort to *force* tragedy into being, by stagecraft alone, has failed so often that we can no longer have faith in it—the suggestion that while we are waiting we cannot know why we are waiting becomes a counsel of helplessness, and we chafe under it. Perhaps we cannot anticipate tragedy, or even know for certain where it has been lately. But can't we, in the meantime, learn something about ourselves as we were while tragedy was away, and so possibly stumble upon the part we played in the estrangement? Tragedy is a concept that keeps at us. We want to be busy about the matter, not blandly content to await the accident of another Pericles, another Elizabeth, another Sun King.

Henri Peyre summarizes the sort of nail-biting that went on during the latter part of the nineteenth century and the beginning years of this one.

The novel was blamed by some critics, and was to be blamed or envied: it had captured the essentials of tragic emotion, while diluting it and often cheapening it. Others thought the fault lay with the modern democratic public, unable to appreciate the structure, the restraint, and the poetry of true tragedy. One of the pervading myths of the age, the myth of progress, seemed moreover to make tragedy superannuated and superfluous, a remnant of an era of violence and of man's undeveloped ability to control and improve his fate.

Mr. Peyre thinks that these were merely fashionable explanations that are now old-fashioned; he does not, in fact, hold that tragedy is dead at all. Yet George Steiner's *The Death of Tragedy* was published in 1961, and the title still seemed to have a certain air of boldness about it; the essential fashion has not changed much. Mr. Steiner, as we have seen earlier, does not confine himself to trivial comparisons with the novel or narrow explications dependent upon one century's notion of "progress." For Mr. Steiner the full tragic spirit was rendered impotent by Christianity's promise of salvation. Forced to explain away the postpromise work of Shakespeare and Racine, Mr. Steiner suggests that Shakespeare was saved by having a remarkably "open" theatrical form, possibly the result of a beginning breakdown of Christian belief in salvation not long before, while Racine, reverting to Greek forms, passed a "miracle of afterlife." There are many who still agree with Mr. Steiner's fundamental premise, which is that tragedy hurls hope back without mercy or justice, and there are many more who subscribe to the principle that tragedy cannot in the foreseeable future be resurrected.

"Once the critical or scientific attitude of mind comes to prevail in a civilization, no arguments in favor of the superiority of art or religion can alter the accomplished historical fact," Hegel has been paraphrased, and it is very easy to turn this general dictum against tragedy. History, for good or ill, has left tragedy behind; its necessary ingredients are no longer viable as beliefs. If the roots of tragedy are in received ritual and believed myth, "man today, stripped of myth, stands famished among all his pasts," Nietzsche insisted. The attempt to restore myth in Hegel's critically oriented age is futile: "no mythology created in the age of rational empiricism," Mr. Steiner warns, "matches the antique in tragic power or theatrical form." If tragedy is conceived as in any way dependent upon given ethical norms, the problem is just as acute. "Today the ethical conventionalism of tragedy seems impossible to adopt," J. L. Styan concludes.

The list of surrenders could, of course, be extended ad infinitum. Name something held to be necessary to tragedy and you will have almost certainly named something that has vanished, as a consensus, from the contemporary world. Perhaps Lionel Abel's analysis of what has happened to the form is more interesting than most. In his tantalizing and exceptionally perceptive little book, *Metatheater,* Mr. Abel contends that in the early seventeenth century—with *Hamlet,* let us say, or with Calderon's *Life Is a Dream*—drama recorded a radical change in human consciousness. Humanity became *self*-conscious, so much so that it was no longer possible for a tragic hero to set about his work directly, confidently, unquestioningly, with his whole being. Previously, tragic man had moved by dark instinct or by what he took to be the command of the gods; in these circumstances he moved without hesitation, without in effect watching his performance or analyzing his motives. "If Antigone were self-conscious enough to suspect her own motives in burying her brother Polynices, would her story be a tragic one?" Mr. Abel asks. The Greek tragic hero is in effect a blind man, doing what his nature and his circumstances order him to do. "Now the Western playwright," Mr. Abel continues, "is unable to believe in the reality of a character who is lacking in self-consciousness. Lack of self-consciousness is as characteristic of Antigone, Oedipus, and Orestes, as self-consciousness is a characteristic of Hamlet, that towering figure of Western metatheater."

Mr. Abel proposes that we substitute the term "metatheater" for "tragedy" because a new descriptive word is needed for a new state of being. Seventeenth-century man's sensibilities had suffered an enlargement; Hamlet cannot simply do what he is told to do, thereby fulfilling his ancient tragic role, he must see himself doing or not doing it, every moment of the time, and the increased insight makes him hesitate, if it does not paralyze him altogether. For the new metahero action is ambiguous, life is indeed something of a dream, the play in which he appears is a play within a play and he is himself at least part author of the interior play. Catching sight of his every gesture in the mirror of his mind, he challenges not simply his integrity but his very identity. Who is he really? If he does not know, he cannot very well act or at least cannot act with a whole heart, for action defines a man—and this new man does not want to be guilty of making a false definition. With Hamlet, we are on our way not only to Pirandello but to Beckett and Genêt. At a certain time in history man peeled one of his outside layers off—this was no doubt an evolutionary inevitability—and with that layer he stripped himself of the power to act tragically.

Much as I admire Mr. Abel's vision, and certainly it is accurate as a description of something that happened to human sensibility at one stage in time, I confess that I have certain niggling first difficulties with it. Antigone, for instance, does not seem to me to be unselfconscious, or incapable of suspecting her motives. She does, at one moment, allow for the possibility that she may be wrong; and I always have the uncomfortable feeling that she is watching herself perform the whole time. Nor do I feel that tragedy is adequately defined by imposing on the hero a degree of obtuseness for which he has no responsibiltiy. Oedipus is rash and stubborn, but not really obtuse; he hears intimations, and fears them, long before anyone else in the play does. His complexity lies, I would say, in his exacerbating self-awareness. Agamemnon, who is truly a kind of blind stalking horse, would fit Mr. Abel's picture of the earlier tragic hero admirably; Agamemnon cannot say what impels him to his various choices, nor does he indicate that reflection on his part would in any way alter his role. But he, it seems to me, is only one kind of Greek tragic hero. There are others, many others, and Pelasgus in *The Suppliants* seems to have no foreordained course open to him, no one tragic command to execute. We do not have the second and third parts of this trilogy; but the first would seem to indicate that only an intense self-searching could provoke its next necessary—or not necessary—step. Isn't Pelasgus an embryo Hamlet?

But these are minor matters for our present purposes, and there is no real point in being finicky about whether Prometheus is or is not intensely conscious of the role he has chosen—and not at all been commanded—to play. Prometheus may be the posturer par excellence. What matters is the eventual disposition Mr. Abel wishes, or is forced, to make of tragedy. Mr. Abel has not proposed that a third kind of play came into existence alongside two earlier kinds. He has suggested, provocatively, that tragedy altered its nature under a fresh set of circumstances and replaced itself by becoming different from itself. We do not now have three forms; we still have two, comedy and metatheater, with metatheater as comedy's twin brother.

Metatheater, then, is what *happened* to tragedy. If I am not entirely persuaded that Mr. Abel's new duality is an ultimate one, or that the term "metatheater" is ever likely to become household coin in the way that "tragedy" has always been, it is because two questions bedevil me. One is this: the evolution of a freshly self-conscious drama from *Hamlet* to Pirandello leads, suspiciously, to something very like comedy or at least to a crossbreed in which comedy figures very importantly. Much of Pirandello is impertinently light, gracefully mocking, in tone, rather as though it were the comedy in *Hamlet*—the comedy *of* Hamlet—that had been pursued all the while, leaving tragic undertones as a somewhat ambiguous residue. The tone continues in Beckett and Genêt, if these are the true heirs of the tradition: nearly everything that is fundamentally serious is perceived through a veil of irreverence that is at first sight, and achingly, comic. We are first made aware of what is preposterous about man, we burrow through absurdity toward a bedrock that may not be there; we laugh at least as much as we fear.

This odd twist of the strand toward comedy—Hamlet the sweet prince is almost entirely taken over by Hamlet the baiter of fishmongers—is, I think, inherent in the stress upon self-consciousness. Self-consciousness, emphasized to the exclusion of all other qualities, is necessarily a symbol of limitation. The purely self-conscious man is a fumbling, uncertain, insecure, awkward, hesitant, ultimately incompetent man. Self-consciousness makes him all thumbs: that is our standard conception of the type, on or off stage. Self-consciousness provokes rigidity, if not paralysis; Bergson would have seen the resulting freezing of responses and called it comedy without further ado.

This means that instead of offering us a substitute form for tragedy, let alone any new third form, "metatheater" actually reduces drama to a single form, which has in fact been drama's drift in recent years. In recent years we have viewed even our sorrows through comic lenses: the despair of *Waiting for Godot,* the human helplessness of *Rhinoceros,* the stupidity of *Mother Courage*'s courage. The fact that the lenses are dark, the comedy bitter enough to be called "black," does not alter its status as comedy: we have seen that blackness has always awaited comedy like an appointment with the dentist. And we shall have to talk about the effect of all this on comedy proper in one more chapter. We must recognize here, I think, that Mr. Abel has not given us an alternative but a surrender. One half of the human instinct for understanding drama as a double impulse, urging man to see himself in two contrary lights, has been waived, allowed to atrophy. Essentially, Mr. Abel is indicating agreement with other theorists that tragedy, "of which we may be incapable," is in fact a dead form, and that we have, since the seventeenth century, been able to see ourselves only in a bleak comic guise.

Self-consciousness has made us essentially comic. My next question: *Need* it have done so? Does the new state of sensibility, real and exacerbating as it is, *force* us into that paralysis which will make us automatons ready for Beckett? As it happens, Hamlet's self-consciousness does not so paralyze him. It inhibits him, delays him, torments him. But it does not prevent him from finally exercising his freedom to act; and by the end of the play in which he appears it is not only apparent that he has acted extensively, we are given to understand that he has somehow acted well. The irresoluteness created by man's awareness of his role is overcome, just as the new crisis of identity—the uncertainty beleaguering man as he discovers himself capable of being several persons at once—is ultimately resolved in Calderon's *Life Is a Dream*. During the seventeenth century a critical development occurred; but the seventeenth century continued to produce tragedy—indeed the seventeenth century is one of the great ages of tragedy. Shakespeare and Racine were able to work themselves through doubt into deed.

Self-consciousness alone does not bring tragedy to its terminal point, because self-consciousness alone does not prohibit action. It brings action into question, severely; but it does not deny it as a possibility.

To account for the "death" of tragedy we need a more chilling development. The development would have to be utterly paralyzing and it would have to be progressive during the eighteenth, nineteenth, and twentieth centuries, the ages that assiduously sought the form without being able to lay hand upon its fundamental energies.

There is only one development chilling enough to have

done the job. Man would have had to press beyond the business of analyzing his freedom to act, beyond watching himself in a mirror as he debated whether or not he might responsibly use his freedom to act. He would have had to come to disbelieve in his freedom to act. He would have had to deny freedom itself in order to kill tragedy.

That is what he has done progressively over three hundred years. It should be obvious, though the obvious is of all things the most easily forgotten, that tragedy has only appeared during those moments in history when man was most exuberantly aware of his freedom. It sounds ironic to insist, though it is not, that tragedy is invariably the product of a fiercely optimistic society. Pericles' Athens was persuaded, temporarily, that it had at last unleashed man's powers toward infinite advancement; Elizabeth's England had discovered to its intense delight that its reach was as great as the great globe itself; Louis's France was confident that the sun in the heavens possessed no more energy, shed no more splendor, than man did.

In such a society the doors of the mind are opened wide. Thought rushes through them, unchecked, free and original, scarcely pausing to take stock of itself and almost bewildered by its infinite options. Deed follows thought and thrillingly confirms it: what had been imagined as possible proves to be possible, so that a belief in freedom becomes an experience of freedom. The world stands at one of its evolutionary thresholds and confidently steps over it. Pain is present, but present as a necessary condition of breaking bonds. Beyond the threshold and beyond the pain lies exhilaration. Exhilaration is *in* the pain, making it altogether endurable, because of what the process promises and can in fact be seen to yield.

Pain can be faced, faced in its most extreme intensity, because the time has come to go through it, to blink nothing, to deny nothing, to avoid nothing. There are terrors inherent in taking any new step, there are plain dangers of failure, there is everywhere the chance that the mind itself will lose footing in such undefined territory. But overriding all of these considerations is a heady conviction: the universe is malleable, and man's hand can do the molding, whether he does it well or ill. Man's energies are felt as infinite, and the same conviction that gives him courage to move forward into the unknown also gives him the courage he needs to face the difficulties and penalties of the passage. The tragic spectacle is endurable because of what lies ahead; it *must* be endured if the advance is to be made. Paradoxically, tragedy thus becomes a necessary form in times of great buoyance. It is the wound the victorious warrior brings home with him as evidence of his triumph, the scar Coriolanus must display in the market place. Tragedy is a sign of strength. It attests to survival and exists as a pledge of indomitability. Tragedy is born of more than hope, it is born of certainty.

Man is rarely so certain of his own coming epiphany as he was in the years of Sophocles, Shakespeare, Racine. The secure optimism that produces tragedy, an optimism so secure that it can embrace the possibility of annihilation without loss of nerve, must be a long and unpredictable time growing. History does not permit man many times of evolutionary passage. The problem of mere survival consumes his energies through agonizingly protracted periods; catastrophe often comes while the foundations are still being laid; there have been many centuries together when the world's disintegration seemed imminent. Clinging to the cliff's edge is a more normal posture for man than boldly taking mountains in stride.

The moment of exuberant release is the result of a prolonged gathering of powers. And there are many near-moments which in the end come to be near-misses, both for social and spiritual confidence and for the tragedy that accompanies it. Spain was clearly on the verge of such a moment in Calderon's time. Having made a strong exploratory thrust forward, and promising itself further gains, it had—in such a play as *Life Is a Dream*—also breached the outer fortifications of tragedy. But the tragic assertion is not quite wholehearted; neither was Spain's social or political energy; at the critical moment a culture's grasp was loosened, its inner resolve weakened. I do not want to go in for fortune-telling by hindsight; but it is almost possible to read Spain's coming national loss of nerve in the wavering structural and stylistic movement of *Life Is a Dream*—the sense of commitment to an absolute is missing.

In the eighteenth century Germany felt its heart leap as it saw its dispersed powers coming together into a single unified power which might prove forceful enough and flexible enough to guarantee a hitherto undreamed-of advance. With this first burst of confidence came a quasi-tragedy, work with enough of the tragic impulse in it to tantalize us still. But the social vision was premature, the dream could not by main force be realized. Tragedy was not fully realized, either. Schiller could to an impressive degree dominate the materials of *Wallenstein,* without flinching from what was unpleasant in the task and with some exhilaration in his new freedom to accomplish it, just as Germany could exult in its recently discovered capacity to dominate, and then productively absorb, a feudal compound of what we would now call robber barons. But the outthrust fist is not firm, which means that not everything can be faced. Put to it, Schiller cannot burn Saint Joan at the stake. Immolation is unthinkable, because there is too much uncertainty as to what lies beyond it. Apparently only the society that is fully and effectively exercising its freedom—that has an experience of freedom's gains rather than an as yet unfulfilled dream about them—is able to record freedom's consequences nakedly.

Certainly the late nineteenth century found itself troubled rather than apotheosized by the burst of quasi-tragic writing offered it. Ibsen reached after tragedy, and on something of our terms. Nora bolts to freedom, slamming all doors behind her; Mrs. Alving would separate herself from a social structure that produced cripples instead of men. The later, less realistic plays openly strain toward transfiguration: The Master Builder climbs his ultimate tower; Rubek, in *When We Dead Awaken,* goes alone to the mountaintop. Strindberg worked himself furiously through that pessimism which identified him for most men toward the transforming power of a kind of capitalized Beauty. But on the other side of these gestures toward freedom or transfiguration there is a curious blank: the question of what Nora went "out there" for has become a commonplace joke, and the symbols of tower, mountaintop, and Beauty seem to stand only for themselves, to lack tangible referents. The age as a whole was not ready to give solidity to these symbols, to imagine an epiphany; the epiphany had to be invented out of whole cloth by playwrights. The playwrights were, quite literally, strangers in town; sometimes they were outcasts. Society itself did not feel close to tragic childbirth.

In the twentieth century, for a brief time, Ireland became conscious of the *fact* of its freedom and did actually give birth to itself; after centuries of aspiration it had exercised its will as a nation irresistibly. Immediately it began to throw off popular and altogether recognizable images on the order of *Shadow of a Gunman* and *The Plough and the Stars,* those images of harshness that accompany achievement as its blind minstrel. But somewhere short of mature tragedy, energy flagged. Ireland had found its power and asserted itself as a nation at the very time when all nationalism was being called into question. The successful first stride could find no second step to take; the new nation could now only suppress its exhilaration while it waited for a thrust much greater than its own, the forming thrust of internationalism, to absorb and virtually deny its successful act of faith. One burst of evolutionary energy had been canceled out by a greater one, still in process and still far from its own ultimate goal.

Tragedy cannot survive a general loss of faith; as the experience of free self-assertion withers away, so does the form meant to record the exhilarating and terrifying thing experienced. In the case of the near-tragedies of which we have been speaking, disillusionment or simple incredulity came too soon: before the adolescent—the social adolescent and the tragic adolescent—could grow to manhood, the role a man might play had been doubted. True, the historical periods which gave us our genuinely great tragedies in the end suffered disillusionment, too; and when they did, tragedy disappeared. But the disillusion that ultimately overtook Athens, London, and Paris was of a different kind: it was not the collapse of spirit that comes from spoiled or doubted promises, it was the exhaustion of spirit that comes from fulfilled ones. All successful impulses must spend themselves; there is nothing too distressing in that. What must be kept in mind about the periods of major advance is that, after a long time of gestation, the human will to assert itself absolutely had burst its womb and literally entered a new state of being, so that the history of mankind would ever thereafter be altered. We have not been the same men since Pericles' time; we have not been the same since Elizabeth's. A mutation of sorts—intellectual in the main—had been brought about by the deployment of man's free faculties. At each such moment tragedy put in its appearance, recording the evolutionary agony and intimating the evolutionary gain.

But just as an affirmation of will can take an unconscionable time flowering, fighting off daily despairs and consuming much of its energy in recovering from interim catastrophes, so a distrust of will and a disbelief in its free exercise can capture the mind of man for extended periods of time. The evolutionary process looks to occasional, rare breakthroughs; it also allows, as a matter of ordinary expectation, for mere adjustment, for surrender to the prevailing environment, a surrender which ends—or may very well end—in dust and bone. A sense of helplessness, of surviving any old way without much conviction that things will get better, can be a long time gestating, too.

Contemporary man is very much the child of such a

gestation, the end product of some hundreds of years of learning to doubt the possibility or the meaningfulness of a free act. During this time man has not been inactive; indeed he has never been busier. But he has come to understand his activity in a new, progressively depressing, and fundamentally untragic way.

With all of his busyness, and allowing for all of the accomplishments he might be thought to take pride in, he lives in a psychological climate which oppresses his heart. The world in which he achieves so much, and in which he cannot stop working, is not for him a vertical one; he is not building a "high rise." His world is horizontal; he can move about on it more flexibly than ever before, but the surface itself is an infinite and barren plain. When he thinks of his productivity, he thinks of it simply as extension and accumulation, as though he were creating nothing more than a coral reef. No, he thinks less of his labor, and of himself, than that. He does not think *he* is creating anything. And if he should be, he does not hold that the construction possesses ultimate value in any case.

Essentially, man has come to see himself not as free but as determined, not as mover but as moved, not as demigod earning his own epiphany through pain but as a blind fungus inching its directionless way—unless death and silence be a direction—over the face of the earth.

The island. A last effort. The islet. The shore facing the open sea is jagged with creeks. One could live there, perhaps happy, if life was a possible thing, but nobody lives there. The deep water comes washing into its heart, between high walls of rock. One day nothing will remain of it but two islands, separated by a gulf, narrow at first, then wider and wider as the centuries slip by, two islands, two reefs. It is difficult to speak of man, under such conditions.

Thus Samuel Beckett. In Beckett, who may speak as well for the twentieth century state of mind as anyone, there is still movement to be recorded. It is the movement of a slug through slime. But this is not intelligible or independently productive movement; it is simply what slugs do in relation to slime, and it is controlled as much by the slime as by the slug; for the slime, after all, is both the source and the last resting place of the slug.

Man's activity is bacterial or chemical activity, not elected activity. It cannot challenge the universe, with or without gods, even though it may explore the universe to find it without gods. Man's activity itself is a by-product of the mindless universe, and hence cosmic waste matter. Prometheus' ancient dare was an illusion, as his act of independence was a lie. Prometheus was bound, is bound, will be bound. There is nothing more to be said. Unsurprisingly, tragedy is silent.

We are not here dealing with an actual state of affairs—evolutionary advances of a most remarkable kind have been made during the past three hundred years—but with a state of mind which refuses to see them as advances of the spirit. Man's image of himself has been diminished by a series of blows to his psyche, blows which may not yet have stopped falling. Under their cumulative force, man has been able to continue *working;* he has not been able to ascribe to the work an absolute value, or to imagine himself as having added a cubit to his stature.

During the century in which Shakespeare was born, Michelangelo could still imagine a titan David, could still create a Campidoglio which suggested that seven-league boots would be required to cross it. In the public places of Florence and of Rome men represented themselves as giants, boldly raiding with their serene profiles the vulnerable province of the sky. In the twentieth century we still call some men great, but we do not figure them forth in any such resolute way. There is no monumental carving anywhere in New York City—or London or Paris or Prague—to show Darwin or Einstein or Freud shouldering the nearly mastered universe.

When we erect a monument to Franklin Roosevelt, as we do, we do not wish to suggest that we are honoring an oversize man; we simply record a movement of sorts from which every trace of purely human power has been quietly removed. We draw a line and let it stand for a momentary surge we do not pretend to understand; it was not a man who moved but an abstract energy which filtered itself through a faintly remembered man while in process of using him up. The man was used by a tide; he did not himself turn the waters back. And when the contours of man become dimly visible, as in certain Henry Moore sculptures, they become visible only as hints imbedded in larger and more dominant contours, the way fossilized fish shapes are often discerned in convolutions of lava which have exercised primal authority and absorbed all organic life into their own inexorable and silent waves. We do not represent men as demigods or, for that matter, as men; we hide them deep inside autonomous equations.

In order to avoid trying to chart the complexities of man's fall from his own grace in day-by-day, or even century-by-century, detail, we may find it simplest to accept Freud's estimate of what diminished in his own eyes the creature who was apparently accomplishing so much. According to W. S. Taylor, Freud held "that there were now three chief offenders of human vanity: Copernicus, who showed that the earth is not the center of things but a satellite; Darwin, that man is not a special creation but an evolved animal; and Freud, that the mind is not a free agent but a product of cause and effect." There is, by the way, no need to express surprise that Freud should have placed himself in such company; he belonged there, and his self-assertiveness is more admirable than the frightened passivity he has tended to produce in his readers.

The rough outline is good enough, and obviously each of these major assaults on man's "vanity" has implications for tragedy, if tragedy is anything like the description of it we have been assembling. The Copernican revolution, which began to make its effect on men's minds as early as 1540, could not help but call into question the tragic hero's sense of direct responsibility for sharing the management of the cosmos. Previously man had stood at the center of things, the cosmos was *his*, naturally ordered to his present good and future advancement. He stood astride a material universe he had been given to rule, answerable only to a spiritual ruler beyond him whose ways were inscrutable but beckoning. God of his own world, man had no equal or rival or true partner but the God of "out there," and his own dignity demanded nothing less than that he wrestle with this other God, this friend and enemy God, to learn the extent of his own powers and the precise character of God's.

But man's role as exclusively privileged combatant was reduced or at least rendered ambiguous by the Copernican surrender of centrality. The sun did not rise to fire the energies of man; man borrowed his energies in passing as he orbited around a magnet more powerfully charged than he. He inhabited one of a number of planets; perhaps he was only one among a number of contenders. Perhaps—the thought was unbearable—he was not a true contender at all but had only dreamed his importance. And perhaps, the powerful but mindless sun aside, there was not really any One to contend with. Man might not only be less than he had imagined. Matters were worse than that. There might be no one greater than he.

It seems to me most likely that these disturbing thoughts were already threatening to play hob with tragedy in Shakespeare's time and that they help to account for that intense self-consciousness Lionel Abel has detected in so many of the principal stage heroes of the transitional age. Yes, man had been dreaming. Yes, the role he had fancied himself playing had in some as yet undefined sense been grounded in an illusion. It was now necessary for man, including man as tragic hero, to take another look at himself. And the only place he could reasonably look was in a mirror. The cosmos no longer reflected his image or promised it completion. Isolated, man would have to study himself, note his gait, examine his stance, make faces at himself to see what face—if any—was truly his. With his identity called into question, he was forced to stare at himself to see what he could make of the strange capering beast that had once passed for a power and a principality. Who was he *really?* But a mirror does not give answers; it only returns the question. A mirror is, in a way, the most confining of cells. When we look into one, we see man bounded by man. Here man is alone with himself while remaining estranged from himself. Multiply the mirrors, as fun houses do, and you create a monstrosity, a world in which the man who is running away from himself is always running toward himself. A man surrounded by mirrors, a man whose eyes are riveted on mirrors, is a man wholly isolated. For him there is no "out there." The new need to study himself has only intensified his remoteness.

Still, Shakespeare's tragedies were written. So were Racine's. To call these plays "failed tragedies" or "miracles of afterlife" does not help us to understand our experience of them: we sense, as we watch them, that they pursue a commitment and exhaust a course that share in some fundamental way the shape of the commitments made and the courses run in Greek tragedy. An intuition compels us to continue calling the plays tragic and to continue to use the word "tragedy" as though it had not been drained of content once and for all by the peculiar world view of the Greeks. It is the same intuition, perhaps, that forces Hamlet, at the last, to drop his agonized attitudinizing before the mirror and to plunge—with infinite relief—into the real dangers of doing. Say, if you will, that Hamlet escapes from himself into action, but remember that action is still a possible option and that Hamlet himself conceives it to be so. Trapped in the crisscrossed mirrors of a fun house, man continues to move forward, even at the risk of bumping into himself, because he still believes that an exit exists. There is an outside somewhere, if he can calm himself sufficiently to find it. Tragic heroes of the early seventeenth century continue to engage in the contest with a residual, if already challenged, conviction that the universe is open-ended and that passage, though hindered by self-doubt, is not prohibited.

It was possible, I think, for the early seventeenth century to absorb its fresh uncertainty about man's standing and to plunge beyond uncertainty into an assertion of freedom simply because the news about man *was* uncertain. The ultimate injury to man's confidence done by the Copernican revolution was as yet not much more than a rumor, a working hypothesis that had by no means been adequately demonstrated. Psychologically and even intellectually, a man could still choose between conceiving himself the isolated tenant of a satellite and the demigod around whom satellites spun. The whisper was there, and sensitive men attended to it; but there was more than a hundred years' work to be done—and thousands of years of traditional thinking to be overcome—before it could be formed into an authoritative word. The physical equipment needed to verify the heliocentric theory was necessarily a long time in the making; meantime, certain of Copernicus' supporting postulates could be flatly disproved. After having been given early encouragement by the Papacy, Copernicus found his work condemned by the Inquisition in 1616, the year of Shakespeare's death. Galileo ran afoul of the same distrust—and also of the same inability to muster sufficient scientific proof of his position—in 1632. Racine was born, seven years later, into an age which held satellitism in formal discredit, and it was not until Isaac Newton was able to provide the theory with essential underpinnings in 1687, some ten years after Racine had abandoned his career as a professional dramatist, that ultimate acceptance of man's diminished cosmic role could be regarded as inevitable. Man was not firmly forced from his ancient throne until the eighteenth century was upon him; the seventeenth, so long as it was permitted to doubt Copernicus, was not compelled to doubt its Prome-thean faith.

Eighteenth-century man, at last assimilating the affront to his ego that had been brewing for so long, behaved admirably for a time. Though the range of his action, the extent of his freedom, had been markedly curtailed, he could still conceive work for the flexible intelligence to do. Putting aside the daring, arrogant, and fundamentally mystical assault on the heavens that had been tragic man's earlier preoccupation, the new age—with its new image of itself as living in a house by the side of the sun—proposed that at the very least it could keep its own house in order. If men were not gods, they were rational beings; as rational beings they could at least make sense of one planet. An age of common sense is not likely to throw up much in the way of tragic heroes; its temper is more nearly that of the resigned and reasonable chorus. But the century worked out surprisingly badly even for this limited, sane objective. One thing reason was obliged to do was prepare for revolution. Man's institutions had been fashioned by a world view that was now an anachronism: if, for in-stance, man was no longer half-divine, it was absurd to talk about the divine right of kings. Revolution came, and with it the reasonable concepts of liberty, equality, and fraternity. But within a very short time, and to the considerable horror of the men who had thought things through, the revolution proved anything but reasonable. Common sense in France turned to chaos, soon to be righted by despotism; and even in the much more promising America, where the rights of a man among men had been so rationally defined, slavery was taken for granted. The management of so much as one planet was not going to be an easy task. Having bravely cut his losses and reorganized his emotional and intellectual economy, eighteenth-century man discovered in himself a propensity for cutting his own throat.

Formerly, when he was at his best, man had felt himself fit to challenge the universe. Now, removed from his position as challenger and reduced to something of a side issue, he found that even when he was at his best he was not quite competent to control the sidelines. Once even in his sin he had been strong; now even in his virtue he was weak. If he had lost his power to confront Zeus directly as a rebellious but favored son, he now saw his power to confront himself—mere man to man—called into question. There was something suspicious about him, something more suspicious than he had been led to believe.

Darwin did nothing to dispel the suspicion. If Copernicus and his successors had displaced man as king of the cosmos, as the giant submissively served by attending sun, moon, and stars, they had not succeeded in making him doubt his lineage. To put the matter as crudely as possible, man still might possibly have been placed upon his planet by the ordering hand of God for the purpose of ruling one sphere as God ruled all. There had been a shift in the balance of things, to be sure: man had been moved out of the town house and into something like a wayside cottage. Nevertheless his position in the cottage was an echo of God's in the cosmos: man could still accept himself as made in the image and likeness of God, a replica in miniature meant to deal with a miniature world. The quality of the likeness had indeed undergone a change, almost a physical change. Man's bulk, man's muscle, was less than it had been, and artists would no longer body man forth in Titan dimensions. Michelangelo, painting God in the act of creating Adam, might have shown the two figures as almost of a size with Adam rather the better-looking of the two. When it would come time to immortalize Nelson, there would once again be a straining for height, an urge to suggest stature: but the height would be in the column supporting the figure, whereas the figure would be no more than a man. Man's likeness to God was now seen not in the breadth of his shoulders but in the play of his mind: the power to reason, the power to know, was the link, and it had been bestowed upon man fully formed, a father's outright gift to his son and heir. Man was still descended from the divine intelligence—he had been born a "noble savage" to begin with—and his legitimacy, however abstract and impersonal its proofs might seem, gave him comfort.

Darwin took these divine blood lines away and showed man descended from an ape. Evolutionary theory does not, of course, trace man's descent from an ape; it derives both man and ape from a common, unidentified ancestor. But the phrase "descended from an ape" is essential here because it was the phrase that lodged in the popular mind and determined its response to Darwin's discoveries. The response was at first one of outraged disbelief, then one of defensiveness, and then, as the truth sank in, one of profound depression.

From our vantage point it is astonishing that something like a hundred years' depression should have followed upon the revelation. Man might well have taken pride in his fresh accomplishment. The working out of the theory was in itself a triumph of human intelligence; it constituted an evolutionary breakthrough of its own. Further, the news might have been read in such a way as to bolster man's vanity rather than injure it further. The nineteenth century might conceivably have attended to the doctrine of "the survival of the fittest" and drawn one clear conclusion from it: man was the fittest. If there was anything to the notion of the process of natural selection, it was that man, after all, had been selected. He might have been selected by an utterly mysterious nature instead of an utterly mysterious God, but that millions of years of evolutionary trial and error had thrown him up as its crowning achievement to date, as its most conscious and most flexible product, was plain enough. The realization that life, in its proliferation of forms, had arrived at *him* as its present masterwork, with all other surviving forms serving him, ought really to have restored some part of the arrogance he had begun to lose. Nor was he urged to think that the process had come to a halt and that his present state, with its

distressing inadequacies, was all that life had ever been working toward; by the end of the century Shaw was telling him
that he might become Superman, indeed that he was obliged
to do so. In short, he was at the top of the heap with no set
limits to how high the heap might be built. The view from
the pinnacle should have been exhilarating.

Psychologically, matters did not work out that way. Only
in our own time—very, very recently indeed—has someone
like Teilhard de Chardin made us feel the especial quality of
exhilaration inherent in the evolutionary evidence. Otherwise, we have at best learned to live with the facts, at worst
averted our eyes from them—as we were still doing, officially,
in Tennessee in the 1920's. As for Shaw, we thought he was
pulling our leg again and appropriated his term for a comic
strip.

The degree to which Darwin's theories depressed us may
perhaps best be suggested by the fact that nowhere in the
popular imagination did the phrase *"ascended* from an ape"
ever take root, though that might have been a more apt
description of what had actually taken place. There had
literally been a growth in consciousness, in complexity, in the
power to control environment, over the long evolutionary
span leading to man; but man insisted upon reading it as a
loss of caste and a diminution of power. Man had been thinking for so long in terms of genealogy, deriving his self-respect
from a guaranteed ancestral line going back to and sometimes
including God, that he could not reverse the direction of his
vision and see himself as rising from the ranks. Growth, even
for the religious-minded the possibility of a continuing
growth toward the fullness of God, could not console him; he
wanted his Father's name and his Father's authorization, not
the fragile, though obviously expanding, body his mother
had given him.

He felt helpless, and—for all that we have said to the
contrary—there was a sound enough reason for his fresh state
of shock, his increased sense of impotence. However far he

had come, he had played no *willed* part in the proceedings. Evolution looked to him like a vast, automatically functioning, machine, a machine which discarded what it could not use, used what it could, and produced what was inevitable. Evolution was using him; he was not using it. In fact, he had exercised no freedom at all, he was simply locked inside a movement which pursued its own ends inexorably. He was being carried along, quite blindly, on the tide of a life force that had not ever consulted him, a life force that was massive, mindless in the human sense, and impervious to any challenge or cooperation he might have cared to offer. From his own point of view he was an accident, a favored one perhaps, but an accident nonetheless: cells had collided, cold and heat had collided, giant jaws had collided, and there—a whim of genes—he stood. What pride could he take in a role he had not written? What exultation could he feel in an achievement that had not been freely won? What assurance, for that matter, did he have that he would not be discarded next? And would resistance to discard have any effect? None that he could see.

There were no tragic possibilities for a man in this state of mind. Such a man could see himself as a lucky throw of the genetic dice; or he could envision himself as pathetic victim, like the Brontosaurus, of the next crunch forward. He could not imagine himself as the true creator of change, as an active contestant, as a force for right or wrong decision.

Only in our own time have we come to realize that the evolutionary step which arrived at the complex intelligence of man was a step which altered the future course of evolution itself. Our grasp of this notion is still dim; but we have begun to see, in the twentieth century, that when evolution freed man to think, to look inward and to understand in part the processes that had gone into his making, it also freed him to participate in his future making. He was handed the opportunity to alter his own development, to rearrange the heat and the cold and even the meeting of genes that con-

290 · TRAGEDY AND COMEDY

stituted both his environment and his nature. Instead of being bound to a blind machine, now that his own eyes were open he was in a position to direct the next activity of the machine. He might remake the machine in a thousand ways if he wished—and if he could summon up enough wisdom to decide how best to remake it. He has not yet, of course, plunged into active direction of the machine in any full sense; he remains apprehensive about results he cannot entirely foresee and about side effects he feels may surprise him. But he *can* now determine, for good or for ill, the shape of human—or superhuman—things to come, and this means that the locked apparatus of which he was formerly a prisoner has been stripped of its inevitability. Man can make a monster of himself or he can arrive at a mastery yet undreamed of, simply by turning keys that are at present in his possession. Furthermore, given the keys, he *must* turn them. There is no going back, now that consciousness has expanded to include the evolutionary processes, to an unconscious, instinctive, mindlessly opportunistic "natural" advance. Evolution as the early invertebrates knew it—or, more precisely, as they did not know it—is over. The change is radical, the situation irreversible. Whatever fears his new freedom to control the patterns of growth may inspire in man, man has got the unfolding future of this planet on his hands, in his hands. The history of the species is his to write.

Alas, even as he has become aware of his power to rule a process that at first seemed to rule him, he has been inhibited from exercising that power confidently by further discovery. Freud, and the whole burden of modern psychology, crossed what might have been an upward thrust of confidence by raising a new question. Yes, science had presented man with a vast new freedom to tamper with himself and his successors, his planet and his universe. Man could act eugenically and arrive at heaven knows what; he could measure light-years, and think in terms of space-time, and begin to test his conclusions by arriving on the moon. But *why* was he doing, or wishing to do, all of these things?

Most men do not much question their motives. They assume them to be good. And any scientist, like any ancient tragic hero, would probably—when put to it—respond to an inquiry about his motives by speaking of the pursuit of truth, the health of the body politic, the alleviation of misery, the creation of a better world. The impulse behind the effort is a beneficent one, readily—if somewhat generally—defined. It is also, quite simply, what it seems to be. A man has entered a situation; he has seen that it contains problems; he has, at considerable cost to himself, struggled to improve the situation by acquiring the knowledge needed to dispose of the problems. One, two, three, plus quite a bit of pain, and all's right with the world, as he meant it to be. The possibility of unearthing the necessary knowledge is not doubted; the desirability of a cleansed situation is not doubted; the motive of the hero engaged in the cleansing process is not doubted. That is, or was, the classic way of looking at "progress."

But contemporary psychology called into doubt the motive of everyman. It pointed a finger at what was thought to be a conscious effort toward some sort of betterment and suggested that it was not conscious at all. The expanding consciousness, the awareness of the workings of the universe about him, in which man might have taken such pride was identified with the ego, that weakest and most suspect part of man's equipment. The great forces that moved man were all buried deep in the unconscious, in an id ancient with instinct. The ego—man's perception of the world and his formalized response to it—was a mere shallow overlay of irresistible impulse, a polite and often self-deceiving evasion of the real. Even the superego, censoriously modifying what might become the unsocial excesses of the id, acted on an unconscious plane, influencing the perception and behavior of the ego without informing it of its manner of functioning. The ego, by means of which man dealt with things outside him, was the least trustworthy and the least powerful of his psychic properties.

In short, it was precisely in the sphere of conscious action that man now found himself least reliable. If he entered an action at all, he had to do so knowing himself part charlatan. He could announce his purpose, but he could not truly believe in it: behind it there lay an unnamed force, a drive not consciously intended, which made his purpose a pretense and himself a tool again. In the midst of his fascinating new freedoms, he was once more locked to a process over which he exercised no substantial control and to which he could not even give a name. Seeing deep into space, he was blinder than ever; ready to manipulate the future, he was forced to acknowledge in a new way that it was he who was being manipulated. Earlier he had been told, in several different ways, that he was not so free as he had thought; but now he was forced to absorb an even harsher piece of news. Freedom itself was not "free."

The discovery resulted in a kind of numb pursuit of action as though at the bidding of the unconscious, action which has continued to produce vast amounts of fresh and valuable knowledge without giving birth to much in the way of pride or confidence. Whereas the tragic hero tends to slap God or his apparent destiny hard in the face in order to see what great leap forward may come of the confrontation, modern man makes his advances like a busy, uncomplaining bee. The "research team" is, in effect, an assembly line. Patience replaces what John Updike has called the "Promethean protest forced upon Man by his paradoxical position in the universe as a self-conscious animal." And it is plain enough by this time that patience has its particular rewards. But there is a dullness of heart in our activity since Freud spoke, too. We do what we can do, do what we must do; but we have little faith that we are going to win what is a mere contest with time. Uneasily, we salvage the elderly and try to feed the underprivileged against the day when the elderly and underprivileged will be blown to bits. We rather assume that those impulses concealed beneath our conscious actions are going to manifest themselves disastrously sooner or later: we feel that they are destructive forces and we know that we are not in charge of them.

It is probably fair to say that Freud's boldest hope was that he would relieve man of fear. Perversely, and once again paradoxically, we have chosen to misread his message as we did Darwin's: the most striking legacy we have taken from Freud is fear of ourselves. Aware that our ids are at odds with our egos, and cringing in apprehension before an unconscious we regard as anarchic, we escape into feverish work, while our spirits wilt. We are all one now, potential victims of a common, incomprehensible heritage, and the great man —the tragic hero—who would risk himself wholly in a direct contest with an absolute is instantly and naturally suspect: he is only doing the bidding of an instinct he fails to grasp, a poor pretender to old and illusory glories.

"Even the Greek tragedy," Philip Rieff says, "was leveled out by Freud; the unique crime of the tragic hero becomes an intention in every heart, and in the most ordinary of plots, the history of every family. Misfortune is not an exceptional possibility, occasioned by rare circumstances or monstrous characters, but is the lot of every person, something he has to pass through in his journey from infancy to old age. The aristocratic bias of the 'heroic' myth is replaced, in Freud, by the democratic bias of the 'scientific' myth: Oedipus *Rex* becomes Oedipus Complex, which all men live through." Mr. Rieff goes on to explain that Freud did not hold a genuinely tragic view of life. "Ordinary men compromise with their instinctual longings and become neurotic; the tragic hero, because he suffers and dies, must be presumed to have carried out his wishes in a way forbidden to most men."

Since Freud we have sometimes proclaimed ourselves liberated from inhibition, though we do know that more and more we have had to seek out the services of psychoanalysts whose partial function is to free us of inhibition. That is to say, our inhibitions seem in some insane way to have increased in proportion to our proclaimed release from them. Perhaps as good an example as any of this inverted development is to be found in John Osborne's perceptive play, *Inadmissible Evidence*. Here the hero—who has typically become an antihero—has long since freed himself of restraints of any sort. The process has not even been conscious. He *was* freed of restraints by the society and the century into which he was born. His sexual liberties have been total; he has not hesitated to make a career of borrowing other men's work; he has accepted no responsibility for the children he has sired. No real limitations have been placed upon his instinctive activity, because all of the social or religious forces that would once have called him "guilty" have been dismantled in the new psychological environment. The old punitive forces were artificial structures built by a community of egos which failed to perceive the degree to which all ego structures are illusory and actually at the mercy of the unconscious. The old rules were hollow rules that failed to reflect the true nature of the psyche. Thus, such rules and structures were incompetent to call men "guilty." Men have learned to brush them aside and live in open harmony with their ids. But a most peculiar thing has happened. The man whom no one calls guilty—no judge on the bench, no priest in the pulpit, no injured wife, no neglected child—now turns in on himself and calls himself guilty. He goes further. Since he has not been called guilty of anything specific, he now feels himself guilty of everything generally. He most literally despises himself, and in Mr. Osborne's play he spends his every waking hour teaching others to detest him. He is, in his own view, altogether loathsome—this is our suspicion of the nature of the id rising to the surface—and because he regards himself as loathsome he cannot bring himself to deal effectively, or even to face, the people with whom he must have relationships. He cannot do business with clients, cannot establish any sort of communication with his daughter, cannot take pleasure in casual sex, cannot meet wife or mistress as a confident man. Apparently he is free to carry out such wishes as he has; nothing is forbidden him. But he can never be a tragic figure, because he can no longer act at all. His kind of freedom has rendered him impotent.

Fundamentally, post-Freudian man has learned to distrust himself. If compromising with one's instincts—making a queasy bargain between ego and id so that both are half satisfied—tends to make a man neurotic, surrendering wholly to instinct seems to destroy the ego utterly. The ego is no longer able to deal with any sort of "out there," its natural terrain. It is incapable of that presumption that is essential to tragedy: the conviction, right or wrong, that one knows what one is doing and that what one is doing is necessary. Forthright action is fatally inhibited, forward movement is halted by man's sense of his inward duplicity. Nothing is what it seems to be. The motive for acting may be a sham. The goal that is apparently sought may not be the goal that is truly sought: it may be sublimation or transference of some shady sort. The ingredients of action are one and all illusory; the face of things is false. Nor is there really much profit to be taken from attacking the false face in the hope of stripping it down to truth. "Something that has not yet been proved false is an illusion, isn't it?" Edward Albee asks, ruminating on the plays he himself writes. What Mr. Albee's question implies is that *everything* is false; any truth we may pretend to hold must in the end be exposed as illusion. Untruth is absolute bedrock. Our progressive explorations, on stage or off, can only lead to the false that underlies the false that underlies the false. The man who would strive toward the vertical in circumstances such as these must soon be incapacitated by vertigo.

The self-doubt that comes of knowing that the unconscious is eternally playing tricks on us is enough to immobilize the tragic hero: how should he make the effort to isolate himself

296 • TRAGEDY AND COMEDY

from the acquiescent crowd and to lift himself up by self-assertion into the arena where ultimates are challenged if he is persuaded that ultimates are only further lies and that the very self he asserts is a non-entity, a façade so spurious that it must in resignation be called No-name? The antihero enters antidrama because values must deny themselves if we are to accept their authenticity. We have learned to work with contradictions rather than correspondences: good is evil masked; evil is innocence misunderstood; aspiration is frustration sublimated; yes is no. Nowhere are we "free" of negation, actual or potential. Nor are we free to think "freedom" free. Freedom may be, probably is, its own opposite.

This last roadblock shutting us off from the tragic heartland of freedom is probably the most formidable that dramatists have yet had to face, though of course Freud and his successors did not imagine that they were erecting barriers to any kind of human activity or human understanding. The earlier blows that had brought tragedy to its knees had seemed external blows. The universe around and about man had been damaged—in his eyes—by the discovery that it did not actually revolve around and about him. Even the change in his lineage that came with the news of evolution remained extrinsic to what he now was: he may once have been an ape, but he was now a rational man. Accepting the fact that, as Amos Wilder says, "the sublime firmament of overhead reality that provided a spiritual home for the souls of men until the eighteenth century [had] collapsed," he might have learned to absorb the damage done to his world view by grappling with it as the responsible, logical, comprehending person he was. But modern psychology snatched the opportunity from his already trembling hands by pointing out to him that something more than the "overhead reality" had gone. The reality inside his head had gone, too. The truth about the universe outside him, and about the past he had left behind him, were only half the horror: his present, and his very person, were dubious as well. With all of his equip-

ment, he had made thundering mistakes about his environment and his ancestry; now he could not trust his equipment
to tell him the truth about what he felt, or thought, or
intended. He stood stunned in his heart and in his intelligence.

This was, however, a state of mind. Man was—and to a
degree still is—in shock, as our novelists tell us in hallucinatory terms, as our sculptors show us in splattered, frag-
mented, and sometimes self-destroying forms. But a near
nervous breakdown, however understandably provoked, is no
accurate reflection of the state of the world in which it takes
place. Shock is a response, not a map or a photograph. In
truth, Freud and his colleagues had increased man's freedoms; they had liberated him from misapprehensions and
indicated a path he might take toward more accurate knowledge of himself. If man has not yet come to the end of the
path, if he feels himself peeling away illusion after illusion
only to uncover further illusion, that is neither surprising
nor ultimately conclusive. The work of getting at roots has
barely begun. If it has taken us a hundred years of psychological regret and intensive research to find in the evolutionary process a cause for rejoicing, who is to say how long it will
take us to embrace the unconscious as something known
rather than feared? That such advances in knowledge can
serve either to depress or to exalt the heart is clear from an
account of the evolutionary span given by J. Nathaniel
Deely:

Let us imagine that the 4,500 million years of our planet's past
are represented by the distance of one hundred miles, and that
we are walking from the time of the earth's origin towards the
present. On the first half of our journey we would encounter no
living thing, and we would traverse a full eighty-eight miles
before even such simple invertebrates as worms and jellyfish
began to appear with any frequency. At ninety-three miles,
certain organisms would begin the invasion of the land masses;

but our own ancestral group, the mammals, would not appear until we were a scant two miles from our goal. The whole of man's physical evolution since the beginning of the Pleistocene epoch would take place over the last sixty yards of our journey, and the span of written history with all its panoply of civilization would be encompassed in the last half of our final stride.

Mr. Deely then quotes Richard Carrington, whose analogy he has adapted in the foregoing paragraph. "The grandeur of our spatial and temporal perspective will seem depressing or exhilarating according to our individual temperaments." If we center our attention upon the millions of years the whole process has taken, we are likely to suffer a sensation of helplessness, to feel the weight of time as an intolerable burden. Our spirits sink under the stretch of the span. If, on the other hand, we focus upon all that has been achieved during a mere half step at the end of the journey, *our* end of the journey, we are quite overcome with a sensation of speed, dizzied by the unbelievable progress made in no time at all. We seem almost supermen now.

The popular view until recently has had eyes for nothing but the endlessly receding, ungraspable past; it has looked backward and asked, in effect, "If it took so long for the very feeblest forms of life to appear, what hope have we?" Lately we have turned our heads in the opposite direction and seen excellent grounds for hope: the moment man appeared he put the long past to shame. We are not yet in a position to place the mysteries of the unconscious in this altered light; we are still digging backward, and in a traumatic state. But past experience suggests that the moment of reversal will come. As we strip the layers of the unconscious away, as we learn to master its depths, we may very well find that our footing is more secure than ever before and that we are free to move about as freshly integrated, unselfconscious beings. Marshall McLuhan insists that the unconscious is already "being eroded at a furious pace; it is being invaded by dazzling investigations and insights; and we could quickly reach a stage in which we had no unconscious. This would be like dreaming awake." The end of our sensation that life is a dream, or that our conscious minds are lying to us, may very well be in sight. Further work is required, but we need not imagine that it will only mire us deeper in quicksand. "This possibility that we are actively engaged in liquidating the unconscious for the first time in history," Mr. McLuhan says, "behooves us to pay some attention to how it is structured, and to what function it serves in human affairs. It may prove to be indispensable to sanity."

Thus, sanity may be the result of what now seems a descent into unreason. Still, we are at present engaged in the descent, and tragedy is possible only in a time of complete confidence. Tragedy, as we have seen, is not dependent upon gains in freedom that are half made; it is not helped by statistics that show mere partial or promised advances. Tragedy needs arrogance. It rises in periods of certainty, when man feels fully sure of himself. It is as much dependent upon feeling as upon facts. No matter if someone learns to construct a steam locomotive or to read hieroglyphs or to devise computers; the announcement of such advances is not enough. Unless man conceives of himself as unquestioned master of all such advances, he will not behave tragically; he may find himself cowering in the face of the advances instead, a frightened innovator.

Twentieth-century man's continuing fear of the freedoms he has won for himself effectively prevents him not from pursuing those freedoms but from presenting himself on the stage or in any other art form as muscular champion of the defiant advance. He labors steadily but speaks softly of himself, terrified lest an excess of action betray a weakness he has not uncovered yet, rather inclined to believe that the end of his researches will reveal him not a power in his own right but the product of an ancestry and an unconscious that dominate him in a manner more demonic than godlike.

How long this cringing posture that prohibits tragedy, this disbelief in a boldly achieved mutation that may prove to be "good," will endure no one can say. The ordinary materials of tragedy lie about us, but are untouched. Anyone who has glanced, say, at Gene Smith's *When the Cheering Stopped* will recognize in it instantly the most conventional of all tragic outlines. Woodrow Wilson has embarked with the best of intentions upon an entirely worthy course: the evolution within our society of an instrument for outlawing war. His early successes, and the quality of his vision, have made him in many eyes something close to a god. He nears his goal only to discover that he cannot have it on his own terms. He must compromise, is denied his absolute. In his arrogance, which is also dedication to an ideal, he refuses halfway measures. His refusal destroys the possibility of the advance for which he has labored. The failure destroys him. As he lies rejected and dying, there is an unexpected gathering in the streets. Spontaneously, people come to cry and to pray for the defeated man who is taking on the contours of something like a "saint." In the end, after he has sacrificed himself, his vision catches hold and the evolutionary instrument he has hoped to fashion comes into being in a new form.

In such an outline there is not only the traditional classroom formula for tragedy: the great man who defeats himself by yielding to a flaw. There are overtones of that larger tragic content we have been forced to take into consideration: self-assertion as an evolutionary sacrifice, followed by epiphany. But though we are fully familiar with this action in all of its aspects, it does not occur to us to place it upon the stage as tragedy. Literally, *it does not occur to us*. Our habit of mind is otherwise. We do not see the narrative as a heroic exercise of freedom, well or ill used. If we probe into its content at all, we probe for another kind of knowledge. When, we ask, did Wilson suffer the first undetected stroke that put him at the mercy of his arteries, that made a helpless victim of him? We try to understand his arrogance as a pathological symptom, not as an intellectual conviction that he possessed the power to act absolutely. Perhaps we are quite right to do so, now that we are so much better informed about the human mechanism. But our present state of knowledge, and our acquired habits of mind, have controlled the beam of light we play over the narrative. We have specifically sought, and found, what was pathetic in it rather than what was tragic in it; we have looked for the conditioned act rather than the free act.

Are there any indications that our habits of mind are in process of being reversed? Perhaps. An impatient existentialism has forced man into the arena of free action again, though not yet in a fully tragic way. It might be better to say that existentialist philosophy has forced man to admit that he *is* in just such an arena, whether he knows it or not, whether he likes it or not. Man has no choice but to act, because it is only in acting that man can be said to have being. Plato had postulated being as a conceptual essence, as something prior to and independent of any individual man. First there was an idea of "man" and then there were men who corresponded to it, like so many samples. The existentialists reject this notion: existence precedes essence, and a "man" discovers who and what he is only through testing his otherwise unknown qualities in a succession of free choices. There is no matrix; there is only an experimental exploration of possibilities. Now this position in no sense relieves contemporary man of his blindness or of his fear of himself. Quite the contrary. He may be *anything*—only what he does will tell him what he is—and there are no helpful hints to guide him in earlier philosophical or religious systems; neither has he a prefabricated conscience or die-stamped instinct to supply him with information before he acts. Modern man must remain forlorn, Sartre says, "for he cannot find anything to depend upon either within or outside himself." He is alone in the universe without excuse, without given commands.

But, unpleasant as the situation may sound, there is for

tragedy some small gain in this uncompromising vision. Tragedy cannot have its intended goal back: nothing is known about any "out there" to provoke a direct challenge. Certainly tragedy cannot here retrieve its sense of exerting godlike powers: in this view there is no available God to serve as a power model, and man himself is without defined resources. "For if indeed existence precedes essence, one will never be able to explain one's action by reference to a given and specific human nature," Sartre insists. Then he adds: "That is what I mean when I say that man is condemned to be free. Condemned, because he did not create himself, yet nevertheless at liberty, and from the moment that he is thrown into this world he is responsible for everything he does."

Freedom is, in this understanding, the whole of man's environment, the one and unavoidable atmosphere in which he must breathe and give himself a name. It is not presented as a precious right or as a tool to be used for intelligible advance. It is seen, rather, as a sentence to be served, as the hard labor meted out to man for the non-crime of having been born. Normally we think of the prison cell as a restraint upon freedom. Here we see the cell *as* freedom. Freedom unconfined becomes the one thing by which man is confined, the condition from which he can never escape. The pressure of infinitely open choices is immediately felt as a burden, as the same kind of nightmare and near-madness that formerly flooded in upon a man placed in solitary confinement. For the new state of awareness *is* solitary. Man is harrowingly alone, completely cut off from his equally solitary fellows, unaccountable to any structure outside himself and undefined by those limits—political or religious—which used to make him feel anchored in space by offering him a map of himself. Discovering himself mobile at the center of a void, man is not free to reject his own horrifying freedom. He must explore the void with a dizzying independence, eternally becoming himself.

The hallucinatory sensation which such a concept of freedom creates in man is readily seen in Camus' *Caligula*. Because there is no one thing which Caligula may not do, and because Caligula cannot become Caligula until he does what Caligula may do, Caligula presses his capacity for action to the extremes of his reach, deliberately and without either emotional or moral reserve. He violates the persons of others wantonly, blasphemes at will. "Before he is slain," Wallace Fowlie points out, "he experiences a nameless solitude . . ." The action has been coldly experimental in character. All possibility has been accepted. The void has been probed for boundaries without yielding any. When Caligula is destroyed, he is destroyed not by a shaped universe whose nature he has violated but by the independent action of other isolates exercising their own unlimited freedoms. When destruction comes, one senses that Caligula welcomes it. Only a vast and desperate weariness can come of never encountering a real obstacle. If we are in any way sickened by the spectacle of Caligula's excesses, he is much more sickened by the experience of exercising a freedom that can never find anything to resist it. If everything dissolves the moment a man puts a fist through it, man's only neighbor in the universe is dissolution itself.

Yet freedom is the area we have entered, and in entering it at all we have made some sort of beginning invasion of the tragic terrain. This emperor is driven mad by the discovery of the extent of his freedom; and existentialist thought is not yet prepared to make sanity of the madness by offering the tragic hero anything actual to contend with, or even to touch. In the circumstances, and by definition, the tragic hero, the play, and the experience of freedom itself must remain essentially shapeless. But to modern man, with his long-standing conviction that freedom is an illusion and his long-standing sensation of being helpless captive of a mechanical process, the very introduction of the notion must come as a reversal and a release. A tide is turning, without promising anything very pleasant; but it does say that swimming is permitted, even commanded.

Nor is the fact that this new insistence upon freedom is presented in terms of dizziness and pain in any way inimical to the promise of tragedy to come. Suffering has, of course, always been a part of the tragic scheme of things, so large a part that we have often mistaken it for the whole. But, as the tide turns, we begin to see suffering in something other than a dark and dispiriting light. As Philip Rahv says, suffering "is the price of freedom, and he who refuses to pay it can only dream of freedom without experiencing it, without substantiating it within the actual process of living." Mr. Rahv adds that this freshly sensed link between freedom and suffering is, in part at least, "close to existentialist thought."

And in his excellent introduction to the central themes of existentialist philosophy, *Irrational Man,* William Barrett makes it plain that the "condemned" man of Sartre's vision is by no means to regard himself as already executed. Rather, horror and hope are intermingled:

Man is doomed to the radical insecurity and contingency of his being; for without it he would not be man but merely a thing and would not have the human capacity for transcendence of his given situation. There is a curious dialectical interplay here: that which constitutes man's power and glory, that which lies at the very heart of his power to be lord over things, namely his capacity to transcend himself and his immediate situation, is at one and the same time that which causes the fragility, the wavering and flight, the anguish of our human lot.

The earlier tragic perception of the Greeks, of Shakespeare and of Racine, is not too far removed from this most contemporary sensation of doubleness, of a necessary effort at transcendence which can only be made through the surrender of all comforts, physical, emotional, and intellectual. The new need to seek identity itself which existentialism has affirmed and the emphasis placed upon free activity as the single guarantor of identity do something more than prod us toward the tragic arena of absolute action. They help man to begin to see himself as heroic once more by defining—or redefining—the essence of the heroic. In a way, we have spent three hundred years wanting to be comfortably heroic. That is to say, we have felt that we could not function as heroes unless we were coddled by a neighborly God, buoyed up by a clear pedigree, certified as clear thinkers by the possession of functioning minds that were plainly rational and not playing tricks on us. Given all, or any one, of these seals of prior approval, we might have been willing to do battle; but we did not quite see how we could issue challenges or explore absolutes without first having passed a fitness test. How could a man be a hero without a hero's license in his pocket?

What we are coming to understand is that heroism itself— any major invasion of the field of action—must be original, presumptive, exploratory, exacerbating, and possibly unrewarding. The hero is not the man who has safely survived and retired to his country estate; he is the man moving forward into a battle he may or may not survive. Heroism itself is a matter of the present tense. It is risk in action. This has always been true, of course—true of Prometheus, true of Oedipus, true of Lear—but, having seen too many monuments and watched too many triumphal parades, we forgot it. We confused the decorated survivor with the man striding blindly through mortar fire, and while our decorations were being stripped away we imagined that our capacities for entering the field were being diminished, too. We are beginning to look at free and forceful action from the point of view of the unproved, uncertain, unrecognized fledgling combatant again, and to see the battleground ahead as all menace but not beyond mastering by the man who exposes himself totally. Though the hero may be killed, he need not cringe; the hero's place is precisely where holocaust looms.

"We deal with a change in quantity," Lionel Trilling says.

"It has always been true of some men that to pleasure they have preferred what the world called unpleasure. They imposed upon themselves difficult and painful tasks, they committed themselves to strange, 'unnatural' modes of life, they sought out distressing emotions, in order to know psychic energies which are not to be summoned up in felicity. These psychic energies, even when they are experienced in self-destruction, are a means of self-definition and self-affirmation." In the past the election of those freedoms which Mr. Trilling calls "unpleasure" has occurred rather rarely: "it is the choice of the hero, the saint and martyr, and, in some cultures, the artist." But "what was once a mode of experience of a few has now become an ideal of experience of many." Our awareness that pleasure, consolation, mere comfort is limiting grows rapidly. Freud noticed that vast numbers of men labored in some mysterious way to free themselves of the pleasure principle and to forge beyond it. But the conclusions he drew from the phenomenon were ambiguous when they were not by implication pessimistic: the impulse was fundamentally an impulse to self-destruction. Philosophic existentialism has, in effect, now altered this to read self-definition. And we are beginning to think—I would like to say hope—beyond existentialism's uncertain promise. "For Sartre," Mr. Barrett says, "the nothingness of the Self is the basis for the will to action. . . . Man's existence is absurd in the midst of a cosmos that knows him not; the only meaning he can give himself is through the free project that he launches out of his own nothingness."

But if he succeeds in giving himself a meaning he will have given himself somethingness. Our minds may be beginning to place the emphasis in this cruel activity upon the *meaning* it may arrive at, not upon the meaninglessness from which it is launched. Existentialism sees man as condemned to action, which is in itself a gain for tragedy. Postexistentialist thought dares to conceive of this action as potentially significant, as a means toward an end which may itself be a good. If we can simply alter our state of mind so that self-definition becomes a sought-after goal, if we can conceive of it as an absolute that might be wrested from a contest with the infinite, we shall be closer again to the temper that once set tragic man in motion. Mr. Trilling looks backward and forward to see this old-new impulse fumbling toward fresh awareness of its nature. Looking backward, he says, "if we consider the primitive forbidden ways of conduct which traditionally in tragedy lead to punishment by death, we think of them as being the path to reality and truth, to an ultimate self-realization. We have always wondered if tragedy itself may not have been saying just this in a deeply hidden way, drawing us to think of the hero's sin and death as somehow conferring justification, even salvation of a sort. . . ." And looking forward from our exhausted notions of comfort and pleasure which have ended only in ennui, we wonder if there is not developing in their place "an ideal of the experience of those psychic energies which are linked with unpleasure and which are directed toward self-definition and self-affirmation."

Our nerves grow somewhat steadier, even in the void, now that we have permitted ourselves to imagine activity in the void yielding a new and much firmer reality. Jung would even urge us to take our very oldest ideals of transcendence— our images of an archetypal God and of an immortality to be won—into the battle with us if we wish to, positing a super-reality "out there" with which we are equipped to make contact. The fact that we must be less precise in describing beforehand the nature of the goals we seek to snatch need not inhibit us. Confidence is a matter of spirit, not of total information, and evolution will never tell us—as it never has told us—where our next suit of clothes is coming from. A man may, and probably must, shape in his mind the look of the things he thinks he is after, whether they bear him out or astound him when he at last has them in his grip. "If he believes in them, or greets them with some measure of credence," Jung reminds us, "he is being just as right or just as wrong as someone who does not believe in them. But while the man who despairs marches toward nothingness, the one who has placed his faith in the archetype follows the tracks of life and lives right into his death. Both, to be sure, remain in uncertainty, but the one lives against his instincts, the other with them. The difference is considerable, and gives the latter an advantage."

Tragedy may return to us, in this time of necessary action and enforced freedom, when man comes to feel once more that he does, or can, bring an advantage with him into the bruising fray. Tragedy, which is affirmation of the will at its fiercest, depends very largely upon the psychology of the historical moment. Doubt will not give it to us. Determination, however hotheaded, may. The philosophical outlook of recent years is in the process of creating a new psychology. Man is reevaluating himself, possibly readying himself for a test of strength that simply cannot be avoided. Certainly, if he is listening, he cannot help hearing the drumbeat of a new theme, a drumbeat which Mr. Barrett paraphrases from Heidegger in this way: "Man . . . is a creature of distance: he is perpetually beyond himself, his existence at every moment opening outward toward the future."

Or, to seize upon Karl Jaspers' formulation, "One can take courage to try to do that which passes beyond his strength from the fact that it is a human problem, and man is that creature which poses problems beyond its powers."

Such news may quite possibly, at some not too far distant time, alert the slumbering tragic hero, who is invariably eager to be the first man beyond himself.

15
COMEDY NOW

I T IS necessary to stress the fact that comedy is at its most vigorous when tragedy is at its most vigorous. Our habit of thought, which has some justification, is to think of tragedy as an occasional visitor descending violently from nowhere and of comedy as a constant companion. Tragedy surprises and then eludes us; comedy, like the poor, can be found at the doorstep every day.

But, because comedy derives its very being from the affirmations of tragedy, to which it plays devil's advocate, it is bound to make its boldest obscene gestures just when the heroic parade is proudest. The size of the hero produces oversize in the buffoon. The clown must expand to the proportions of the presumptuous man he is parodying.

This provides us with the extravagance we call farce, just as it makes farce the fundamental comic form. We do not particularly wish to acknowledge farce as the fundamental comic form nowadays, principally because we live in one of those softer and somewhat rueful ages from which tragedy is absent and in which comedy must perforce modify the brazenness of its assault. We have preferred, for some time now, to distinguish between farce, conceived of as a sort of clumsy country cousin whose table manners are notoriously coarse, and that more refined member of the family we like to call comedy proper. Comedy proper, for us, is proper indeed.

The distinction is meant to be prejudicial. George Meredith, for instance, was quickly embarrassed whenever farce came to table, distressed that Oliver Goldsmith should have stooped so low to conquer: "And how difficult it is for writers to disentangle themselves from bad traditions is noticeable when we find Goldsmith, who had grave command of the Comic in narrative, producing an elegant farce for a Comedy." Meredith reserved his highest praise for the writer who could keep laughter "impersonal and of unrivalled politeness, nearer a smile; often no more than a smile." If Goldsmith can be faulted for grossness, Aristophanes is all but beyond the pale. Because we must deal with Aristophanes, we do so, holding in high esteem his lyric gifts and overlooking as best we can the coarser texture of his plotting and his improvised tomfooleries. These last, Gilbert Norwood says, "are often ignored because of a widespread notion that farce must be bad, and we are too loyal to attribute farce to a great writer."

Yet there is no ignoring the fact that "some of the finest work included under the convenient title of 'Greek Comedy' should in strictness be called farce," any more than there is any escaping the *commedia dell' arte* base of Molière's stories, characters, and idle tricks. Nearly everything in Molière is what we should now call farce if we were freshly confronted with it, and only Shakespeare lends any support to our nation that true comedy is a gentler, more lyric thing. Shakespeare, much of the time, *is* gentler and more humane than either Aristophanes or Molière; the degree to which he has tempered the farce assault can easily be seen by comparing his work with that of his contentious rival and friend, Ben Jonson. At the same time we must not be misled into thinking him all domestic kindliness and romantic glow. Putting to one side such an obvious—and durable—farce as *The Taming of the Shrew,* and not bothering for the moment with those curiously two-toned and sometimes grotesque pieces we call the "dark comedies," we are obliged to recognize in the lightest and least savage of his comedies a farce substructure that stands in constant tension with the surface tenderness accorded the people. Olivia and Viola may be winning in a way that *Les Précieuses* are not; nevertheless they live in a world of shipwrecks, mistaken identities, drunkenness and practical jokes that is bold in outline and essentially skeptical in attitude. Portia may be warm and Lorenzo may be capable of the music of "in such a night"; but Portia has been wooed by casket and wed only after cunning deceit, while Lorenzo has got his girl by plain theft. The plot of *The Merchant of Venice* is the plot of any improvised Italian farce. *A Midsummer Night's Dream* is sheer accident from dusk till dawn: love is mocked in the play, not mooned over, and the most nearly gossamer of the entertainment's many heroines is passionately in love with a jackass, who is, as it happens, someone else. The fork-tongued Beatrice and the fatuous Benedick, appealing as they are, can be brought together only by a series of overhearing scenes, farcical in themselves, in which everything overheard is calculated fraud. All of these "comedies" embrace, without difficulty, the lechers and tosspots and senile fantastics who first did duty under Aristophanes, almost as though Sir Toby and Dogberry, Sir Andrew and Bottom were required as ballast to keep the Olivias and the Rosalinds from straying, lyrically, too far from the comic root; and the comic root itself is always there in the narrative, a gnarled protuberance over which even Rosalinds and Olivias must trip. Not just the bumpkins, but the bones, are farce; the radiance of Viola is flesh wrapped around the fortuitousness of twinness and the chicanery of disguise. Shakespeare's tone is his own, but there is a skeleton in the closet, and it is the same skeleton that Meredith scolded Godlsmith for rattling so many years later.

It should surprise no one that farce is capable of lyric extension, or that broadly conceived characters should be made to yield great complexity and in some cases to command affection. The lyric extension is already present in Aristophanes' choruses, without being ill suited to the low violence of the principals' pranks; and we know from Molière that it is possible to begin with a gross caricature and then to fill the enormous cartoon with so many rich and varied shadings that we come to know the monster, and even to like him, better than we do the somewhat simpler and more plausible people he persecutes. Orgon is more interesting than his good wife; and Arnolphe, in *The School for Wives,* is the rogue we watch with real interest and respect, however much we may wish the young lovers to elude him.

By virtue of its very broadness, its anxiety to parody the tragic hero in scale, farce possesses an amplitude that is denied to the gentler and homelier form we now call "comedy." Farce puffs itself up to the greatest possible proportions, somewhere just short of bursting with the effort, and in doing so it makes room for every sort of effect: it can inhale lyric beauty, a degree of kindliness, even tears if it cares to, because its lungs are so powerful and because all of these other things can be properly proportioned in a ballooning so vast. Farce is forced to increase its stature if it is to stand next to tragedy and make its humbling point: it must make its action extravagant as the tragic hero's action is extravagant, it must carve the clown's profile as boldly as though Aeschylus were at work on the lifted head of Prometheus. Its purpose, of course, is to render such high aspiration absurd; but it acquires a height of its own in the process of stretching to mock. Farce is the largest comic form we know, potentially the most dimensional; it offers us the greatest spaces to be filled in. If a playwright, or a period in history, fails to fill in the spaces and chooses instead simply to reproduce the cartooned outlines in a mechanical way, that is not the form's fault. It has matched the thrust of tragedy as best it could and left us the directions for making lunacy out of nobility; what we do with the legacy will depend upon our own capacities.

What we have always done is to scale down the outlines the

moment tragedy vanishes. Once the Greek tragic impulse is broken, comedy is diminished to the soft and solacing domesticities of Menander. The change is startling: at first glance it is difficult to believe that a form so fantastic, so far-reaching, so bizarre and so brazen could, in a very few years, shrink its scope so. Suddenly we are denied access to Cloud-Cuckoo-Land or to Hades and confined to the kitchen, or at least to the limits of everyman's household. The problem of keeping a cook becomes important; the problem of dealing with house guests, invited or uninvited, becomes important; a love story leaps to the foreground, with a degree of sentiment attached to it, and becomes the thread on which these lesser and somewhat incidental comic difficulties are hung. We begin to have the kind of "comedy" which we now distinguish from farce. It is fond, paternal in feeling, observant enough about the crotchets of human behavior, but in no sense savage about man's failure to become more than he is. From Menander to the routine domestic comedy on Broadway today, with its cheerful exposure of frailties which we readily recognize and just as readily forgive, is no very great step.

The tragic impulse breaks because a society has, through one experience or another, lost confidence in its capacity to overmaster the universe. What the society now asks is to be comforted. Further tragic sacrifice is, for the moment, beyond such a society. The massive insult offered to tragedy by farce is equally beyond it; indeed it would be gratuitous now, when men make fewer pretensions. "Comedy" contrives a kind of comfort, arranges a realistic adjustment to the new state of affairs. It does not abandon its purpose, which is to call attention to cracks in the human façade; but it has a much less imposing façade to deface, and can therefore afford to lower its voice. It lets on that it rather *likes* people, poor things that they are; and if it is by nature obliged to point at the dust on the furniture and at the slipshod manner in which dinner is served, it does so with a new degree of

314 • TRAGEDY AND COMEDY

tolerance, with "no more than a smile." The new realism is realistic in two ways: it is realistic about man's failings, and it is realistic about the fact that he isn't pretending not to have them just now. Comedy cannot severely attack a creature who does not think too highly of himself.

Since the first change of tone from Aristophanes to Menander, comedy has had ready to hand two available attitudes: it could be blunt or reserved, raucous or refined, harsh or gentle, extravagant or domestic. It would return to something like its original outrageousness whenever tragedy returned; and when tragedy had begun to expire again it would once more permit itself to be tamed and kept as a near-pet. The softening from Shakespeare to Fletcher and Dekker is plainly evident; there is a revitalized arrogance in Congreve and Wycherly at the same time that Dryden is trying desperately to restore tragedy, but once that effort has failed we are well on our way to the homespun pieties of eighteenth-century "sentimental comedy." After Molière, we may well expect Marivaux.

Comedy extends itself, then, in the presence of tragedy, achieving its own greatest stature when it has occasion to taunt stature. But though it is dependent upon tragedy for its inspiration and even for its carefully inverted incidental effects, it is not forced to disappear the moment tragedy disappears. There are several reasons why comedy can continue to do its work after its source fades from sight, but the most obvious of these lies in that aspect of action it has elected as its own. It has, from the beginning, chosen to display the thousand and one limitations that inhibit free action. Limitation is its domain, and, though the tragic assertion of total freedom may no longer shake the heavens, limitation as a human experience continues without interruption. If anything, the experience is intensified in the absence of tragedy: man is sharply aware that he is more limited than he formerly thought he was. In theory, this might even seem a gain for comedy, though it is not. Comedy is a parasitical form, and no absolute; it needs a richer form to feed on. Limitation too much multiplied will in the end devour, or obscure, the thing to which it adheres. We speak of a limitation *on* something, or of a limit *to* something; but the limitation must not loom so large that we can no longer see its referent. Comedy can survive in an age which feels its feebleness all too keenly because there is a clear correspondence between what comedy has always been saying and what the age now feels; but it cannot perform at its very best, because there is not enough light to make for a thoroughly satisfying shadow dance.

Still, comedy can feel at home with the disheartened, and so long as there are some small goals to make sport of it will still have a referent. Men do continue to have goals after transcendent goals have been abandoned. If neither Olympus nor the nether world of the Furies is to be reordered by tragic force, everyman continues to pursue ideals of order in his now narrower domain. He wants to get a good wife, to rear a good family, to establish himself in a good business, and perhaps to be respected in council, academy, and church. These aims engage his freedom and lure him into thinking he has used it well. Thus comedy is provided with a target. The target is smaller than it had been, which means that the darts must be smaller, too, but the relationship between an aspiration and the clumsy limitations life imposes upon it persists—for just so long as there *is* an aspiration, a belief in the effective use of freedom, about.

No doubt we should also remember that comedy survives the collapse of tragic practice because even in the collapse of its practice tragedy itself is not lost. It is there, on page and stage, for us to visit. We know it now; it is one half of our accumulated theatrical experience; if we find ourselves unable to write it, we can nonetheless take ourselves into its presence. Comedy profits from old acquaintance when new acquaintance proves impossible. The tragic heritage, as a shaper of comedy, is so much with us that to this day schoolboys have not stopped parodying *Hamlet*. It might be noticed as well, without making too much of the point, that when better-than-hack comedies appear they often appear in environments saturated with the production of old tragedies. Sheridan and Goldsmith both worked in an age heady with the rejuvenation of Shakespeare: while Samuel Johnson was busy freshly justifying the old tragedies, Garrick and Macklin and Siddons were busy acting them. And, as we know all too well, Shaw wrote with Shakespeare much on his mind. The afterimage of tragedy serves as a continuing invitation to comic intrusion.

It is conceivable, however, that comedy's life can, under certain circumstances, be threatened; and we must now deal with that possible threat. Let us suppose that an age comes to disbelieve in psychic freedom altogether, as our own age has very nearly done. Let us suppose that the same age begins, as a consequence, to doubt the value of activity of any sort, and learns to see itself as essentially static or as plodding through motions which are blind and gratuitous, without intelligible direction. Let us suppose that the earlier tragic library is at the same time called into question, so that plays we had once thought true tragedies are seen as no such thing but as manifestations of an unconscious drift toward inhibition and then impotence. And let us suppose that we are given to understand that *if* any such thing as valid tragedy did once exist it *cannot* return at any future time; the book, such as it was, is closed.

That is to say, both in life and in the theater, philosophically and aesthetically, we are told that we are now, and forever will be, denied access to the proving ground of transcendent free activity. In this understanding, and supposing that we are persuaded by it, what must become of comedy? With tragedy finally dead, can comedy continue its caper? Has it anything to caper about? "I know that when I set about writing a comedy the idea presents itself to me first of all as tragedy," Christopher Fry has said, adding that "if the characters were not qualified for tragedy there would be no comedy." Is there to be no comedy?

That comedy has been exposed in recent years to just the sort of intellectual weather described above is plain. For us the tragic landscape has become virtually invisible, the sun that shone on it having grown progressively feebler over three hundred years. The clown, staring at it for inspiration and knowing that he must take all of his own sustenance from what he sees outside himself, can only have had the sensation of going slowly blind. The landscape has darkened. What can comedy do but grow darker with it? Perhaps that is not so bad: comedy has worked in darkness before. Shakespeare wrote "dark" comedies only to discover dawn again; and darkness rather confirms comedy's prophetic pessimism in any case. But what drives comedy to desperation in our own time is something deeper than darkness. The tragic landscape is now described as a place that never truly existed, or at least a place that is not going to exist in future. Thus it claps down into utter blackness. On the instant comedy turns black with it.

Black comedy is a phenomenon of the moment that derives from the complete absence of any tragic aspiration. Non-black comedy looks at affirmation, or the pretense to it, and finds it faulty. Black comedy acknowledges the disappearance of affirmation altogether and—fighting for its life—tries to work with the proposition that no motive is ever good and that no man would care to deceive himself into thinking that one might be. Joe Orton's *Entertaining Mr. Sloane* is a reasonably representative sample of the form. An obviously shifty young man comes looking for lodgings. The lady of the house, an amorous but frustrated spinster, accepts him on the spot so that she can make advances to him. Her successful-businessman brother drops by and at first scolds her for what she is up to. The lodger, however, "camps" just enough to suggest that he is available on other sexual terms, and the brother warms to him quickly. Shortly brother and sister are in fierce competition for the lodger's sexual favors. Their aged and testy father, meanwhile, has had an intuition about the young man; pursuing it, he discovers that the lodger is in fact a murderer. He is careless enough to disclose this fact to his children, who kill him. The surviving three, brother, sister, and lodger, now meticulously and heartlessly arrange for the death to appear an accident and, bound as they are by their shared guilt, contrive an accommodation among them: henceforth brother and sister will divide the lodger's love-time between them, six months each. The curtain falls on a satisfied household.

In all of this, or nearly all of it, there is no pretense. Motives are neither concealed nor rationalized, they are candidly acknowledged. Each member of the group is greedy in his own way and willing to spell out his greed without affectation. There is no shock at any disclosure; universal venality is taken for granted. There is no false mourning for the murdered father; before his feet are cold they are being laced into new, slippery shoes which will account for his "accidental" fall. Hypocrisy is ruled out as a subject of possible ridicule. All cards are on the table; and they are all deep black spades.

How much of this is funny? Not too much. It is difficult to produce laughter where no incongruity exists, where no real vulnerability exists. The people are invulnerable because they are open with one another, and with us; there is no façade to be brought down. And they cannot behave incongruously, since their actions are always in strict accord with their appetites; logic moves them absolutely and without interruption. Indeed, the only way in which the play can be regarded as funny is by comparison *with something that is not present in the play*. Outside the play, hovering over it like a race memory, is a set of affirmations formerly believed in: women are ideally not sluts; sexuality is ideally male-female and then associated with affection; murderers are rarely regarded as desirable companions; and fathers are not coolly dispatched when they interfere with the urgencies of the flesh. The play *as a whole* will seem funny in proportion as we bring to the theater with us a habit of seeing life in terms of ancient aspirations. In effect, we must have in our heads a landscape for the play to deride and we must hold it there as best we can while its negations are independently acted out upon the stage. If *we* do not supply the light against which the dark can be seen as dark, we shall not laugh at all. And if, at some future time, we find that we have effectively erased from our minds the standard affirmations now lodged there, the play will in no sense seem a comedy; it will seem a perfectly straightforward play about people who go about exercising their instincts sensibly. We now *do* laugh at the moment in which the three figures strike their final, preposterous bargain—but only because it is preposterous by standards we still hold and which the play does not mention.

This is comedy making friends with the enemy and hoping that someone will remember its true allegiance and see incongruity in its behaving as it does. It is a tricky, troubled, daredevil business, an attempt to paint a shadow on absolute night by depending upon the audience to bring a kind of cat's-vision with it; it is comedy showing no mercy, while begging it. There is fear in it, certainly on comedy's part, frequently on the audience's. What if the last remembered glimmer of aspiration, now precariously contained only in the eye of the beholder, should go out? There is none of it on stage; nothing can be kindled there. And the longer the audience watches the stage the harder it is to keep the necessary antithesis in mind. The threat that black comedy poses for comedy is that it may succeed all too well in persuading the audience that its vision is a complete one and that no contrast need be set beside it, in persuading the audience to suppress or to forget the counterpoint which is stored in its head and which alone guarantees the light-dark relationship upon which laughter depends. As things stand, the laughter that greets black comedy is sporadic, uncertain, often ill at ease; it is sometimes, to alter Meredith, "no more than a groan." A laugh begins because we see the contradiction between what is happening on stage and what we hold to be true; then it falters, descends into hollowness, because we cannot be certain that what we hold *is* true and because what is happening on stage has the grim authority of a recorded event. Our confidence, which comedy is counting upon to save it in the dark, is easily shaken.

Yet comedy has no choice but to try to make something of the situation. It cannot turn its back on the pervasive bleakness of an age; it must contend as best it can with what occupies the minds of men, using one dodge or another to supply the doubleness it requires. Having been so long the gleeful urchin calling out that the emperor had no clothes, it cannot really retire from a society which sees neither clothes nor emperor. It must go down into the pit, clawing furiously and, with luck, entertainingly the whole way down, even if the pit at last proves so deep that it can never emerge to flaunt daylight again. Here is the pit, and what may happen to comedy in it, sketched out for us by Martin Esslin in his synopsis of Samuel Beckett's *Act Without Words:*

The scene is a desert onto which a man is "flung backwards." Mysterious whistles draw his attention in various directions. A number of more or less desirable objects, notably a carafe of water, are dangled before him. He tries to get the water. It hangs too high. A number of cubes, obviously designed to make it easier for him to reach the water, descend from the flies. But however ingeniously he piles them on top of one another, the water always slides just outside his reach. In the end he sinks into complete immobility. The whistle sounds—but he no longer heeds it. The water is dangled in front of his face—but he does not move. Even the palm tree in the shade of which he has been sitting is whisked off into the flies. He remains immobile, looking at his hands.

The clown is defeated now. He may be dying. He was still funny in some sense just so long as he was trying to do what his tragic brother had taught him to do: reach. But with the possibilities of free action exhausted, and with aspiration rendered finally and wholly absurd, he is forced at last into stillness. No light from the tragic landscape penetrates the pit. He closes his eyes.

Can comedy survive this ultimate experience? Is the vision meant to be comic? If not, is it meant to be anything else? If the universe, wholly limited, cannot be seen as anything *other* than comic, must comedy—which is an echo, and needs an other to mock—fall silent?

Or, as Nigel Dennis asks after coming from a performance of Beckett's *Happy Days*, "in what state of mind should we look at a stage that is empty save for a half-buried wife and the back of a husband's bald head?" The wife is imbedded in a mound of sand which is steadily growing higher; at the beginning she is immobilized from the waist downward, toward the end from the neck downward. The husband, reading an out-of-date newspaper and looking at faded "dirty pictures," lolls behind the mound, turned away, incapable of any motion other than crawling. Before the play is finished, the husband has crawled around the mound and toward his wife, though with what purpose we cannot say. In any event, he does not reach her. The curtain falls on universal immobility. Now Mr. Dennis can imagine various states of mind in an audience watching the spectacle. Some playgoers will feel simply depressed; others will sternly nerve themselves to a useful lecture on the human situation. "But," he goes on to say, "both these attitudes seem almost inexplicable. For is it possible, *really*, to half-bury a *diseuse* and en-tunnel her hubby and still demand that the spectacle inspire the sadness of a train-accident in the Simplon Tunnel, or the gravity of a sociological conference? Surely the situation before us is entirely ludicrous and demands an entirely humorous response?"

Yet it does not. People who are confronted with Beckett "realize that he is not a satirist—that he has no quarrel with any persons or institutions, that he holds nobody and nothing up to ridicule. They know that he is a considerable preacher— a sort of unfrocked parson who no longer believes in a Christian salvation, but only feels that much worse in consequence. They know that he is a pessimist and that all his plays, no matter in what terms he couches them, are emphatic in regard to the sadness and regrettableness of human affairs."

The situation can scarcely be anything but a joke; at the same time we cannot freely respond to it as to a joke. This disjunction between the image and the response Mr. Dennis sees as the secret of Samuel Beckett's particular kind of power: "Is there any other dramatist who could present the ludicrous so frankly and get back such a heart-rending groan? Moreover, it *is* in large part the true nature of Mr. Beckett's power: he does in truth sorrow with the humourless and mourn with the sad. It is the humorist who suffers most at Mr. Beckett's hands, because the humorist is always seeing in a Beckett play whole jokes that are only really half-jokes, and funny situations that may have been intended otherwise. The humorist, indeed, tries to strike a bargain with Mr. Beckett, saying: 'Sad underneath, by all means. But funny in expression, no?' But the bargain is refused. Mr. Beckett denies the working agreement that Chekhov accepted . . ."

Mr. Dennis deserves to be quoted at length because he seems to me to have described without flaw the wavering needle we watch now in the theater, or even at home as we read. There is considerable doubt in my own mind as to whether Mr. Beckett is truly a dramatist; he affects me as a lyric poet does, and I enjoy him best at short length and in privacy. Reading *Happy Days* at home I find myself moved by its autumnal ache, by the foolish, prattling gallantry of its heroine, by its sense of powers irretrievably lost; in the theater nothing happens to me at all. The wavering needle is so delicately poised, however, that the effect can be very different for Mr. Dennis. Reading the play, Mr. Dennis "began to smile at the very first line and went on smiling to the bitter end." In the theater his smile "fled like a chalk mark, leaving only a blackboard behind." He asks: "How can such a thing be possible? Is the human mind, or voice, such that *any* line and *any* words can be spoken in an infinite variety of ways, so that the most ridiculous remark can sound tragic and the most tragic cry ridiculous? We know, in fact, that this *is* so, but is there not a limit somewhere?"

The needle wavers because we stand at the center-point, now, of two pressures. As we noticed in discussing Lionel Abel's *Metatheater,* tragedy has, since *Hamlet,* been working toward comedy: self-consciousness has driven it into the illusionism of Pirandello, Genêt, Edward Albee. At the same time, comedy, precisely because it has been deprived of its tragic master plan, has had to descend into a blackness so impenetrable that its own identity is in question. *Two* lost identities meet and grapple in the dark. As tragedy turns into comedy, comedy is not quite there. And comedy is not quite there because of what tragedy has done.

The dizzying implications of the situation were made most real for me one day as I watched, at very close range, the comedy team of Nichols and May play out their "Pirandello" sketch. The sketch has now become quite celebrated, and most justly so. At the time it had not been done publicly; by happenstance I was present in the offices of a television studio when the comedians quietly auditioned it. The sketch begins with two children quarreling. In the course of the quarrel they begin to mock their parents. Imperceptibly, they turn into the parents, so that we are now engaged in the parents' quarrel, which is a bitterer and much more ominous thing. But as the parents become more real, something worse happens. The reality reaches out to embrace Nichols and May, so that, in sudden alarm, we feel that the performance has got out of hand and that Nichols and May are using an imitated spleen to vent their actual spleen upon one another as performers. The needle wavers again: we cannot be certain which angry insult may have been prepared in advance for the sketch and which may have popped out, with quite personal malice, in the heat of the moment. Quickly the engagement becomes so intense that we are embarrassed: Nichols and May themselves have crossed the border line between art and actuality and we are present, humiliated, at a fiasco. We have been exposed to the performers *as* performers at a time when their concealed hatred of one another could no longer be concealed.

On the first occasion, when Mr. Nichols spat out his last word and left the room, slamming the door behind him, the three or four of who were listening feared, for a fraction of a second, that the partnership had been broken and that we might never see the team perform again. By the time that Mr. Nichols had reopened the door, grinning, we had recovered from the first sharp sensation of vertigo: the word "Pirandello," mentioned earlier but forgotten in the increasing intensity of the experience, had come back to us, and we were already feeling somewhat sheepish for having been so thoroughly taken in. I have never seen the sketch work quite so effectively in the theater, perhaps because the theater itself prevents our awareness of form from dissolving. In an office, however, we *were* taken in. Comedy had cracked in two and fallen into the abyss.

Now what the present situation means for comedy is that it must assume a double burden. It must be willing to accept the weight placed on it by the transformation of what was once a part of tragedy into something closer to its own tone: it must absorb the very large degree of seriousness that is left in Pirandello, Genêt, Beckett, *et al.* This seriousness, which is sometimes savagery, has nowhere else to go; there is no tragic form available to house it. And comedy must do this at a time when its own heart is heavy, when its own devices are near exhaustion for want of a tragic landscape, a tragic aspiration, to stimulate them into fresh and impertinent activity. Comedy is now the vessel that must contain disillusioned tragedy and the deflated comic impulse at once, and the pity of it is that comedy is the narrower of the two vessels we began with so long ago. Into a channel designed to accommodate the corrective afterthought of limitation must be poured the whole of contemporary experience. Comedy, as a form, was ordained to coexist with tragedy and to find certain aspects of its behavior absurd. Now it must do all the work, for everything is absurd. Small wonder that its voice sounds small, and its tricks seem halfhearted, some nights.

Its resources are, nonetheless, most remarkable. When it is not flogged too hard, when it is not pressed face down into the void by a hand motivated more by pique than by honest curiosity, when it is not forced to make humor of the philosophies of essentially humorless men, it exhibits an extraordinary capacity for shouldering its twin burdens simultaneously. I think it is too little noticed how resolutely comedy has preserved our *seriousness* for us these days.

Nearly every recent play we choose to regard as fundamentally serious, nearly every play we welcome for its uncompromising harshness, nearly every play we regard as the breakthrough of an authentic new voice, is conveyed to us in the language of laughter. The most vigorous and perceptive talent to have erupted in England during the past ten years or so is that of John Osborne; *Look Back in Anger* was the declaration of war. We know that Mr. Osborne's first play, like each of his succeeding plays, was altogether serious about challenging the social and philosophical preconceptions of the audiences that came into the playhouse. Yet *Look Back in Anger,* ruthless and uncompromising, is an evening of virtually uninterrupted laughter. In America the most abrasive newcomer has been Edward Albee; at the time of writing, *Who's Afraid of Virginia Woolf?* is Mr. Albee's most fully developed, and also his most "serious," play. From the rise of

326 • TRAGEDY AND COMEDY

the first curtain laughter explodes in the auditorium, relaying a vision of life seen as obscene with expletives arranged for maximum comic impact.

Both plays do their work in much the same way. Mr. Osborne's hero, Jimmy Porter, means to sting us into an awareness of the emptiness of contemporary life. The stinging is done with fancifulness, with outrageous exaggeration, with wit. Without the wit, Jimmy would be a whine and a bore. Mr. Albee's married couple mean to persuade us that living on illusion is a dangerous, probably disastrous, business. But the persuasion is not done with straightforward rhetoric; it is done with a fast, low curve that hits the catcher's mitt with a crackle. The few straightforward sequences are the least effective in the play.

In both plays it is comedy that takes care of all of the theater's vital needs: comedy commands us to listen to what is going forward; it creates our recognition that there is some truth to what is going forward; it even provides us with a sensation that we are going forward when we are not. This last may be its most ingenious contribution, for it is here that comedy supplies seriousness by sleight of hand, almost by default. Jimmy Porter has no defined objective. He is not a serious person in the sense that he has seriously analyzed the malaise that animates him or seriously conceived an alternative to simple vituperation. He rages to no purpose he would care to discuss; he rages simply to articulate his distemper, and one feels that he would be vastly disappointed if his world ever threatened him with a promise of coherence. He loves being free to despise; contempt is his candy. Yet, when the play is finished, we infer something serious from what we have seen and heard. Its hero has thrashed against a cage which is actually an infinitely receding nothingness. But the existence of a cage that cannot be grappled with is an exceedingly serious matter. We can only know the cage as the absence of anything defined. We know it, in fact, as the absence of anything Jimmy Porter can take seriously. But we have arrived at a negative affirmation: the play is serious because Jimmy cannot be. Comedy has kept seriousness alive by refraction. It has intimated aspiration by Jimmy's anger at not having any.

In short, comedy is supplying by indirection the light against which it would cast its shadow if it could. This is, to be sure, an exhausting thing for comedy to be attempting, implying a tragic landscape through the fury of people who cannot bear being unable to see one. Yet Mr. Albee brings off the effect as readily. At the end of his play all illusions have been destroyed. Over the dead bones of dreams his husband and wife sit down down together, last survivors in a slaughterhouse. From a serious point of view, this last image does not promise much. It does not promise that when man's last illusion has been shattered he will be any happier or more confident or more at home in his surroundings. It simply promises that he will be free of lies, however dry his mouth may seem to him. But if man himself is no longer lying, then he will be taking at least himself seriously. During the battle that has gone on, comedy has been the killer, the one effective hired gunman; it has ridiculed dreams until they were reduced to so much dust. Being comedy, it could not replace the loss with anything substantial, and the end of the play is stringently neutral if it is looked at honestly, spurious if it is looked at hopefully. But once again comedy has implied an ultimate seriousness by noisily emptying every comic cartridge it could lay hand on. For it is when we are deafened by noise that we remember silence.

Tennessee Williams' harrowing effects are often filtered through a grotesquerie we must laugh at: we laugh at the son's most violent denunciation of his mother in *The Glass Menagerie,* at Blanche du Bois's most pitiful pretensions in *A Streetcar Named Desire.* Harold Pinter is all nightmare; most often we laugh at what secretly terrifies us. Friedrich Duerrenmatt turns to a play about the diabolic struggle for atomic power and writes it out in the form of a comic strip.

In none of this is comedy called upon because it is "commercial." Neither is it used as a crutch, to do part-time or merely incidental work. Comedy is now used as the only door open to us, no matter what it is we mean to say. With tragedy lost to us as a working form, we lack an adequate vessel for our seriousness. Though our thoughts are mainly sober, we shy away from phrasing them naturally. We sense that to speak our serious minds openly would be to speak them inadequately, naïvely; the container for such things is nowhere to be found. Of the two forms bequeathed us in the beginning—and there have been just two, no matter how much we have mixed them—comedy, the vessel of limitation, is the only one shaped to our hand. Having a profound, and profoundly disturbing, sense of our own limitations, we reach for the form that suits us. Comedy responds as best it can, straining to play jester and Jeremiah at once.

It succeeds surprisingly often, as we have seen. And, at the same time that it is behaving with such devious tenacity, it keeps looking about for some means of rediscovering and reasserting its own independent unburdened identity. It would like to find, if possible, a real pretension that it might parody, a new aspiration at which to thumb its nose. *Surely* men are still taking themselves more seriously than they ought, even at a time when they are proclaiming that nothing can be taken seriously and that all activity is futile. *Surely* men are somehow still putting on airs.

Looking about, comedy discovers what it needs in the very despair that has nearly robbed it of a target. What if despair itself is the new heroic posture, the new pretense to greatness? What if there is, after all, an aspiration open to ridicule: contemporary man's aspiration to be known as the most wretched of all beings? What if one freedom is still being exercised—the freedom to deny that freedom exists? That would give comedy something to challenge and bring down again: man glorifying himself as groaner, man freely denying his freedom, man fancying himself godlike by inventing his own cross. Murray Schisgal has quickly taken the hint.

In Mr. Schisgal's comedy *Luv,* Milt and Harry are comparing despairs on a park bench. Harry has just finished telling the tale of his blighted childhood, but Milt is not to be bested:

MILT. Paradise. . . . It was paradise compared to my childhood. Picture this. It's late at night. The wind's blowing outside. A small undernourished boy sits by the cold kerosene stove, feeding his toy wooden horse a bit of bread that he stole during dinner. The parents are quarreling. "If you don't like it here, get the hell out," the father shouts. "You're telling me to get out," the mother shouts back, and with savage hysterical fury she picks up the boy's toy wooden horse and throws it at the father. He ducks and it smashes against the wall. The boy drops down beside his broken toy horse, the only thing he ever loved, and he cries quietly.

HARRY. (*Moves right, then whirls back to Milt; pugnaciously.*) Did you ever get beaten?

MILT (*Emphatically*). I did.

HARRY. With what?

MILT. A strap, a stick, a radiator cover.

HARRY. A chain?

MILT. How thick?

HARRY. As thick as my wrist.

MILT. (*Foiled; moves away, turns.*) What did you get for breakfast?

HARRY. At home?

MILT. At home.

HARRY. A glass filled with two-thirds water and one-third milk.

MILT. Coffee grounds, that's what I got.

Milt is temporarily victorious in the sorry-for-myself sweepstakes. But Harry has a hideous tale to tell, the tale of the incident that blighted his life. He had been a promising student, full of plans and prospects. He had been sitting on a park bench, daydreaming in the hot Sunday sun, when a small fox terrier approached him, raised its leg, and urinated:

All over my gabardine pants. And they were wet, through and through. I could swear to that! Then he turned right around and walked off. The whole thing was . . . It was all so unreal, all so damn senseless. My mind . . . I thought . . . (*Emotionally*) Why me? Out of everyone in that park, out of hundreds, thousands of people, why me? What did it mean? How do you explain it? . . . That started it; right there was the beginning. From that minute on, it changed, everything changed for me. It was as if I was dragged to the edge of the cliff and forced to look down. How can I make you understand? What words do I use? I was nauseous, Milt. Sick to my soul. I became aware . . . aware of the whole rotten senseless stinking deal. Nothing mattered to me after that. Nothing.

As a consequence of this profound descent into the void, Harry gave up his plans to go to medical school, gave up the book he was writing, gave up his Greek studies:

I couldn't go on. . . . No roots. No *modus vivendi*. I had to find some answers first. A reason. I traveled, went everywhere, looked everywhere. I studied with a Brahmin in Calcutta, with a Buddhist in Nagoya, with a Rabbi in Los Angeles. Nothing. I could find nothing. I didn't know where to turn, what to do with myself. I began drinking, gambling, living in whorehouses, smoking marijuana, taking guitar lessons. . . . Nothing. Still nothing. Tonight . . . Milt, tonight I was going to end it all, make one last stupid gesture of disgust and . . . that would be it!

But why end it all, comedy asks with a happy smirk, when all is so gloriously exacerbated, so romantically ravaged, so gloriously shot through with the most fashionable *angst?* A pride of pain swells in Harry, a comforting certainty that he has missed no malaise prescribed for the age by philosopher or poet. Kierkegaard would know him, Kafka would greet him warmly. He is important, representative, glamorous, sick in all the right ways. And he is certainly not going to kill himself, for all his threats and his several cautious attempts; he is much too content with the dramatic scope of his pain.

The humor of the moment is only partly dependent upon a little dog's triggering such a big despair, though it does mean to suggest that Harry was looking for despair and might well have found it in something less shattering still. For the most part Harry's comedy is the product of his ambition, his determination to excel all other men in the suffering he is capable of sustaining, his vision of himself as an up-to-date Prometheus crying out "I am wronged!" In the void itself, deep down in the pit, comedy has come upon an aspiration that will serve it as the old tragic aspirations did, as a heroic declaration to be derided. It has become itself again, rather than a mixed thing, by rendering the absurd absurd.

This last little trick is a considerable accomplishment. I would like to think that it is something more than a trick, without imposing upon Mr. Schisgal a prophet's mantle he has laid no claim to. To say that the posture of absurdity is absurd is to imply that the man inside the posture is not truly absurd, no matter how strenuously he chooses to writhe under his fiercely imagined bonds. If despair is an illusion then despair is no longer real.

Now this could be mere whistling in the dark on comedy's part, though I rather doubt that if it were no more than wishful thinking it would be greeted with very much laughter. Audiences demand substantial truth in an image before they offer it open response. Conceivably, the portrait of *angst* as a preposterous self-delusion *could* also be a beginning echo of that change in the philosophical climate we spoke of in the preceding chapter. Just possibly the news that man is literally nothing but his own freedom, that he can only define himself by asserting himself and that the pain involved in such potentially tragic action is to be preferred to the comfort of remaining a nonentity, is in process of invading the public mind, so much so that comedy can build confidently upon it. If a real change in our habits of thought is taking place, and we are on the verge of overcoming our long-standing sensation of diminishment and unfreedom, then the spectacle of men imprisoned by feelings of diminishment in the face of the void will at last come to seem funny. If the pain of growth is to be welcomed as something good and necessary, not groaned over as an unjust imposition of fate upon the helpless, then two men who compete to say how painfully helpless they are can be laughed at. A fool who makes heroism of his haplessness is a proud fool; and pride can be brought to heel once more.

Comedy may have sensed that we are slightly past *angst* now—not altogether, only slightly—and that from our earlier quailing before the void we have turned toward active investigation of the void. The void itself has not gone away. We have simply altered our attitude toward it. The very fact that *Luv* is a satirical comedy suggests that we have advanced a bit from our former position. Satire always comes into being a few minutes after the thing being satirized has lost its hold upon us. We think of satire as a corrective in the present tense, as a weapon calculated to expose the foolishness we are engaged in *now*. But it is not. Satire cannot begin to function effectively until we have all grasped how foolishly we *have been* behaving; we could not respond at all unless we had begun to wake up. When Fletcher's delightful *The Knight of the Burning Pestle* was first produced in London, it failed. The play satirizes the pushiness of the new middle class, but the new middle class was at that time so new that it had not begun to see itself as pushy. It was merely offended by the play, and ruled it off the boards. A few years later, when the same class was secure enough to look back and understand how boorishly it had behaved, the play became an enormous success in revival. Audiences could laugh now, because, if they were not altogether through with that sort of cloddish self-assertion, they had come to realize just how cloddish it was. "It is not until after skepticism about a ruling 'way' has formed in the minds of a large section of the masses," William Graham Sumner insists, that the satirist "makes himself the mouthpiece of it." In 1906 Mr. Sumner wrote that "a protective tariff is a grand object for satire, but so long as the masses believe in it satire is powerless. The same is true of any folkway so long as it is not yet doubted. Satire is then blasphemy. While a way is prevalent there is pathos about it . . . as there is now amongst us about democracy, but there never can be satire and pathos at the same time, in the same society, about the same thing."

Or, as cartoonist Al Capp confessed in 1963,

McCarthy was coming to power when I created shmoos, and those were inconceivably terrible times. They got worse and worse, until eventually the only satire possible and permissible in this democracy of ours was broad, weak domestic comedy. That's why I married off Li'l Abner and began to concentrate on him again. I was absolutely sure that to keep on with political satire—with things like shmoos—would be to commit suicide, and I asked myself, seriously, "Al, what use would you be dead?" I really believe that it's the duty of the satirist to stay alive—to duck—until it's safe to come out and possible to be useful again. Society's finally free for satire now, and that's one reason I brought back shmoos.

We have certainly had our pathos—to use Sumner's word for belief—about the plight of man, that plight in which, as painter Francis Bacon says, "we watch ourselves from the cradle, performing into decay. Man now realizes that he is an accident, a completely futile being, that he has to play out the game without reason." And comedy has had to deal with this deeply credited pathos, sometimes at the expense of its own identity. The pathos—the belief—is not wholly done with. For all anyone can say, a new shock may intensify it for us tomorrow. But if, in a commercial Broadway play, we have taken a first tiny step from pathos to satire, from belief in futility to laughing at a belief in futility, then the winds have changed somewhat. That the step should have been taken in a commerical Broadway play is significant: it means that Mr. Sumner's skepticism has indeed taken form in "a large section of the masses." The changed tone is not the province of a few philosophers; it has penetrated, however faintly and intuitively, the public ear.

If it is possible that we are nerving ourselves to tragedy again—we cannot be certain, we can only watch tentative marks being made on a graph that will always surprise us—it is possible also that comedy will be relieved of the ennui that has threatened it with stillness, that has forced it into every sort of counterattack including a willingness to do at least part of tragedy's serious work for it, that has placed it in the odd position of having to be all things to all men. It is possible that comedy will once more be free to be thoroughly insulting about freedom—to be itself.

Comedy waits for tragedy as a lover waits for a girl he cannot very well do without. It *will* wait, so long as it has a memory to go by and legs to stand on. Waiting, it will pass the time somehow. If it is impatient, it is impatient partly out of love and partly because it has a few sharp things to say.

And there is one last dissatisfaction that helps to keep comedy kicking. That is its dissatisfaction with itself. Comedy is by nature schizoid. It wants to attack, and it despises itself for succeeding.

Comedy cannot help finding the flaw in free, proud, vaulting activity. Its eyes are trained in that direction, its habits of mind are compulsive. Let a clown loose anywhere and he will unerringly detect the least trace of spuriousness in an otherwise confident posture. The clown cannot help himself; he was born to bring ambition down. He will do it to his own mother, he will quickly be caustic about the children he loves, he will put his own body on the firing line if he has to. His pessimism is reflexive, unpremeditated, uncontrollable. In the presence of Michelangelo's David, he will see only the idealized pubic hair. With a quick and gleeful whoop, he will make use of the single subterfuge he has seen to call the whole vast image into question. He focuses exclusively upon the prettying-up that can be ridiculed and makes the rest of the soaring architecture a mere appendage to the tiny pretense he has pointed out. He devalues by instinct, and his inverted vision is 20–20.

Yet he detests his own accuracy and secretly wishes, in great anguish, that his eye could be proved false. He really keeps at his work in the hope that one day he *will* be proved mistaken. He yearns, with all his heart, for the perfection he is constantly exploding. One day, one day perhaps, he will cast his cunning eye on an image of aspiration that will defy him; the blemish will not be there, he will look feverishly and not find it, he will feel his talent is failing him. That is his unacknowledged hope, the hidden affinity for greatness that keeps him working so hard, the secret of his tagging forever after the tragic hero whose failures he taunts. He keeps close on the heels of the man-god he has long since disposed of. He has had so many successes in ridiculing this pretentious fellow that he might well have washed his hands of him, long since. But he hasn't. He doesn't now. With the expression of an anxious spaniel, he begs to be permitted to come along on the journey. He will be a nuisance on the journey, he will mock it and make a mess of it; but he wants to be there. He is driven by his need to demoralize; he is also driven by the same ideal of perfection—future perfection, possible perfection, somewhere, somehow—that animates the tragic man he doubts so. He has inherited his furtive, constantly denied, dream of perfection from the tragic hero because he has inherited his very being from the tragic hero. It is just his bad luck that he happens to notice, all of the time, the stupid impediments the tragic hero is trying to forget. He really hates himself for his own perceptiveness.

Thus, there is always an element of exasperation with *self* in the clown, in comedy. A comedian is rarely exasperated by the situation in which he finds himself. He rarely permits himself to be too much exasperated by others; that would suggest bitterness, anger, those qualities that unfailingly turn comedy sour. What fills the clown with occasional, usually briefly displayed, disgust is not the fact of hurricanes in the sky or haplessness in other people's conduct, but his intense awareness of his own nature. He is the dour one who *sees* what is wrong. He is the advocate of impediments. He can find something inadequate in everyone he meets, in everything he touches. And because he has doggedly hoped all along to find someone or something that would not yield to his iconoclastic investigations, that would not further encourage his doubts, he becomes—now and again, and very slightly —fed up. He becomes fed up, as we all do, with a mind that functions in only one way, however effectively.

He does not let us see this impatience with his own nature too often. He does not want to betray an underlying streak of futile optimism that his own talents are committed to denying and destroying; he must not give more than an inch to the affirmative temperament of the tragic hero, it is not his business to do so. Yet the streak sometimes shows, in the form of contempt for his own task. It is there in the strange little gasp, accompanied by a rattled shake of the head, that Buster Keaton permits himself perhaps once in each film. He wants to say something else, and can't. He wants himself to be better, and cannot quite bear the knowledge that he never, never will be. The streak is present at once in Feste, whose very first words are "Let her hang me," when he hears that his mistress is angry with him for being dilatory about his fooling; it is covered over with great effort by the nearly exhausted clown during the rest of the play. It is defined without evasion by Jaques. "They say you are a melancholy fellow" is Rosalind's greeting to him in the forest. "I am so," Jaques replied, "I do love it better than laughing." When Rosalind quickly points out that the extremes of gaiety and melancholy are both to be avoided, Jaques stands his sorry ground.

"Why, 'tis good to be sad and say nothing."

"Why, then, 'tis good to be a post."

"I have neither the scholar's melancholy, which is emulation; nor the musician's, which is fantastical; nor the courtier's, which is proud; nor the soldier's, which is ambitious; nor the lawyer's, which is politic; nor the lady's, which is nice; nor the lover's, which is all of these: but it is a melancholy of mine own, compounded of many simples, extracted from many objects; and indeed the sundry contemplation of my travels, in which my often rumination wraps me in a most humorous sadness."

"A traveller! By my faith, you have great reason to be sad. I fear you have sold your own lands to see other men's. Then, to have seen much, and to have nothing, is to have rich eyes and poor hands."

"Yes, I have gained my experience."

Jaques' experience, his use of his eyes, has robbed him of Touchstone's exuberant animation and left him both cynic and introvert. The strain, almost a strain of madness, erupts as W. C. Fields slashes out with his stick in undisguised fury, not bothering for the sudden second to keep himself attractive, or as Bert Lahr, in a burlesque sketch, fiercely snatches from a woman a package of pork chops he doesn't want. For this woman's purposes, and for comedy's, he has had to descend into feigned, but nearly real, madness, in order to pursue the matter of who is going to pay for the pork chops. When he snatches them away he does so abruptly, with his teeth set and with a kind of moral perspiration showing plainly on his forehead; he wishes to terminate violently the playful nonsense that has supported him as a clown. Groucho Marx lurches to the footlights in the middle of a sequence to look directly at the audience and remark, "Well, you can't expect all the jokes to be funny." The remark itself becomes funny in the circumstances. It is not a snarl. But it is the candor that short-circuits a snarl by anticipating it. The clown is here absolving himself of his own hatred for his work. Similarly, Groucho must insist, as a professional comedian, that the figure in the wheel chair headed directly for a stone wall must be a real old lady. The clown feels a meanness inside himself that can only be exorcised by being acknowledged. "You think I'm kidding," the clown says. "I'm *not*."

The clown suffers deeply for the meanness his work entails. We pay virtually no attention to the problem of suffering in comedy, largely because the moment we think of "suffering" we think of tragedy. We quite forget that the comic miser who has lost his money is genuinely racked with a pain that is to him intolerable, that the comedy coward dies a thousand times each time he fails to fight, that even at the lightest level the thwack of a slapstick *hurts*. In *The School for Wives*, one of the most artificial of great comedies, the old fool who has carefully reared a girl to be as stupid as possible so that she will not hesitate to marry him is presented throughout as an obvious, though incredibly ingenious, fool. He earns no sympathy from us; we want to see him hoodwinked and despoiled. Yet there comes a moment—one only—in the play when this man reveals the hurt that has lodged all along inside him. The girl is still his prisoner. He can have her. But he is, in a burst of unlooked-for anguish, suddenly beside himself. He can no longer repress the *self* that he simultaneously coddles and despises:

> Look at me; see the torture in my face;
> . . . no love can match the love I offer.
> Ingrate, what is the proof you ask of me?
> You want to see me weep? And beat my breast?
> You want to have me tear out half my hair?
> Or shall I kill myself? Is that what you want?
> Oh, cruel girl, I'm ready to prove it so.

Shylock suffers so deeply that we still cannot decide whether he is a comic figure or a tragic figure or possibly a playwright's mistake. The fact of the matter is that the central contest of *any* play—comic or tragic—engages its principals in a kind of agony; Sir Giles Overreach, in what is certainly a comedy, suffers so much that he does go mad.

Pain is common to both forms and is so far from being a distinguishing mark between them that it actually attests to their close relationship. The contest that is going on in a play—its *agon*—is an agony whether in a comedy or a tragedy. It so happens that the theatrical use of the term *agon* derives from comedy rather than tragedy.

But the pain of comedy is possibly more protracted and more frustrating than that of tragedy, because it does not know how to expel itself. Tragedy's pain is productive; it comes of the abrasiveness of moving forward toward transformation. Comedy, making capital of the absurdity of seeking transformation, must forever contain its pain. By denying freedom it denies release. Tragedy *uses* suffering; comedy can only live with it. Comedy can only live with it, that is to say, against the possible day when tragedy, in an ultimately successful transformation, frees them both. Comedy, hugging the fox to its breast, stays close to tragedy against that possible, eternally doubted, day.

But this interior anguish of comedy, this intense impatience and exasperation with self, in itself becomes an energy. Dissatisfaction with self is a goad, perhaps the most powerful goad man knows. The tragic hero courageously, sometimes presumptiously or even wrongly, takes up arms to advance the self; the clown, holding back as he must if he is to be a clown, retains the dissatisfaction as a canker which can neither be expelled nor quieted. Impatience kicks and thrashes inside the clown, like a violent baby in the womb that cannot bring itself to term.

It is just this powerful agitation that is, in the end, comedy's strongest assurance of survival. Detesting its work while half despising itself for being so good at it, finding its limited situation intolerable even while it is being applauded for the hilarity it provokes in so accurately describing the situation, comedy burns with a fever that may prove unquenchable. Transforming anger into laughter abates the anger temporarily, slightly; it does not remove its causes. The causes fester, seek expression in any which way, generate activity. If we have seen comedy cropping up on all sides in all hues in our time, willing to offer itself as a sacrifice to seriousness or to paint itself black where it was once too carelessly thought to be a painter of rainbows, it is because it can never be content to lie fallow in the face of the contempt it feels for itself. Comedy may keep kicking, because it cannot help kicking out at itself. And because it owes everything to tragedy, both the original gift of a thing to be parodied and also the only ultimate promise of a new state of being in which all private exasperations and secret despairs will be melted away in the annealing passage through time and space, it must keep kicking to see if it can kick tragedy awake.

The clown screams at his sleeping companion. He wants him up and on with it. Once he has got him up, if he ever succeeds, he will of course tell him that his activity is absurd. But he wants it to be absurd. Only the tragic absurdity is capable of transcending itself.

What a good man the clown is, to endure so much, to survive so relentlessly, to keep us company in all weathers, to provide us with a way of looking at the worst that enables us to take a temporary joy in the worst! For that is what he does: he stands horror on its head to keep us tolerably happy against the day when tragedy will look horror straight in the eye and stare it down.

He knows what it is that he secretly wants, and he is wonderfully ingenious about doubling us up as he displays his—and our—combined anguish and desire. Chekhov's Platonov is a marvelously wretched fool: he is so naturally attractive to women that he has quite exhausted himself in the process of satisfying the lovely, predatory creatures. Fighting off the latest swarm of conquests that have so conquered him, he turns in desperation to his wife, the wife he has endlessly betrayed. She, however, has had her fill of his revelry and is leaving him.

"Sacha, stay here!" he cries out in mortal pain. "I don't want happiness. I just want you."

That is what comedy is forever saying to tragedy. And that is its funny way of saying it.

REFERENCES

MODERN PLAYS AND TRANSLATIONS

Aeschylus, *Agamemnon*. Translated by Richmond Lattimore. In *Greek Plays in Modern Translation*. Dial Press, New York, 1947.

Aeschylus, *Eumenides*. Translated by George Thomson. In *Greek Plays in Modern Translation*. Dial Press, New York, 1947.

Aeschylus, *Prometheus Bound*. Translated by Edith Hamilton. In *Greek Plays in Modern Translation*. Dial Press, New York, 1947.

Aristophanes, *Lysistrata*. Translated by Dudley Fitts. Harcourt, Brace, & World, Inc., New York, 1954.

Aristophanes, *The Acharnians*. Translator anonymous. In *The Plays of Aristophanes*. Everyman's Library, J. M. Dent, London; E. P. Dutton, New York, 1909.

Aristophanes, *The Birds*. Translated by Dudley Fitts. Harcourt, Brace, & World, Inc., New York, 1957.

Aristophanes, *The Clouds*. Translator anonymous. In *The Complete Greek Drama*, edited by Whitney J. Oates and Eugene O'Neill, Jr. Volume 2. Random House, New York, 1938.

Aristophanes, *The Clouds*. Translator anonymous. In *Aristophanes, The Eleven Comedies*. Immortal Classics, no date.

Aristophanes, *The Frogs*. Translated by Dudley Fitts. Harcourt, Brace, & World, Inc., New York, 1955.

Aristophanes, *The Knights*. Translator anonymous. In *The Plays of Aristophanes*. Volume 1. Everyman's Library, E. P. Dutton, New York, 1909.

344 • REFERENCES

Chekhov, Anton, *A Country Scandal (Platonov)*. Translated and adapted by Alex Szogyi. Coward-McCann, New York, 1960.

Chekhov, Anton. *The Cherry Orchard*. Translated by Stark Young. In *Best Plays by Chekhov*. Modern Library, Random House, New York, 1956.

Eliot, T. S., *The Cocktail Party*. Harcourt, Brace, & World, Inc., New York, 1950.

Euripides, *Alcestis*. Translated by Richard Aldington. In *The Complete Greek Drama*, edited by Whitney J. Oates and Eugene O'Neill, Jr. Volume 1. Random House, New York, 1938.

Euripides, *Iphigenia in Aulis*. Translated by F. M. Stawell. In *The Complete Greek Drama*, edited by Whitney J. Oates and Eugene O'Neill, Jr. Volume 2. Random House, New York, 1938.

Euripides, *Medea*. Translated by Gilbert Murray. In *Ten Greek Plays*. Oxford University Press, New York, 1935.

Euripides, *Medea*. Translated by Frederic Prokosch. In *Greek Plays in Modern Translation*. Dial Press, New York, 1947.

Euripides, *The Bacchae*. Translated by William Arrowsmith. In *Euripides III*. Modern Library, Random House, New York, 1959.

Euripides, *The Cyclops*. Translated by E. P. Coleridge. In *The Complete Greek Drama*, edited by Whitney J. Oates and Eugene O'Neill, Jr. Volume 2. Random House, New York, 1938.

Fry, Christopher, *A Phoenix Too Frequent*. Oxford University Press, New York, Toronto, 1959.

Ionesco, Eugene, *Rhinoceros*. Grove Press, New York, 1960.

Machiavelli, Niccolò, *The Mandrake*. Translated by Frederick May and Eric Bentley. In *The Classic Theater*, Volume 1. Doubleday Anchor, New York, 1958.

Molière, *School for Wives*. Translated by Morris Bishop. In *Eight Plays by Molière*. Modern Library, Random House, New York, 1957.

Molière, *Tartuffe*. Translated by Richard Wilbur. Harcourt, Brace, & World, Inc., New York, 1961.

Molière, *The Critique of the School for Wives*. Translated by

Morris Bishop. In *Eight Plays by Molière*. Modern Library, Random House, New York, 1957.

Molière, *The Misanthrope*. Translated by Richard Wilbur. Harcourt, Brace, & World, Inc., New York, 1954.

Molière, *The Miser*. Translator anonymous. In *Plays by Molière*. Modern Library, Random House, New York, no date.

Molière, *The Physician in Spite of Himself*. Translated by Morris Bishop. In *Eight Plays by Molière*. Modern Library, Random House, New York, 1957.

Molière, *The Would-Be Gentleman*. Translated by Morris Bishop. In *Eight Plays by Molière*. Modern Library, Random House, New York, 1957.

Plautus, *The Braggart Warrior*. Translated by George E. Duckworth. In *The Complete Roman Drama,* edited by George E. Duckworth. Volume 1. Random House, New York, 1942.

Plautus, *The Pot of Gold*. Translated by Lionel Casson. In *Six Plays of Plautus*. Doubleday Anchor, New York, 1963.

Schisgal, Murray, *Luv*. Coward-McCann, New York, 1963.

Shaw, Bernard, *Man and Superman*. In *Selected Plays*. Dodd Mead, New York, no date.

Sophocles, *Antigone*. Translated by Dudley Fitts and Robert Fitzgerald. In *Greek Plays in Modern Translation*. Dial Press, New York, 1947.

Sophocles, *King Oedipus*. Translated by William Butler Yeats. In *Greek Plays in Modern Translation*. Dial Press, New York, 1947.

Sophocles, *Oedipus at Colonus*. Translated by Robert Fitzgerald. In *The Oedipus Cycle*. Harvest Books, Harcourt, Brace, & World, Inc., New York, no date.

Sophocles, *Oedipus Rex*. Translated by Dudley Fitts and Robert Fitzgerald. In *The Oedipus Cycle*. Harvest Books, Harcourt, Brace, & World, Inc., New York, no date.

Sophocles, *Philoctetes*. Translated by Thomas Francklin. In *The Complete Greek Drama,* edited by Whitney J. Oates and Eugene O'Neill, Jr. Volume 1. Random House, New York, 1938.

Yeats, William Butler. *Calvary*. In *Collected Plays*, Macmillan, New York, 1953.

OTHER SOURCES QUOTED

Abel, Lionel. *Metatheatre*. Hill and Wang, New York, 1963.

Agee, James. *Agee on Film*. McDowell, Obolensky, New York, 1958.

Albee, Edward. Interview, *New York Post,* November 4, 1962.

Anouilh, Jean. Interview, *The New York Times*, Sept. 13, 1964.

Aristotle, *Poetics*. In *The Basic Works of Aristotle*. Edited by Richard McKeon. Random House, New York, 1941.

Bacon, Francis. "Art." *Time,* November 1, 1963.

Barrett, William. *Irrational Man*. Doubleday Anchor, New York, 1962.

Barthes, Roland. *On Racine*. Hill and Wang, New York, 1964.

Baudelaire, Charles. *The Essence of Laughter*. Translated by Gerard Hopkins. Introduction by Peter Quennell. Meridian Books, New York, 1956.

Beckett, Samuel. *Malone Dies*. Grove Press, New York, 1956.

Beckson, Karl and Ganz, Arthur. *A Reader's Guide to Literary Terms*. Farrar, Straus and Cudahy. New York, 1960.

Bergson, Henri. *Laughter*. Macmillan, New York, 1913.

Bradley, A. C. *Shakespearean Tragedy*. Macmillan, London, 1912.

Brodrick, Alan Houghton. *Father of Prehistory*. William Morrow, New York, 1963.

Capp, Al. In "Talk of the Town," *The New Yorker,* October 26, 1963.

Chaplin, Charles. *My Autobiography*. Simon and Schuster, New York, 1964.

Charlton, H. B. *Shakesperian Comedy*. Methuen, London, 1938.

Chekhov, Anton. *The Selected Letters of Anton Chekhov*. Translated by Sidonie K. Lederer, edited by Lillian Hellman. Farrar, Straus & Giroux, Inc., New York, 1955.

Cornford, Francis Macdonald. *The Origin of Attic Comedy*. Cambridge University Press, New York, 1934.

Cox, Harvey. *The Secular City*. Macmillan, New York, 1965.

Crane, Stephen. *The Collected Poems of Stephen Crane*. Knopf, New York, 1932.

Danby, John F. *Shakespeare's Doctrine of Nature, A Study of King Lear.* Faber and Faber, London, 1949.

Deely, J. Nathaniel. "Evolution: Concept and Content." *Listening,* Autumn, 1965.

Dennis, Nigel. "No View from the Toolshed." *Encounter,* January, 1963.

Duchartre, Pierre Louis. *The Italian Comedy.* Translated by Randolph T. Weaver. John Day, New York, no date.

Eastman, Max. *The Sense of Humor.* Scribner's, New York, 1921.

Esslin, Martin. *The Theatre of the Absurd.* Doubleday Anchor, New York, 1961.

Fergusson, Francis. *The Idea of a Theatre.* Doubleday Anchor, New York, 1949.

Fowlie, Wallace. *Dionysus in Paris.* Meridian Books, New York, 1960.

Fry, Christopher. "Comedy." *Vogue,* January, 1951.

Hazlitt, William. *English Comic Writers.* Everyman's Library, J. M. Dent, London; E. P. Dutton, New York, 1910.

Hegel, Georg Wilhelm Friedrich. *Hegel on Tragedy,* edited by Anne and Henry Paolucci. Doubleday Anchor, New York, 1962.

Jaeger, Werner. *Paideia: The Ideals of Greek Culture.* Oxford University Press, New York, 1945.

Jaspers, Karl. *Tragedy Is Not Enough.* Gollancz, London, 1953.

Jones, John. *On Aristotle and Greek Tragedy.* Oxford University Press, New York, 1962.

Jung, C. G. "Jung on Life After Death." *The Atlantic Monthly,* December, 1962.

Kitto, H. D. F. *Form and Meaning in Drama.* University Paperbacks, Methuen, London; Barnes & Noble, Inc., New York, 1956.

Kitto, H. D. F. "Greek Tragedy and Dionysus." In *Theatre and Drama in the Making,* edited by John Gassner and Ralph G. Allen. Houghton Mifflin, Boston, 1964.

Kitto, H. D. F. *Greek Tragedy.* Doubleday Anchor, New York, 1954.

Knox, Bernard. "Sophocles' Oedipus." In *Tragic Themes of Western Literature,* edited by Cleanth Brooks. Yale University Press, New Haven, 1955.

Kronenberger, Louis. *The Cart and the Horse*. Knopf, New York, 1964.

Kronenberger, Louis. *The Thread of Laughter*. Knopf, New York, 1952.

Lea, K. M. *Italian Popular Comedy*. Russell & Russell, New York, 1962.

Leacock, Stephen. *Humor, Its Theory and Technique*. Dodd, Mead, Toronto, 1935.

Mack, Maynard. "The World of Tragedy." In *Tragic Themes in Western Literature*, edited by Cleanth Brooks. Yale University Press, New Haven, 1955.

Mandel, Oscar. *A Definition of Tragedy*. New York University Press, 1961.

Martz, Louis L. "The Saint as Tragic Hero." In *Tragic Themes in Western Literature*, edited by Cleanth Brooks. Yale University Press, New Haven, 1955.

McCarthy, Mary. "General Macbeth." *Harper's*, June, 1952.

McLuhan, Herbert Marshall. "Address at Vision 65." *The American Scholar*, Spring, 1966.

Meredith, George. *An Essay on Comedy*. Scribner's, New York, 1897.

New Century Classical Handbook. Edited by Catherine B. Avery. Appleton-Century-Crofts, New York, 1962.

Nicoll, Allardyce. *Masks, Mimes, and Miracles*. Harcourt, Brace, & World, Inc., New York, 1931.

Nietzsche, Friedrich. *The Birth of Tragedy and the Genealogy of Morals*. Translated by Francis Golffing. Doubleday Anchor, New York, 1956.

Norwood, Gilbert. *Greek Comedy*. Methuen, London, 1931.

Parker, Dorothy. *Enough Rope*. Boni and Liveright, New York, 1926.

Peyre, Henri. "The Tragedy of Passion, Racine's Phèdre." In *Tragic Themes in Western Literature*, edited by Cleanth Brooks. Yale University Press, New Haven, 1955.

Plato. *Symposium*. Translated by Benjamin Jowett. In *Great Books of the Western World*, Volume 7. Encyclopaedia Britannica, Chicago, London, Toronto, 1952.

Plutarch. *The Lives of the Noble Grecians and Romans*. Translated by John Dryden. In *Great Books of the Western World*,

Volume 14. Encyclopaedia Britannica, Chicago, London, Toronto, 1952.

Raphael, D. D. *The Paradox of Tragedy*. Indiana University Press, Bloomington, 1960.

Repplier, Agnes. *In Pursuit of Laughter*. Houghton, Mifflin, Boston and New York, 1936.

Richards, I. A. *Principles of Literary Criticism*. Harcourt, Brace, & World, Inc., New York, 1948.

Rahv, Philip. *The Myth and the Powerhouse*. Farrar, Straus & Giroux, Inc., New York, 1965.

Rieff, Philip. *Freud: The Mind of the Moralist*. Doubleday Anchor, New York, 1961.

Sartre, Jean Paul. "Existentialism." In *Philosophy of Existentialism*. Philosophical Library, New York, 1965.

Schlegel, August Wilhelm. *Lectures on Dramatic Art and Literature*. Translated by John Black. George Bell, London, 1894.

Simmons, Ernest J. *Chekhov, a Biography*. Little, Brown, Boston, 1962.

Sprague, Arthur Colby. *Shakespeare and the Actors*. Harvard University Press, Cambridge, 1944.

Steiner, George. *The Death of Tragedy*. Knopf, New York, 1961.

Styan, J. L. *The Dark Comedy*. Cambridge University Press, New York, 1962.

Sumner, William Graham. *Folkways*. Dover paperback, New York, 1959.

Taylor, W. S. "Psychoanalysis Revised or Proschodynamics Developed?" *The American Psychologist*. November, 1962.

Trilling, Lionel. "The Fate of Pleasure." *Partisan Review*, Summer, 1963.

Trilling, Lionel. "The Modern Element in Modern Literature." *Partisan Review*, January–February, 1961.

Updike, John. Book review of Denis de Rougement's *Love Declared: Essays on the Myth of Love*. *The New Yorker*, August 24, 1963.

Warshow, Robert. *The Immediate Experience*. Doubleday, New York, 1962.

Welsford, Enid. *The Fool*. Farrar and Rinehart, New York, no date.

Whitman, Cedric H. *Aristophanes and the Comic Hero.* Harvard University Press, Cambridge, 1964.

Wilder, Amos. "Art and Theological Meaning." In *The New Orpheus: Essays Toward a Christian Poetic.* Sheed & Ward, New York, 1964.

INDEX

(Names in small capital letters are those of fictional characters.)

About the Author

WALTER KERR was born in Evanston, Illinois, in
1913. He received his B.S. and M.A. from North-
western University and from 1938 to 1949 taught
at the Catholic University of America in Washing-
ton, D.C. From 1950 to 1952 he was drama critic
of *Commonweal* magazine and in 1951 he became
the drama critic of the New York *Herald Tribune,*
a position he held until 1966 when he became
drama critic of *The New York Times.* His previous
books include *How Not to Write a Play, Pieces at
Eight, The Decline of Pleasure,* and *The Theater
in Spite of Itself.* He, his wife (playwright-humorist
Jean Kerr) and their six children live in Larch-
mont, New York.